THE CUBAN STORY

Books by Herbert L. Matthews

The Cuban Story (1961)

The Yoke and the Arrows (1956; *revised edition,* 1961)

Assignment to Austerity (*with Nancie Matthews*) (1950)

The Education of a Correspondent (1946)

The Fruits of Fascism (1943)

Two Wars and More to Come (1938)

Eyewitness in Abyssinia (1937)

Herbert L. Matthews

The Cuban Story

GEORGE BRAZILLER

NEW YORK   1961

© *1961 by Herbert L. Matthews*

Library of Congress Catalog Card Number: 61-17381

FIRST PRINTING, SEPTEMBER, 1961
SECOND PRINTING, MARCH, 1962

Printed in the United States of America

To Eric and Bobbie

Acknowledgment is due, as always, to The New York Times *in whose service all my information was gathered. Some material from a series of three lectures for the Third Annual Lectures in History at the City College of New York in March, 1961, has also been used.*

Contents

THE CUBAN STORY

The Sierra Maestra Story

JOURNALISTS RARELY make history. This is not our function. We are the chroniclers of our times; at best we provide material for history.

It was an accident that my interview with Fidel Castro in the Sierra Maestra on February 17, 1957, should have proved so important. There was a story to be got, a censorship to be broken. I got it and I did it—and it so happens that neither Cuba nor the United States is going to be the same again.

I am not accepting, for myself or for *The New York Times*, either blame or credit for having started Fidel Castro on his meteoric rise to fame and power. He was a man of destiny who would somehow have made his mark, sooner or later. Cuba was ripe for revolution.

The United States had a reckoning to pay for past policies. What Adlai Stevenson had called "the revolution of rising expectations" was exerting dangerous pressures

15

It is indicative of u.s. Influence, for Matthews to assume that a u.s. newspaper would have the power to influence the Cuban people, into backing the revolutionary of the N.Y. Times choice.

throughout Latin America. And the world was ready to come in on us, on our Western Hemisphere, safe for so long, still untouched by the cold war.

A bell tolled in the jungles of the Sierra Maestra that gray, sodden dawn, but how or why should a newspaperman, out after a scoop, know it?

I have never done a story that gave me more professional satisfaction. From the technical point of view, all I claim credit for is having interpreted what I saw and heard correctly, for having realized that the extraordinary young man pouring his heart out to me in whispers for three hours was the one around whom the hopes and passions of Cuba would gather to a flood tide of victory.

Fidel Castro has flair. He needed publicity in the strict sense of calling public attention to himself. Having studied his country's history he must have known the remarkable use to which the Cuban rebel General Máximo Gómez had put the attention he was able to get from the American newspapers in the insurrection of 1895–98. "Without a press we shall get nowhere," General Gómez had said. With a press he got American intervention.

Without a press Fidel Castro was a hunted outlaw, leading a small band of youths in a remote jungle area of eastern Cuba, isolated and ineffectual. He was believed to be dead by most Cubans (even General Batista thought him dead) and none except a small group in his 26th of July Movement could be sure that he was alive.

His band was surrounded by Government troops. There was a rigid censorship. The odds against the rebels seemed insuperable, but Fidel Castro was never dismayed by odds. Look at him today, confidently embarked on a war to the finish with the United States! He has a supreme faith—in himself, only himself.

He had landed at a swampy stretch of the western coast of Oriente Province, below Niquero, with eighty-one men, on December 2, 1956. The leaky sixty-two-foot yacht, Granma, had sailed from Mexico eight days before. (The true spelling of the name was "Granma" but it was always pronounced and usually spelled "Gramma.") The departure was hasty, for the Mexican authorities were after him. There was little food; the boat—which could comfortably accommodate no more than a dozen men—was dreadfully overcrowded; the Granma's engines were bad.

Everything seemed to go wrong. It had been arranged that his 26th of July followers in Santiago de Cuba would rise on November 30, the day Fidel and his band were supposed to land. There was a brave, but of course, futile uprising on November 30, with Fidel far out to sea.

In a typically flamboyant gesture, Fidel had announced that he was coming before the end of the year, so Batista's men were on the lookout for him. The yacht could not be unloaded in the swampy ground and all the equipment was lost.

The eighty-two men landed safely, but only a dozen, including Fidel, his younger brother, Raul Castro, and the Argentine doctor who had joined them in Mexico, Ernesto (Che) Guevara, escaped into the mountain jungle whose name is now so famous—the Sierra Maestra. It took a Fidel Castro to convert such a complete disaster into a triumph.

It was given out—and widely believed—that Fidel, himself, had been killed. The United Press even had told where he was buried, and stuck to its story until my interview was published months later.

For the Cuban people, Fidel was a myth, a legend, a hope, but not a reality. He had to come to life, and like General Gómez, he must have been saying to himself, "without a press we shall get nowhere."

Toward the last week of January, 1957, a survivor of the eighty-two, René Rodríguez, arrived in Havana with a message for the acting chief of the 26th of July Movement in the capital, Faustino Pérez. Rodríguez said that Fidel would like to see a foreign correspondent—not a Cuban correspondent, for the censorship was on, and Fidel never trusted the Cuban press, anyway.

A Havana University student leader was present at the meeting—Javier Pazos, son of Felipe Pazos, economist, banker and a former president of the National Bank of Cuba. (Father and son are examples of the best type of Cuban citizen and patriot. The father has for many months been one of the Cuban exile leaders seeking to overthrow the Castro regime; the son remained a loyal Fidelista.)

Rodríguez's instructions did not contain concrete details as to the way a meeting could be arranged. Fidel was to send further instructions, because his situation in the Sierra at that time was so precarious that he, himself, did not know how he would be able to manage the interview. It was typical of Fidel that he first decided what he

18

wanted to do and then had no doubts that he would do it, however impossible it seemed.

Faustino Pérez delegated Javier Pazos to make the necessary contacts, and since Javier's father was already actively cooperating with the 26th of July Movement, the son sought his help. The only foreign correspondent Felipe Pazos knew personally was Mrs. R. Hart (Ruby) Phillips of *The New York Times.* He went to see her at the *Times* office on Refugio Alto and explained his problem.

From that moment, the lives of a certain number of Cubans were in the hands of Ruby Phillips and a little later, of me and my wife Nancie. Edward (Ted) Scott of the Havana *Times* and the National Broadcasting Company was consulted the first day by Ruby, as he shared the *Times* office and was knowledgeable and discreet.

"I must say that this was one of the best projects I have ever been informed of, with respect to security," Ted Scott wrote me long afterwards. "I am sure you did not know that I was informed of what was going on and no one else in Ruby's organization knew what you and Nancie were conspiring to do.

"I saw you minutes before you left for the hills and said *'Buen viaje!'* or something like that. I remember you and Nancie looking quickly at each other as if to say, 'What does the fat bastard mean by that? Does he know what we are doing?' "

Americans had no conception in those last two years of the Batista dictatorship of the fierceness and viciousness with which the General was fighting back against the terrorism and the rising wave of revolutionary opposition.

Death for plotters was not only the normal rule; in cases like this torture always came first, since the police would want to extract whatever information they could get. It was going to be necessary to exercise the utmost discretion and to keep down to an absolute minimum those who knew anything about the venture.

The last place to get the slightest inkling of what was happening had to be the American Embassy, whose Ambassador, Arthur Gardner, was closely identified and very friendly with the dictator, President Fulgencio Batista. Except for Cuban Government circles and the American and Cuban business community, Gardner was hated by the Cubans. No word, therefore, was breathed about the project to him or to any member of the Embassy staff. In fact, the only foreigners who knew anything about the project were Ruby and Ted, until the story broke in *The Times*. The only Cubans let in on it were those who took an active part in organizing and carrying through the plan. Knowing Cubans as I did, it was a miracle that the secret was kept and the elaborate project carried off without a hitch.

On the journalistic side, this was an operation that had to be done by an outsider coming in to get the story and going out to write it. This eliminated Ruby and Ted, who were resident correspondents. By coincidence, I had written Ted telling him that my wife and I were going to Havana in a few weeks. I had been getting reports of considerable ferment and discontent, and was intrigued by the mystery of Fidel Castro, whose name kept cropping up in persistent reports that he was not dead, as the Government had announced and everybody seemed to believe.

Fidel had been a heroic figure, especially for the youth of Cuba, ever since the suicidal attack he had led on the Moncada Barracks in Santiago de Cuba on July 26, 1953. It was from this incident that the 26th of July Movement got its name.

A message from Ruby Phillips to Emanuel R. Freedman, our Foreign Editor, simply suggesting that I get to Havana as soon as possible, took me and Nancie down there in a few days. Ruby had had a talk in Felipe Pazos' office with René Rodríguez, who was attended by two fierce-looking bodyguards. Javier Pazos and Faustino Pérez, who was being hunted by the police, were also present.

The day after our arrival I had a meeting in the *Times* office with Felipe Pazos and his son. I asked Felipe in 1960 to give me his recollections of the whole incident. In connection with our first meeting he wrote:

"I remember your asking me whether I had met Fidel, whether I believed him alive and what did I think of the contention that Fidel had abandoned his men at Moncada, fleeing for his life. My answers were no to the first and third, and yes to the second. I remember telling you that I had been strongly inclined to believe in his death (in spite of the personal testimony of Faustino Pérez to the contrary: I thought him sworn with all the others to hide the truth) and that the first convincing indication I had had of his being alive, which I now believed, was the message that he wanted to see a foreign correspondent. With regard to the story of his betraying his men at Moncada, I told you that if he had done this, he would not have kept the fanatical loyalty that he seemed to inspire in his men.

"After that, I asked whether you would send for someone from New York, and you answered that you, yourself, would go. Without sufficient care not to show my surprise, I asked whether you were apt at mountain climbing, and you just repeated dryly, but softly, that you would go."

As if any newspaperman would pass up an opportunity like that! Felipe Pazos could not have known what makes a journalist tick. A newspaperman who will run a big risk for a mediocre story is a fool; one who will not run a big risk for a big story should go into the public relations business.

The account was picked up at this point by Javier Pazos, who likewise wrote me his recollections in 1960. A name comes in here which was not mentioned before—Liliam Mesa. The young, attractive Liliam, who comes from a well-to-do, upper class Havana family, was a fanatical member of the 26th of July Movement, typical of the young women who risked—and sometimes lost—their lives in the insurrection. The extent to which the women of Cuba were caught up in the passion of the rebellion was extraordinary, for like all Latin women they were brought up to sheltered, non-public and non-political lives. Liliam posed as Faustino's wife on our trip to Oriente Province. We knew them simply as "Luis" and "Marta."

"More or less coinciding with these events," Javier Pazos wrote, "another messenger had come from Manzanillo requesting Faustino's presence in the Sierra and giving the date on which the interview would take place, plus the necessary contacts in Manzanillo. For the first time since he had landed, due to the disposition of Batista's troops and the revolutionary organization of the Manzanillo zone, Fidel was in a position to hold a meeting with all the national leaders of the revolutionary movement. He thus wanted to use this opportunity for, besides seeing the foreign correspondent, a talk for the first time since he had landed with Frank País García, Faustino Pérez, Armando Hart, Vilma Espín and Haydée Santamaría, on questions concerning the general strategy of the movement.

"After I saw you, the coordination of everything else was very simple. Faustino had only to make sure that some arms we had just received were properly hidden and we would leave by car (Liliam Mesa, Faustino and I) starting from his hide-out, picking up you and your wife at the Sevilla Biltmore Hotel and continuing to Manzanillo. My presence was due, primarily, to the fact that Faustino wanted me to help him convince Fidel that a second front be opened in Las Villas province with the armament we had just received in La Habana. This was later discarded because of the more realistic necessity of re-enforcing Fidel's troop with everything the movement could afford. I must confess that within myself, I had doubts about Fidel's presence in the Sierra until we saw him."

Nancie and I had been told to stand by on Thursday and Friday—February 14 and 15. The precise time Javier called me at the office and told me to get ready in an hour was five thirty on Friday afternoon. The moment was fixed, when we looked back afterwards by my wife, who remembered that she had started to do her hair when I called and had to stop. From the beginning I had had the idea of taking Nancie along as "camouflage."

At the hotel I told them we were going on a fishing trip, and I had bought suitable clothes for such a purpose. At the office, Ruby told her two Cuban assistants that we were going to Santiago de Cuba for a few days to see what the situation was like at the other end of the island.

All I knew was that the rendezvous with Fidel Castro had been fixed for midnight the next night in the Sierra Maestra. I knew who Javier Pazos was, but aside from that I did not ask, nor did I want to know, the names of any of the Cubans who were risking their lives to take me to Fidel. It was not until after we started that I even knew our destination and jumping-off point in Oriente Province—Manzanillo.

Nancie wrote an account of the trip for *The New York Times* house organ for March, 1957—*Times Talk*. This is how it went from Havana to Manzanillo:

I should have remembered that most Cubans, however gloriously brave, are consistently unpunctual. It was almost ten o'clock that bright moonlight night before we started. The delay gave us our last chance for a pair of frozen daiquiris at the Floridita and some delicious Moro crab, a combination to stouten a timorous heart. My queasiness changed to excited anticipation.

I will call our young companions Juan [Javier Pacos] and Paco [Faustino Pérez]. Paco had brought his wife, Marta [Liliam Mesa], to do part of the driving. Marta and Juan sang an international repertoire of songs.

Herbert had told me that the utmost discretion was neces-sary, but in the sixteen hours our journey took we stopped so many times for thimblefuls of Cuban coffee that a long trail of people had every chance to examine us in detail. By 5 A.M. we were cold. I was hideously depressed.

As day broke we were well into Oriente Province and the sugar country. We decided to breakfast in a large town (Camaguey—there are about two million people in Oriente Province). Marta, driving, had no sense of direction. She circled the same handsome, pleasant policeman three times to ask him the way to a good hotel. That charming girl, I thought, is a dangerous wife for a revolutionary. Café au lait, fresh rolls and the warmth of the sun gave us all the lift we needed as we approached the Sierras and the troop road blocks we knew would come.

My heart missed a beat as a soldier stepped into the road and signaled us to stop, but he merely peered at us in friendly fashion. One look at the white chimney-pot hat put on to cover the wreck of my hair and we were waved on. "The absolute dope," I exclaimed, feeling almost let down. Juan shrugged. "Why should they care?"

We now ran parallel to the Sierra Maestra—a fine fertile country. At the next road block, soldiers were searching a car. Now, I thought, one examination of Herbert's passport marked "Journalist" and we will at least be turned back. But we were not stopped then or at any other patrol point. It was after 2 P.M. February 16, when we got *there* [Manzanillo]. For obvious reasons I cannot say where or what house, nor could Paco for a while. We circled and circled. Paco seemed to shrink into himself, speechless. He would point a finger in some direction, now and again, to the bewildered Marta. No one dared ask directions. I didn't know until later that Paco was one of the eighty-one youths who had landed with Fidel Castro in the yacht, Gramma, from Mexico on December 2.

I dare not give too many details, but after an agonizing hunt we located the preliminary rendezvous. We found ourselves surrounded by the kind of men and women you might meet

25

at any Cuban tea party. Incongruously, someone asked me in English if I wanted my dress pressed.

Our hosts in Manzanillo could not keep their names secret from us since they were known to everyone in town. They were Pedro and Ena Saumel, both teachers, and both typical of the middle-class intellectuals who made the Cuban Revolution as they have made all modern social revolutions since France in 1789.

There was an irritating wait of some hours at the Saumels' little house, where I was to leave Nancie overnight. It gave me a chance to rest and, being fifty-seven years old at the time and having been up all night in the drive from Havana, a rest was useful. Others from the 26th of July Movement were gathering in Manzanillo, some from Santiago de Cuba. They were intent on their own purposes and, in fact, most of them went off during the afternoon to join Fidel, leaving me behind. Javier was upset, fortunately for me. The young man who was to drive us to the foot of the mountains in his jeep, a resident of the neighborhood named Felipe Guerra Matos (Guerrita, he was called) was balky.

"I was very disturbed with the organization of the whole thing in Manzanillo," Javier wrote in his letter to me, "and being very conscious of the importance of your seeing Fidel, thought the merry way in which everybody else went in on the first trip leaving us in Manzanillo quite irresponsible. Later when Guerrita arrived he called me apart to tell me we had to wait till the next day because army patrols had been stationed in the road we had to take. I had a discussion with him telling him that I didn't care how we got there, but that I knew the only excuse Fidel would accept for our not going on that day was our getting killed trying. Finally, he unwillingly agreed to take us. The other thing that had me upset, was the presence of René Rodríguez and Liliam, with whom I must agree I acted very harshly, stopping her from going. I didn't want you to get the impression that it was a country fair; as things go, next day she was right up there with us."

We got off at about seven o'clock in the evening of February 16 and I was back at the Saumels' house about five o'clock the next afternoon.

This is the story, complete and word for word, that I wrote for *The Times*. It appeared on Sunday, February 24, 1957, as the first of three articles on the Cuban situation.

Fidel Castro, the rebel leader of Cuba's youth, is alive and fighting hard and successfully in the rugged, almost impenetrable fastnesses of the Sierra Maestra, at the southern tip of the island.

President Fulgencio Batista has the cream of his Army around the area, but the Army men are fighting a thus-far losing battle to destroy the most dangerous enemy General Batista has yet faced in a long and adventurous career as a Cuban leader and dictator.

This is the first sure news that Fidel Castro is still alive and still in Cuba. No one connected with the outside world, let alone with the press, has seen Señor Castro except this writer. No one in Havana, not even at the United States Embassy with all its resources for getting information, will know until this report is published that Fidel Castro is really in the Sierra Maestra.

This account, among other things, will break the tightest censorship in the history of the Cuban Republic. The Province of Oriente, with its 2,000,000 inhabitants, its flourishing cities such as Santiago, Holguin and Manzanillo, is shut off from Havana as surely as if it were another country. Havana does not and cannot know that thousands of men and women are heart and soul with Fidel Castro and the new deal for which they think he stands. It does not know that hundreds of highly respected citizens are helping Señor Castro, that bombs and sabotage are constant (eighteen bombs were exploded in Santiago on February 15), that a fierce Government counter-terrorism has aroused the people even more against President Batista.

Throughout Cuba a formidable movement of opposition to General Batista has been developing. It has by no means reached an explosive point. The rebels in the Sierra Maestra cannot move out. The economic situation is good. President Batista has the high officers of the Army and the police behind him and he ought to be able to hang on for the nearly two years of his present term that are still left.

However, there are bad spots in the economy, especially on the fiscal side. Unemployment is heavy; corruption is rife. No one can predict anything with safety except that Cuba seems in for a very troubled period.

Fidel Castro and his 26th of July Movement are the flaming symbol of the opposition to the regime. The organization, which is apart from the university students' opposition, is formed of youths of all kinds. It is a revolutionary movement that calls itself socialistic. It is also nationalistic, which generally in Latin America means anti-Yankee.

The program is vague and couched in generalities, but it amounts to a new deal for Cuba, radical, democratic and therefore anti-Communist. The real core of its strength is that it is fighting against the military dictatorship of President Batista.

To arrange for me to penetrate the Sierra Maestra and meet

28

Fidel Castro, dozens of men and women in Havana and Oriente Province ran a truly terrible risk. They must, of course, be protected with the utmost care in these articles for their lives would be forfeit—after the customary torture—immediately if any could be traced. Consequently, no names are used here, the places are disguised and many details of the elaborate and dangerous trail in and out of the Sierra Maestra must be omitted.

From the looks of things, General Batista cannot possibly hope to suppress the Castro revolt. His only hope is that an Army column will come upon the young rebel leader and his staff and wipe them out. This is hardly likely to happen, if at all, before March 1, when the present suspension of constitutional guarantees is supposed to end.

Fidel Castro is the son of a Spaniard from Galicia, a "Gallego" like Generalissimo Francisco Franco. The father was a pick-and-shovel laborer early in this century for the United Fruit Company, whose sugar plantations are on the northern shores of Oriente Province. A powerful build, a capacity for hard work and a shrewd mind led the father up in the world until he became a rich sugar planter himself. When he died last year each of his children, including Fidel, inherited a sizable fortune.

Someone who knew the family remembers Fidel as a child of four or five years living a sturdy farm life. The father sent him to school and to the University of Havana, where he studied law and became one of the student opposition leaders who rebelled against General Batista in 1952 because the General had staged a garrison revolt and prevented the Presidential elections of that year.

Fidel had to flee from Cuba in 1954 and he lived for a while in New York and Miami. The year 1956, he announced, was to be the "year of decision." Before the year ended, he said, he would be "a hero or a martyr."

The Government knew that he had gone to Mexico and,

last summer, was training a body of youths who had left Cuba to join him. As the end of the year approached the Cuban Army was very much on the alert, knowing that something would be tried and that Fidel Castro was coming back. He was already, in a measure, a hero of the Cuban youth, for on July 26, 1953, he had led a band of youths in a desperate attack on the Moncada Barracks in Santiago de Cuba.

In the fighting then about 100 students and soldiers were killed, but the revolt failed. The Archbishop of Santiago, Monseñor Enrique Pérez Serantes, intervened to minimize the bloodshed and got Señor Castro and others to surrender on promises of a fair trial. Fidel Castro was sentenced to fifteen years in prison but there was an amnesty at the time of the Presidential elections of November 1, 1954, and he was let out. It was then he crossed to the continent and began to organize the 26th of July Movement. It is under this banner that the youth of Cuba are now fighting the Batista regime.

The blow, which at the time seemed an utter failure, was struck on December 2, 1956. That day a 62-foot diesel-engined yacht, the Gramma, landed eighty-two young men, trained for two months on a ranch in Mexico, on the Oriente shore below Niquero at a spot called Playa Olorado. The idea had been to land at Niquero, recruit followers and lead an open attack against the Government. However, the Gramma had been spotted by a Cuban naval patrol boat. Planes flew in to strafe and the men on the yacht decided to beach her.

Playa Olorado, unhappily for the invaders, was a treacherous swamp. The men lost their food and most of their arms and supplies and soon were being attacked by army units. They scattered and took to the hills. Many were killed. Of the eighty-two no more than fifteen or twenty were left after a few days.

President Batista and his aides were remarkably successful from then on in hiding what happened. The youths they captured were forced to sign statements saying that they had been told Fidel Castro was on the Gramma with them but that they had never seen him. Thus doubt was cast that he had ever come to Cuba.

Because of the complete censorship, Havana and the other Cuban cities crackle with the most astonishing rumors; one constantly encouraged by the Government has been that Fidel Castro is dead. Only those fighting with him and those who had faith and hope knew or thought he was alive—and those who knew were very few and in the utmost peril of their lives if their knowledge was traced.

This was the situation when the writer got to Havana on February 9 to try to find out what was really happening. The censorship has been applied to foreign correspondents as well as Cuban. What everybody, even those who wanted to believe, kept asking was: "If Fidel is alive, why does he not do or say something to show that he is?" Since December 2 he had kept absolutely quiet—or he was dead.

As I learned later, Señor Castro was waiting until he had his forces reorganized and strengthened and had mastery of the Sierra Maestra. This fortunately coincided with my arrival and he had sent word out to a trusted source in Havana that he wanted a foreign correspondent to come in. The contact knew as soon as I arrived and got in touch with me. Because of the state of siege, it had to be someone who would get the story and go out of Cuba to write it.

Then came a week of organization. A rendezvous point and a time had to be fixed and arrangements made to get through the Government lines into the Sierra Maestra.

After the first few weeks the Army had given out the report that the remnants of Señor Castro's forces were being starved out in the Sierra. In reality the Army had ringed the Sierra with fortified posts and columns of troops and had every road under heavy guard. The reports reaching Havana that frequent clashes were taking place and that the Government troops were losing heavily proved true.

31

By verifying that Castro was Alive And in Cuba, Matthews overcame the Batista government's attempts To censure Castro's voice and leave doubt that he was in Cuba. This was the Time's true contribution To the Revolution.

The first problem was to get through the Government road blocks and reach a nearby town that would be a jumping off place. Late on the afternoon of Friday, February 15, Señor Castro's contact man got in touch with me in Havana with the news that the meeting was set for the following night in the Sierra and that Señor Castro and his staff would take the chance of coming a little way toward the edge of the range so that I would not have to do too much climbing. There are no roads there, and where we were to meet, no horses could go.

To get from Havana to Oriente (more than 500 miles away) on time meant driving all night and the next morning, so as to be ready Saturday afternoon to start for the Sierra.

The plan worked out to get through the Army's road blocks in Oriente was as simple as it was effective. We took my wife along in the car as "camouflage." Cuba is at the height of the tourist season and nothing could have looked more innocent than a middle-aged couple of American tourists driving down to Cuba's most beautiful and fertile province with some young friends. The guards would take one look at my wife, hesitate a second, and wave us on with friendly smiles. If we were to be questioned a story was prepared for them. If we were searched the jig would be up.

In that way we reached the house of a sympathizer of Señor Castro outside the Sierra. There my wife was to stay amid warm hospitality, and no questions asked. I got into the clothes I had purchased in Havana "for a fishing trip," warm for the cold night air of the mountains and dark for camouflage.

After nightfall I was taken to a certain house where three youths who were going in with me had gathered. One of them was "One of the Eighty-two," a proud phrase for the survivors of the original landing. I was to meet five or six of them. A courier who owned an open Army-type jeep, joined us.

His news was bad. A Government patrol of four soldiers in

a jeep had placed itself on the very road we had to take to get near the point where we were to meet the Castro scouts at midnight. Moreover, there had been a heavy rain in the Sierra in the afternoon and the road was a morass. The others impressed on him that Fidel Castro wanted me in there at all costs and somehow it had to be done.

The courier agreed reluctantly. All across the plain of Oriente Province there are flat lands with sugar and rice plantations, and such farms have innumerable dirt roads. The courier knew every inch of the terrain and figured that by taking a very circuitous route he could bring us close enough.

We had to go through one Army road block and beyond that would be the constant risk of Army patrols, so we had to have a good story ready. I was to be an American sugar planter who could not speak a word of Spanish and who was going out to look over a plantation in a certain village. One of the youths, who spoke English, was my "interpreter." The others made up similar fictions.

Before leaving one of the men showed me a wad of bills (the Cuban peso is exactly the same size and value as the United States dollar) amounting, apparently, to 400 pesos, which was being sent in to Señor Castro. With a "rich" American planter it would be natural for the group to have the money if we were searched. It was interesting evidence that Fidel Castro paid for everything he took from the guajiros, or squatter farmers, of the Sierra.

This was contradicted in later reports

Our story convinced the Army guard when he stopped us, although he looked dubious for a little while. Then came hours of driving, through sugar-cane and rice fields, across rivers that only jeeps could manage. One stretch, the courier said, was heavily patrolled by Government troops but we were lucky and saw none. Finally, after slithering through miles of mud we could go no farther.

It was then midnight, the time we were to meet Castro's scouts; but we had to walk some first and it was hard going.

33

At last we turned off the road and slid down a hillside to where a stream, dark brown under the nearly full moon, rushed its muddy way. One of the boys slipped and fell full length into the icy cold water. I waded through with the water almost to my knees and that was hard enough to do without falling. Fifty yards up the other slope was the meeting point.

The patrol was not there. Three of us waited while two of the men went back to see if we had missed the scouts somewhere, but in fifteen minutes they returned frustrated. The courier suggested that we might move up a bit and he led us ahead, but obviously did not know where to go. Señor Castro's men have a characteristic signal that I was to hear incessantly—two low, soft, toneless whistles. One of our men kept trying it, but with no success.

After a while we gave up. We had kept under cover at all times, for the moonlight was strong, and we knew there were troops around us.

We stopped in a heavy clump of trees and bushes, dripping from the rain, the ground underfoot heavily matted, muddy and soaked. There we sat for a whispered confab. The courier, and another youth who had fought previously with Castro, said they would go up the mountainside and see if they could find any of the rebel troops.

Three of us were to wait, a rather agonizing wait of more than two hours, crouched in the mud, not daring to talk or move, trying to snatch a little sleep with our heads on our knees and annoyed maddeningly by the swarms of mosquitoes that were having the feast of their lives.

At last we heard a cautious, welcome double-whistle. One of us replied in kind and this had to be kept up for a while, like two groups meeting in a dense fog, until we got together. One of our party had found an advance patrol and a scout came with him to lead us to an outpost in the mountains.

The scout was a squatter from the hills, and he needed to know every inch of the land to take us as he did, swiftly and

34

unerringly across fields, up steep hills, floundering in the mud. The ground leveled out blessedly at last and then dipped suddenly. The scout stopped and whistled cautiously. The return whistle came. There was a short parley and we were motioned on, sliding down into a heavy grove. The dripping leaves and boughs, the dense vegetation, the mud underfoot, the moonlight—all gave the impression of a tropical forest, more like Brazil than Cuba.

Señor Castro was encamped some distance away and a soldier went to announce our arrival and ask whether he would join us or we should join him. Later he came back with the grateful news that we were to wait and Fidel would come along with the dawn. Someone gave me a few soda crackers, which tasted good. Someone else stretched a blanket on the ground and it seemed a great luxury. It was too dark in the grove to see anything.

We spoke in the lowest possible whispers. One man told me how he had seen his brother's store wrecked and burned by Government troops and his brother dragged out and executed. "I'd rather be here fighting for Fidel, than anywhere in the world now," he said.

There were two hours before dawn, and the blanket made it possible to sleep.

With the light I could see how young they all were. Señor Castro, according to his followers, is thirty, and that is old for the 26th of July Movement. It has a motley array of arms and uniforms, and even a few civilian suits. The rifles and the one machine gun I saw were all American—discarded models. The captain of this troop was a stocky Negro with a black beard and mustache, a ready brilliant smile and a willingness for publicity. Of all I met, only he wanted his name mentioned—Juan Ameda [Almeida], "One of the Eighty-two."

Several of the youths had lived in the United States and spoke English; others had learned it at school. One had been

35

The only Afro-Cuban in Castro's army.

a professional baseball player in a minor league and his wife is still in the United States.

The part of the Sierra we were in grows no food. "Sometimes we eat; sometimes not," one rebel said. On the whole they obviously keep healthy. Supporters send in food; the farmers help, trusted couriers go out and buy supplies, which the storekeepers sell them at great risk and against Government orders.

Raul Castro, Fidel's younger brother, slight and pleasant, came into the camp with others of the staff, and a few minutes later Fidel himself strode in. Taking him, as one would at first, by physique and personality, this was quite a man—a powerful six-footer, olive-skinned, full-faced, with a straggly beard. He was dressed in an olive gray fatigue uniform and carried a rifle with a telescopic sight, of which he was very proud. It seems his men have something more than fifty of these and he said the soldiers feared them.

"We can pick them off at a thousand yards with these guns," he said.

After some general conversation we went to my blanket and sat down. Someone brought tomato juice, ham sandwiches made with crackers and tins of coffee. In honor of the occasion, Señor Castro broke open a box of good Havana cigars and for the next three hours we sat there while he talked.

No one could talk above a whisper at any time. There were columns of Government troops all around us, Señor Castro said, and their one hope was to catch him and his band.

The personality of the man is overpowering. It was easy to see that his men adored him and also to see why he has caught the imagination of the youth of Cuba all over the island. Here was an educated, dedicated fanatic, a man of ideals, of courage and of remarkable qualities of leadership.

As the story unfolded of how he had at first gathered the few remnants of the Eighty-two around him; kept the Government troops at bay while youths came in from other parts of

Oriente as General Batista's counter-terrorism aroused them; got arms and supplies and then began the series of raids and counter-attacks of guerrilla warfare, one got a feeling that he is now invincible. Perhaps he isn't, but that is the faith he inspires in his followers.

They have had many fights, and inflicted many losses, Señor Castro said. Government planes came over and bombed every day; in fact, at nine sharp a plane did fly over. The troops took up positions; a man in a white shirt was hastily covered up. But the plane went on to bomb higher in the mountains.

Castro is a great talker. His brown eyes flash; his intense face is pushed close to the listener and the whispering voice, as in a stage play, lends a vivid sense of drama.

"We have been fighting for seventy-nine days now and are stronger than ever," Señor Castro said. "The soldiers are fighting badly; their morale is low and ours could not be higher. We are killing many, but when we take prisoners they are never shot. We question them, talk kindly to them, take their arms and equipment, and then set them free.

"I know that they are always arrested afterward and we heard some were shot as examples to the others, but they don't want to fight, and they don't know how to fight this kind of mountain warfare. We do.

"The Cuban people hear on the radio all about Algeria, but they never hear a word about us or read a word, thanks to the censorship. You will be the first to tell them. I have followers all over the island. All the best elements, especially all the youth, are with us. The Cuban people will stand anything but oppression."

I asked him about the report that he was going to declare a revolutionary government in the Sierra.

"Not yet," he replied. "The time is not ripe. I will make myself known at the opportune moment. It will have all the more effect for the delay, for now everybody is talking about us. We are sure of ourselves.

"There is no hurry. Cuba is in a state of war but Batista is hiding it. A dictatorship must show that it is omnipotent or it will fall; we are showing that it is impotent."

The Government, he said with some bitterness, is using arms furnished by the United States, not only against him but "against all the Cuban people."

"They have bazookas, mortars, machine guns, planes and bombs," he said, "but we are safe in here in the Sierra; they must come and get us and they cannot."

Señor Castro speaks some English, but he preferred to speak in Spanish, which he did with extraordinary eloquence. His is a political mind rather than a military one. He has strong ideas of liberty, democracy, social justice, the need to restore the Constitution, to hold elections. He has strong ideas on economy too, but an economist would consider them weak.

The 26th of July Movement talks of nationalism, anti-colonialism, anti-imperialism. I asked Señor Castro about that. He answered, "You can be sure we have no animosity toward the United States and the American people."

"Above all," he said, "we are fighting for a democratic Cuba and an end to the dictatorship. We are not anti-military; that is why we let the soldier prisoners go. There is no hatred of the Army as such, for we know the men are good and so are many of the officers.

"Batista has 3,000 men in the field against us. I will not tell you how many we have, for obvious reasons. He works in columns of 200; we in groups of ten to forty, and we are winning. It is a battle against time and time is on our side."

To show that he deals fairly with the guajiros he asked someone to bring "the cash." A soldier brought a bundle wrapped in dark brown cloth, which Señor Castro unrolled. There was a stack of peso bills at least a foot high—about $4,000 he said, adding that he had all the money he needed and could get more.

38

"Why should soldiers die for Batista for $72 a month?" he asked. "When we win we will give them $100 a month, and they will serve a free, democratic Cuba."

"I am always in the front line," he said; and others confirmed this fact. Such being the case, the Army might yet get him, but in present circumstances he seems almost invulnerable.

"They never know where we are," he said as the group arose to say good-by, "but we always know where they are. You have taken quite a risk in coming here, but we have the whole area covered, and we will get you out safely."

They did. We ploughed our way back through the muddy undergrowth in broad daylight, but always keeping under cover. The scout went like a homing pigeon through woods and across fields where there were no paths straight to a farmer's house on the edge of the Sierra. There we hid in a back room while someone borrowed a horse and went for the jeep, which had been under cover all night.

There was one road block to get through with an Army guard so suspicious our hearts sank, but he let us through.

After that, washed, shaved, and looking once more like an American tourist, with my wife as "camouflage," we had no trouble driving back through the road blocks to safety and then on to Havana. So far as anyone knew, we had been away fishing for the week-end, and no one bothered us as we took the plane to New York.

In this interview were all the elements out of which the insurrection grew to its ultimate triumph. So was the true figure of Fidel Castro, before power taught him realism and worked its intoxicating spiritual corruption, before the ideals of democracy and freedom presented themselves as impossibilities if he was to make a drastic social revolution. The essence of the social revolution was there on February 17, 1957, in the words of a hunted youth in the heart of the jungle fastnesses of Cuba's Sierra Maestra. History was speaking, and it will be for history to say whether, by and large, he betrayed the grandiose ideal for which he was fighting.

The true idealism of the revolution was certainly there on that day. It gave Fidel and his men faith. It won the hearts and souls and the allegiance through torture and death of uncounted thousands of Cuban men and women throughout the island. Some of it—even much of it—remains in this late summer of 1961 as the heart and the appeal of the Cuban Revolution. But so much was lost!

I could not claim, myself, at the time to have had any idea of the terrific impact my story was going to have, or the chain reaction it was going to set up in the whole Western Hemisphere. I knew I had a sensational scoop. I exulted at the fact that at the age of fifty-seven I could still show a younger generation of newspapermen how to get a difficult and dangerous story, and how to write it. And I was moved, deeply moved, by that young man.

Anyone who thinks that Fidel Castro did not passionately believe every word he said to me would completely fail to understand him. As I learned in the course of time, one could say of Fidel what a contemporary said of Robespierre: "That young man will go far; he believes every word he says."

It was true that Fidel then had "strong ideas of liberty, democracy and social justice, the need to restore the Constitution [of 1940], to hold elections." It was also true, as I said, that he was leading "a revolutionary movement that calls itself socialistic." These were not necessarily incompatible, as the European Socialist movements have proved.

I had taken a minimum of notes in the Sierra—about six pages—which I still have. Among the phrases I did not use textually were these: "He inspires confidence . . . a born leader . . . an enormous faith and confidence."

Fidel had said of the civic resistance: "Outside of the Sierra we have a support in high social and business circles that would be startling if the names could be given." This was true—and these are the men and women now in exile in Miami or in the Cuban underground.

At one point I jotted down: "How young!" I little realized the importance of that ejaculation.

For the historic record, a few minor errors in the *Times* story should be noted. It was not true that the Archbishop of Santiago de Cuba, Monseñor Enrique Pérez Serantes, saved Fidel's life. This is a myth that still persists. Orders had been given to kill Fidel on sight when captured after the 26th of July attack. The man who caught him, Lieut. Pedro Sarría, disobeyed orders and brought Fidel in alive.

I overestimated the size of Fidel's forces in the Sierra Maestra at the time. When asked, I said I had seen about twenty-five rebels and knew there were others nearby— perhaps forty in all. This was correct, but I was wrong to think the group I saw was a part of a large force. As Fidel revealed in a speech to the Overseas Press Club in New York in April, 1959, he had only eighteen men under arms at that time. The number I saw was swelled by those from the 26th of July Movement who had come in with me.

My story, in fact, came at the ebb tide of the flood that was to lead Fidel on to fortune.

41

Fidel and his men had done more than come down "a little way toward the edge of the range," as I wrote. They had come a long way—from Pico Turquino—and, as those who went up later to see him discovered, it took about two days of walking and climbing, not three hours, to reach him.

He had, in fact, put himself well into the region controlled by Batista's troops, taking a really great risk to contact me. The whispering was not histrionics; it was a necessity. Fidel told me years later in Havana that they did not wait a minute after I left to dash back toward the mountain tops and they heard they had narrowly escaped an ambush.

My estimate that the rebels had "something more than" fifty telescopic rifles was way off the mark. At all times in the next two years the size of Fidel's forces was greatly exaggerated. He neither needed nor wanted large fighting forces. The technique he used was explained so well after the victory by Che Guevara in his *La Guerra de Guerrillas (Guerrilla Warfare)* that the book is now used as a text by the United States Special Forces units.

Finally, I would never again call Raul Castro "pleasant."

Having got the story, I had to get it out. Javier Pazos went back with me to Manzanillo where the Saumels gave me something to eat and Pedro drove us at top speed to Santiago de Cuba. There was one scare when a soldier stopped us and looked us over too suspiciously, but by then we were in our guise of middle-aged American tourists.

In Santiago, there was just time for a hasty snack at the

home of a woman teacher, Señora Caridad Pérez Cisneros
—who was efficient, kind and brave. She had arranged for
three professors from the University of Oriente to join us.
I mention this because all were members of the 26th of
July Movement and one of the professors happened to be
Regino Boti, who has been and still is, Fidel's Minister of
National Economy. The civic resistance was impressive
as early as that, which helps to explain why I gave so much
importance to it in my account.

We took the direct flight that night to Havana, Javier
traveling with us as our son, "Albert." In Havana, Ruby
and Ted tried hard to get us to leave immediately, for we
were sitting on a keg of dynamite and if anyone had
talked, it would have gone hard with us.

However, I had some loose ends to tie together, especially
the secret rendezvous with leaders of the Student University Federation (FEU), whom I had promised to see.
That meeting also, in its way, proved historic because the
President of the FEU was none other than José Antonio
Echevarría who was to die gloriously in the brave and
almost successful March 13 attack on the Presidential
Palace in Havana. The students told me they had a plan
which would put a definitive end to the dictatorship.

I was taken to the rendezvous by Gonzalo de Varona.
The other three present were Victor Bravo, José Luis
Gómez Wanguemert and Fauré Chomón. Gómez was also
killed in the March 13 attack on the Palace. Fauré Chomón
(the original family name was Chaumont) became a
leader of the Directorio Revolucionario, which opened a
fighting front in the Sierra de Escambray, and he is now

the Cuban Ambassador to Moscow. Fauré was badly wounded in the assault of March 13.

José Antonio was right when he said to me that day: "Cuban students were never afraid to die."

That night we went out to visit the Hemingways at the Finca Vigía in San Francisco de Paula.

We were to fly back to New York on Tuesday morning, February 19. The customs inspection at the airport would be our last hurdle. Papers were sometimes examined and we could not know whether our secret had been kept. The pages of notes from the Sierra Maestra and on the meeting with the students were dangerously revealing, especially as Fidel had signed and dated my notes.

"Let me carry them," Nancie said that morning. She put them inside her girdle and, when we were well out of Havana, retired to the lavatory and extracted them.

I started working on the plane. The series was held up until Sunday, February 24, in order to give the Promotion Department time to advertise the articles and to give play to the interview. Our Sunday circulation is twice that of the daily.

In 1960, when the attacks on me reached a high pitch, William Buckley's reactionary *National Review* printed a clever cartoon. It showed a happy-looking Fidel Castro, sitting on a map of Cuba. Underneath was our famous advertising slogan:

"I got my job through *The New York Times*."

CHAPTER TWO

The Insurrection

THERE IS NO thrill in journalism like getting a scoop, and this was the biggest scoop of our times. Professionally speaking, no one can ever take that away from me. No one could even try, because it was more than two months before anyone else could get in to see Fidel Castro and three months before the public had incontestable proof that what I had written was true. This was when Robert Taber and Wendell Hoffman of the Columbia Broadcasting System televised a filmed interview with Fidel that was presented on May 19, 1957.

The first reactions to my interview were outraged official denials in Havana. Unfortunately for Batista, he had hired a former CBS executive, Edmund Chester, as public relations counsel in 1953. Chester generally managed to do Batista more harm than good, and this time he surpassed himself. Like the others, he was convinced that Fidel was dead. It followed that my interview was a fake. So Chester drew up a statement that was put out by the Minister of National Defense, Santiago Verdeja, on February 27, the day after my series of three articles was completed.

We published the text of Santiago Verdeja's denial in *The Times* on February 28, along with my reply and a photograph of me and Fidel in the Sierra Maestra. Fidel was lighting a cigar and I was making notes. The statement read:

The Minister of National Defense, Santiago Verdeja Neyra, replied to a cable sent by the New York *Herald Tribune* to the Chief of State requesting some clarification upon the report of Matthews in relation with a supposed interview with the pro-Communist insurgent Fidel Castro.

The President has handed to this Ministry the cable for reply and the Minister makes the following statement:

Before anything else, let me assure you that the opinion of the Government, and I am sure, of the Cuban public also, is that the interview and the adventures described by Correspondent Matthews can be considered as a chapter in a fantastic novel. Mr. Matthews has not interviewed the pro-Communist insurgent, Fidel Castro, and the information came from certain opposition sources.

It is noted that Matthews published a photograph saying that it was of Castro. It seems strange that, having had an opportunity to penetrate the mountains and having had such an interview, Matthews did not have a photograph taken of himself with the pro-Communist insurgent in order to provide proof of what he wrote.

The Government does not know whether Fidel Castro is alive or dead, but if he is alive, the Government takes the full responsibility for stating that no such supporting forces as Matthews describes actually exist and, with the same responsibility, the Government reiterates that at no time did the said correspondent have an interview with the individual to whom he ascribes so much force and so many non-existent followers.

Even the political opposition to the [Batista] regime, in almost its entirety, repudiates the methods followed by the pro-Communist Castro and at no time has he been able to build a popular organization to win public support for his unsuccessful terroristic attempts.

As to the poor economy to which the reporter refers, I assure you that never in history has the nation's economy been sounder or more efficiently administered. It was precisely for the purpose of eliminating malfeasance and clearing up the Administration, as well as reconstructing the economy of Cuba, that the revolution of March 10, 1952, was carried out against those who afterwards furnished money, arms and war materials, to be used against the nation and against the people of Cuba.

The Times followed this with my reply:

The story about Fidel Castro surely speaks for itself. It is hard to believe that anyone reading it can have any doubts.

So far as the photographs are concerned, there is one of Fidel Castro and myself which was not clear enough for good newspaper reproduction but which is very clear to the eye on a glossy print.

[The picture which showed me and Fidel Castro was reproduced on the same page of *The Times*.]

Knowing the doubts that would be cast on my story, I also took the precaution to get Fidel Castro to sign his name on a sheet of paper that I had, giving the place, "Sierra Maestra," and the date, February 17. This was reproduced in the final editions of *The New York Times* on Sunday. This edition does not go to Cuba, which gets an early airplane edition. Appar-

47

ently the Minister of Defense did not see it and did not realize
the extent to which he had made himself incredible.

The truth will always out, censorship or no censorship.

The next day, General Martín Díaz Tamayo, military
commander of Oriente Province, whose troops were hunt-
ing for Fidel and his rebel group, also issued a statement
denying that the interview could possibly have taken
place:

Statements of that North American newspaperman are
totally untrue due to the physical impossibility of entering the
zone in which the imaginary interview took place. No one can
enter the zone without being seen. In my opinion this gentle-
man was never even in Cuba. Someone furnished the imaginary information and then his imagination did the rest. It is
totally impossible to cross the lines where there are troops
and it is foolishness to pretend that a sentry would let anyone
pass against the orders which he has received. This interview
is prefabricated with the purpose of aiding the psychological
war which is going on in the country. I do not know where
we will go if we listen to *bolas* (rumors) of this type which the
public have named "radio bombs." With regard to Fidel
Castro, I must refer to what the President of the Republic said,
that is, he may or may not be here. Up to date, no one knows
for certain. If we have captured so many men, is it that Fidel
will be the last one?

Chester was confirmed in his disbelief by the fact that
President Batista himself did not believe my story. In
the memoirs the General wrote in exile, entitled *Respuesta*
(Reply), published in Mexico in 1960, he had this para-
graph:

In this atmosphere of doubt, the newspaperman Herbert Mathews (sic), of *The New York Times,* published an interview held with Fidel Castro and, to confirm it, inserted a photograph which, because of the darkness caused by the foliage, was not very clear. The military commanders of the province affirmed with such emphasis to the High Command that such an interview had not taken place, that the Minister of Defense made a public statement denying the existence of this event and I, myself, influenced by the statements of the High Command, doubted its authenticity. The interview, in effect, had taken place and its publication gave considerable propaganda and support to the rebel group. Castro was to begin to be a legendary personage and would end by being a monster of terror.

"Ed Chester, of course, is fit to be tied," Ted Scott of the Havana *Post* wrote me. "He had told Ambassador Gardner that Castro was killed and buried on December 9, which was a week after McCarthy's United Press despatch reporting Castro's death. . . . Yesterday I was told that Ambassador Gardner is simply furious with you and *The Times* and that he will get into the act today with some kind of statement. He is being pressed by the [Cuban] Government to make a statement and probably will do so."

Mr. Gardner, fortunately for him, did not issue any statement, as it would have made him look as foolish as the others. The Castro interview came as a complete surprise to him and everyone else at the American Embassy.

It was therefore incredible and inexplicable to me that long afterwards, on August 27, 1960, Arthur Gardner should have testified under oath before the Senate Internal Security Subcommittee that I had gone to him in advance and asked his help to get up to see Fidel. He had then, said Gardner, got General Batista to help arrange the trip on a promise from me that on my return I would report back to the Ambassador on what I had found.

For the historic record, and because my reputation for never writing anything that is not true—or to the best of my knowledge true—is sacred to me, I am recording here in black and white that every word Arthur Gardner said before the Subcommittee on this subject was false.

It is amusing and ironical to look back now on the enthusiastic flood of praise and—on the Cuban side—joy that was heaped upon me after my articles on Cuba appeared. The tide of letters and telegrams that kept coming in for months had no precedent in my career or in anything I had heard. I would say the proportion of enthusiastic support to criticism was about fifty to one. Because the photograph of Fidel and me showed us both smoking cigars I was inundated with enough Havana cigars by grateful, and to me anonymous, Cubans to last a year and a half.

Cubans and Americans wrote poems in my praise. The Sevilla Biltmore Hotel in Havana, where we always stayed, put a page advertisement in a magazine as late as February, 1960, proudly announcing that: *"En este Gran Hotel se hospedó* HERBERT MATTHEWS, *el eminentísimo Periodista Americano."* (In this Grand Hotel, Herbert Matthews, the eminent American journalist stayed.)

When I went back to Cuba for a visit in June, 1957, I learned in Havana and Santiago de Cuba what it was like to be a famous Hollywood actor. It was excruciatingly embarrassing, as a matter of fact.

History, like life, has its little ironies. The very Cubans who were most grateful and enthusiastic—the middle-class elements of the civic resistance—are now the most violent in their criticisms. The humble people who thanked me then are still thankful.

The history of the revolution was shaping up in this period of gestation. No one could know what form it would take—no one, not Fidel Castro, not the civic resistance and, of course, not Fulgencio Batista. So far as the President was concerned, Fidel was "an agent of the Soviet Union" and his followers were Communists.

The accusation was false, but it is another irony that Batista now says: "I told you so," and many ill-informed Americans will go on believing to their dying day it was all a Communist plot.

Professor Juan Marinello, head of the Communist *Partido Socialista Popular,* wrote me a letter at this time explaining the official party line. His letter was written on March 17, 1957, four days after the students had made their heroic and almost successful assault on the Presidential Palace in Havana.

"In these days," wrote Marinello (in my translation), "and with reference to the assaults on barracks and expeditions from abroad—taking place without relying on popular support—our position is very clear; we are against these methods."

He went on to say that it was not necessary to make

"a popular insurrection" and that what Cuba needed was "democratic elections."

"Our posture with regard to the 26th of July Movement," he went on, "is based on these criteria. We think that this Group has noble aims but that, in general, it is following mistaken tactics. For that reason we do not approve of its actions, but we call on all parties and popular sectors to defend it against the blows of tyranny, not forgetting that the members of this Movement fight against a Government hated by the entire people of Cuba."

What the Communists wanted, said Dr. Marinello, was "a government of a Democratic Front of National Liberation."

This was, and this remained, the party line until the autumn of 1958, when the Cuban Reds saw that Fidel and the 26th of July Movement were certain to win. They then sent their shrewdest brain, Rafael Rodríguez, a newspaperman, up to the Sierra Maestra to join the rebels. They never helped Fidel. On the contrary, in the crucial attempt at a general strike on April 9, 1958, they stood by General Batista. At no time did they embarrass the Batista regime, and in all the brutal counter-terrorism that the Dictator carried out the Communists were spared. Very few Reds were among the many thousands of political prisoners in jail.

General Batista was playing the same old game that all dictators play so successfully with the United States. They claim to be—and sometimes even are—anti-Communist, and this will generally get them tolerance, if not support, from American interests. In reality, dictators pave the way for the Communists, and if Cuba has not taught the United States that lesson we will never learn it. The only sure protection against the Communists is democracy.

Batista had been sitting on a lid ever since he seized power by his garrison revolt in 1952. It was easy for a while, but by the time Fidel Castro made his apparently disastrous landing at the end of 1956, a heavy ground swell of discontent had built up. It was widespread, popular and bourgeois in content, as well as youthful and revolutionary.

What it needed was a symbol of hope, a rallying point, a leader. Fidel Castro provided all this. He had it in him. Nothing could have stopped him at that time. He was Cuba's man of destiny. All I did was recognize these facts. By my interview I turned the spotlight on him. He has held the center of the stage ever since, but that was where he belonged. The Muse of History wrote that play, not I.

Batista, naturally, could not see this, nor could he see how unpopular—in fact, how hated—he was. It is notorious that a dictator who is settled in power and who has surrounded himself with self-seekers and sycophants does not know what is really happening in his own country. Above all, he loses touch with the masses. No one dares to tell him the truth. He is told what he wants to hear. He deludes himself and is deluded by those around him. Unpleasant truths are rejected as lies or the product of ignorance. Opponents are criminals, Communists, paid agents.

(This, alas, is what has happened to Fidel Castro, although his opponents are "counter-revolutionaries and agents of Yankee imperialism.")

The Cuban Revolution came out of the past. On March 10, 1952, which was close to the fiftieth anniversary of the formal birth of the Cuban Republic, Major General Fulgencio Batista turned the clock back with his garrison revolt. Between 1902 and 1906 Cuba had her first President and her only honest one—Tomás Estrada Palma. He was driven out in the so-called "Revolution of August," 1906, because a lot of politicians wanted to get jobs and, above all, loot the treasury of the 20,000,000 pesos that Estrada Palma's administration had saved. History went on repeating itself in the next six decades.

The birth pains of the Cuban Republic had been exceptionally long and severe. Other Latin American colonies of Spain had won their independence generations before. Cuba remained a colony so much longer partly because the Spanish-Creole plantation owners were afraid of the Negroes and mulattoes, and partly because it was in the United States' interests that Cuba be in the weak hands of Spain rather than a volcanic source of disorder just off American shores. There had been sporadic movements to annex the island, and it almost happened a few times. To our eternal credit, we refrained from annexing Cuba after the Spanish-American War, when we had our best chance.

On the Cuban side the struggle for independence was constant and often heroic. It was carried on by Cubans who fought a desperate and bloody "Ten Years War" between 1868–78, which was lost through eventual exhaustion. On balance, the United States helped Spain. In 1895 the Cubans rose again, led by their "Apostle," José Martí. Their version of the rebellion is that they were just about to win when we moved in to "frustrate" their victory in 1898. In considering Cuban-United States relations this must always be kept in mind. History is often what you believe.

The idea that politics is a spoils system and that political office is a means of enriching the individual rather than of serving the public was one of the evil inheritances of Spanish rule. It remained the prevailing attitude in Cuba, despite many honorable exceptions. Padding of public payrolls, bribing of legislators, graft in public expenditures of all kinds (Batista's regular cut on all public works was 35 per cent), open raids on the national lottery funds and cuts on illegal lotteries, outright theft of public funds —these were the rule in Cuba for nearly six decades.

Both the government and the opposition were coalitions of splinter parties. To be elected as a Representative to the Government coalition (naturally the more lucrative) a candidate would have to spend from $100,000 to $150,000. His salary during his four-year term would be $48,000. A Senate seat never cost less than $250,000; the salary for the term would be $96,000.

The difference—and a lot more besides—had to come out of graft. Since all congressmen had parliamentary immunity, they did not need to fear investigation. The successive Presidents (Batista's predecessors, Ramón Grau San Martín and Carlos Prio Socarrás were among the worst) and Cabinet Ministers got their spoils mainly through manipulation of the lotteries and padded costs of public works. Most American companies moving into Cuba to invest (this was especially true of public works) had to pay large bribes to government officials and turn a blind eye to subsequent graft.

Batista's regime differed from preceding administrations only in the prevalence of high Army officers among the grafters. The General had seized power with their help or forbearance and he kept the officers happy by cutting them in. Some made huge fortunes through smuggling and the proceeds of the wide-open, enormously profitable gambling, with prostitution and narcotics on the side. Some of our most notorious American gamblers had a stake in Cuba. The great luxury hotels built in the 1950's centered around the expected profits from their gambling casinos.

A *Times* correspondent, Robert Alden, was taken at Christmas time, 1957, "to a new gambling casino frequented by many persons high in the Cuban Government or Army. The automobiles that drove up to this place were the longest and shiniest that money could buy. The women wore chinchilla capes and sported diamonds as big as robins' eggs. Thousands of dollars changed hands at each throw of the dice."

The next day Alden was taken to La Llaguas, "a section of Havana hard by a city dump where people lived in almost unbelievable squalor in shacks made of palm fronds."

At the end of the first twenty-five years of independence Professor Charles E. Chapman of the University of California wrote a "History of the Cuban Republic," in which he said: "It is doubtful if the most notorious political rings in the United States, whether national, state or municipal affairs, have gone as far in bad practices as the usual government in Cuba."

Writing on the fiftieth anniversary, I could only say that the record between 1927 and 1952 had continued as bad or worse. In the succeeding seven years of the second Batista dictatorship, it was still worse.

On March 10, 1952, the Cuban people were preparing peacefully and—by relative standards—democratically for a general election on June 1. They had had Presidential elections in 1940, 1944 and 1948, and Congressional elections in between. To have passed another milestone in 1952 would have been a big achievement.

It was then that Batista struck. He had been the most powerful figure in Cuban politics since he engineered the "Sergeant's Revolt" in 1933 after the brutal dictator, Gerardo Machado, had peacefully departed. There had been three Presidents between Estrada Palma and Machado (1924–33), one worse than the other. The peculations of Alfredo Zayas, Machado's predecessor, were astounding.

Cuba was as ripe for a social revolution in 1933 as she was in 1959, but the United States, which still had ultimate control of Cuba's internal affairs through the Platt Amendment to the Cuban constitution and through its economic domination, worked successfully to forestall a revolution. The result was another twenty-six years of corruption, violence and inefficiency culminating in a revolution far more drastic and dangerous than anything that could have happened in 1933. For President Kennedy to say in 1961 that the United States favored social reforms in Cuba was too late. We will be fortunate if we are not too late in other countries of Latin America.

Fulgencio Batista was a candidate in the 1952 Presidential elections. He knew he could not win by the polls, so he took power by his garrison revolt. The Cubans have always fought for their liberties—as they are now doing—but in between convulsive upheavals there was always a pall of defeatism and cynicism, the more or less patient shrug of the shoulders, the acceptance of violence, graft and mismanagement as if they were the normal order of events. When the Batista coup came along too many Cubans said: "Well, what else could you expect? That's the way things happen here."

One who did not say so was a young lawyer, Fidel Castro.

Batista was a self-made man of great native capacities, shrewdness, a tigerish courage and ferocity. He was a beast of prey, as ruthless and as predatory as any dictator in Latin American history. The fortune he amassed in his career, and especially in his last period of dictatorship, was estimated by Cubans in the hundreds of millions of dollars. His cruelty was animal-like; it was not performed out of sadism or viciousness—simply the law of the jungle. It was perhaps not paradoxical that he could be, and often was, charming. There was an attractiveness about him for which there is an untranslatable Spanish word—*simpatico*.

He had what Cubans call "character." What he did not

have—and what Fidel had in overwhelming measure—was charisma, that magnetic, mystical quality which wins fanatical popular support. Batista, in fact, was only tolerated by Cubans when he was in favor. He was loved by none, and those who hated him did so because of his brutality and greed.

There was no respect in which he operated like Fidel Castro, and it is ridiculous for Americans, State Department officials included, to compare them. Batista was of Spanish, Indian, Negro and Chinese blood. He was orphaned at thirteen and taken into a school operated by American Quakers. Before he ended up as an enlisted soldier, he had been a cane-field laborer, a grocery clerk and a railroad fireman.

The key to fame and fortune in his case was stenography, which he learned after his first enlistment. At the time Machado was driven out in 1933, Batista was a headquarters stenographer with the rank of sergeant. Morality and patriotism never interested him; politics he acquired. Batista had nothing to do with the fall of Machado. He picked up the pieces afterwards when he led the "Sergeant's Revolt" that made him master of Cuba —a position he held, in and out of office, for twenty-five years.

Fulgencio Batista could not know it, but his importance in the history of the Western Hemisphere did not lie in his shoddy, brutal, corrupt reign of a quarter of a century. His unwitting role was to be the precursor of Fidel Castro.

It was infuriating to him that I and other American, European and Cuban journalists were presenting Fidel

Castro and the 26th of July Movement as a growing and formidable, as well as heroic and patriotic, threat to his power. There was Fidel, holed up in the Sierra Maestra with a small group of poorly armed followers, and so far as the civic resistance was concerned, how could they overthrow a government backed by an army of 30,000 men, the police and a Military Intelligence Service (SIM) whose ruthless counter-terrorism could be—and was— stepped up to fearsome proportions?

Logic was on the side of General Batista, the Cuban ruling classes, U.S. Ambassador Gardner, the State Department and the Pentagon. History, Fidel Castro and the Cuban people were on the other side. What I saw first and what others echoed with virtual unanimity, was that the best elements of Cuban society and its entire youth were at last getting together to create a new, decent, democratic Cuba.

As it happens, the result in 1961 is as far from democratic as it can be. That is another story, which we will come to later. In 1957–58, Fidel Castro's ideal was a free and democratic Cuba. Neither he, nor any other Cuban, would have fought with such passion and courage for anything else.

The story of the insurrection belongs to another book and to scholars who have access to the Cuban Government archives and, above all, to the records kept by the rebels in the Sierra Maestra. Celia Sánchez, the appealing young daughter of a physician in Pilón, Oriente Province, who joined Fidel in the mountains even before I went up to see him, and who has remained by his side ever since, has all the documentation—every order, every letter, every broadcast, every message and proclamation. For history's sake one must hope they survive the inevitable end of the revolution.

I was always in touch with the rebels in the Sierra Maestra and with the civic resistance. No Cuban came to New York without seeing me or trying to see me. They never got advice or more than their journalistic due, but at least *The Times* was kept informed, and no one could say, when the rebellion triumphed, that readers of *The Times* had been kept uninformed.

Cubans never could understand, and never would believe me, when I said that my trip to the Sierra Maestra and everything else I wrote was professional journalism. The facts and the truth were their best allies in those two years of struggle.

Jaime Benitez, Chancellor of the University of Puerto Rico, writing in May, 1961, made a distinction between what he called "the two Castros, the two Cuban revolutions, each appreciable on its own and yet simultaneous and inter-acting.

The first we shall call the Cuban Revolution: it was made by Castro with the support of the Cuban people, and be it said in fairness, of *The New York Times*—whose stories and editorials helped to make Castro and his movement acceptable to as yet undecided Cubans—and of all the liberal press and progressive opinion throughout the United States. It had in back of it the best Cuban traditions of courage and idealism and enjoyed the endorsement and best wishes of free men throughout the world.

Dr. Benitez called the second revolution "Fidelismo" which, he said, "was also part of Cuba's background, traditions and infirmities." As I said before, we will get to this "revolution" later. If its embryo lay in the womb of Cuban history as early as 1957–58, it could not be seen. It need not ever have been born.

Faustino Pérez and Liliam Mesa, the young couple who took us to Oriente Province with Javier Pazos, were arrested by the SIM on March 19, 1957. I learned this in a letter from someone named Dolores Montero, a friend of theirs in the 26th of July Movement, who wrote me from Havana. Incidentally, this was the first time we learned their true names and that they were not husband and wife. Dolores Montero said that they had been maltreated to get them to confess that they had taken us to the Sierra Maestra but had refused to talk. Somebody had talked, but it was not either of us. Cubans are as little able to keep a secret as any people in the world. The Central Intelligence Agency was to discover this when it was preparing for the invasion of April, 1961.

Javier Pazos went underground at the time and later joined Fidel in the Sierra Maestra. On January 12, 1958, he, Armando Hart, a young lawyer, and Dr. Antonio Buch, of a prominent Santiago de Cuba family—all important lieutenants of Fidel's—were captured. Havana Army headquarters telephoned Santiago that they were to be executed. The telephone operator handling the call in Santiago listened in and passed the word to the 26th of July leaders in the city. Through the Buch family they got on to me in New York and to the State Department.

Washington had inquiries made through the Embassy in Havana and we made our inquiries through Ruby Phillips, our Havana correspondent. The executions were called off.

This was the way the rebellion had its links to the United States. Our inquiry was legitimate journalism, but it helped save the lives of three young Cubans, one of whom became—and still is—Minister of Education.

(I had discovered during the Perón dictatorship in Argentina that Latin American dictators fear *The New York Times* more than they do the State Department, and that publicity in *The Times* would get political victims out of jail where recourse to the local courts was hopeless. In 1955, I penetrated the Villa de Voto jail in Buenos Aires, under the guise of an Argentine relative, interviewed a group of students who had been held without trial for months, wrote a story about them for *The Times* and got them released in a few days.)

In order to keep "law and order" Batista used some of the toughest killers and sadists available in key Army and police posts, where they could meet terrorism with counter-terrorism. It was what President Gerardo Machado had done in 1928–33. The American press in general (not *The New York Times*) has the shameful record that it printed almost nothing of this slaughter of thousands by Batista while it has chronicled in the most lurid way the execution (without torture, incidentally) of hundreds by Fidel Castro—nearly all "war criminals" in the first weeks of the revolution.

I had been getting authentic information of the brutality and the revolutionary ferment, so I went back to Cuba in June, 1957. I started out with a long interview that General Batista gave me and that we front-paged. It was one of Batista's virtues that he never allowed his personal feelings to interfere with the business of government. I had done him more harm than all other journalists in his career combined, and he was sharp in some of his answers, but we sat and talked off the record in friendly fashion for three-quarters of an hour. He would not, or could not concede that his regime was unpopular, but he wryly agreed with me that it is easier to seize power than to give it up.

In Santiago de Cuba, the underground approached me, although I was living in a goldfish bowl. Some of the most respected citizens provided the cover and the contacts that enabled me to have long talks with men and women whose lives would have been forfeit if the SIM had been as well organized as the 26th of July Movement. The operation consisted in leaving the hotel with some prominent and unsuspected person, driving around to be sure we were not followed, then switching cars swiftly, sometimes twice. At the assignation point a youth would be standing or walking as a lookout and would give the signal that all was clear and we had not been followed.

In this way I saw, among others, Frank Pais, Fidel's second in command, Celia Sánchez, whom *Time* magazine was later to call "Fidel's Girl Friday," Vilma Espín, Raul Castro's girl friend and now his wife, and Manuel Urrutia, the judge, who was to become the first, tragic President of revolutionary Cuba. Dr. Urrutia had stood out against the other judges of the Urgency Court of Santiago de Cuba the month before in refusing to condemn a large group of young insurrectionists, among them twenty-two who had been on the Granma with Fidel. He argued that it was legitimate to fight against a government that violates civic liberties. The Judge was promptly relieved of his post, and when I saw him he was planning to flee to the United States. The judgment he rendered as a *voto particular* (a personal sentence) was to become heresy in the Castro regime.

The next time Frank Pais came down from the Sierra Maestra to Santiago de Cuba the police caught up with him and killed him. He was a great loss to Fidel and to Cuba, as was later the tragic death of Camilo Cienfuegos. These were two young, very able, moderate and anti-Communist patriots whose death left the field clear for the radical young Argentine doctor, Che Guevara and Fidel's younger brother, Raul.

As a result of my talks in Santiago de Cuba and Havana I was able to tell *The Times* in a despatch on June 8 that Fidel Castro "is stronger than ever, his prestige has risen throughout Cuba and he is today far and away the greatest figure in the nation-wide opposition to President Fulgencio Batista."

The next day I sent an article from Santiago de Cuba saying the city was "in open revolt" and the whole Province of Oriente was up in arms against Batista. I told of the reign of terror, of the risks people took to see me and how "dozens of humble persons accosted me on the streets and elsewhere to shake hands, partly to thank *The*

New York Times for what it considered its effort to present the truth about Cuba in its news and editorial columns, and partly as a gesture of defiance against the authorities."

"Everybody I saw was convinced that the police authorities had orders from Havana to refrain from any act of terrorism during the three days I was here," I wrote. "For this reason, *The Times* gets credit for having given Santiago de Cuba three days of peace, such as this tormented city has not known for many months."

A week later I summed up my experiences in two despatches from Havana.

"In analyzing the elements of this situation," I wrote, "it seems evident that two men must be satisfied or one or the other must withdraw or be killed before a solution is possible. Both represent powerful forces in Cuban life and they are deadly enemies.

"The first is General Batista, who holds the reins of power primarily through his command of the army and the police forces. Important business, banking and landowning elements, Cuban and American, desire peace and continued prosperity, and they fear the consequences of an overthrow of the regime. These elements also support General Batista. Finally, the President has until now had the open support and friendship of the United States, as represented by the retiring Ambassador, Arthur Gardner, who is leaving Havana.

"The other national figure is Fidel Castro, the rebel who leads a fighting force in the Sierra Maestra at the eastern end of the island. The Cuban army has thus far been powerless to liquidate him and he has a widespread following through his 26th of July Movement and supporters of that Movement everywhere in Cuba."

I went on to describe these supporters, among the youth, the middle class, the civic organizations and the Roman Catholic Church.

"This combined force," I said, "is fighting, literally or metaphorically, to oust President Batista and all he stands for. It proclaims ideals of democracy, freedom and honesty in government."

These despatches, and others I sent on subsequent visits in the next year and a half, and the editorials I wrote in New York, undoubtedly helped to make Fidel Castro and his Movement acceptable to Cubans and liberals all over the world, as Chancellor Benitez was to say. It so happens that every word I wrote was true. These were the facts. This was, and is, and always will be the history that no scholar with any judgment will be able to ignore.

It was at this time that my connections with the two United States Ambassadors who represented us during the entire seven years of Batista's dictatorship came to what might be called a climax. These relations were the subject of a generally nonsensical pair of hearings by the Eastland-Dodd Subcommittee of the Senate Judiciary Committee, held on August 27 and 30, 1960.

In my despatches in February and June, 1957, I had pointed out how excessively friendly Ambassador Gardner was with General Batista and how bitterly Cubans felt about him and Washington. On June 16, 1957, I wrote: "Ambassador Gardner left Cuba today with the relations of the Cuban people toward the United States gravely impaired."

Of this there could be no doubt. Gardner was possibly right in blaming me for his removal from the Havana post, although I would like to believe that the State Department realized his shortcomings. I had seen Secretary of State John Foster Dulles in Washington a month before, and he told me they had had the worst time trying to force Gardner out. He wanted desperately to stay and even went over Dulles' head to the President to try to remain indefinitely. Gardner said Batista would be very upset as he, Gardner, was so close to Batista and that it would be a sign we were changing our policy toward Cuba and acknowledging the rightness of the criticism of himself. Therefore, he could not be persuaded to offer a genuine resignation. However, he had, like all ambassadors, submitted a *pro forma* resignation when President Eisenhower started his second term in January, 1957. Dulles told me that he dug that resignation out of the files and had the State Department get out a press statement that Gardner had resigned and the resignation was being accepted with regret. This, he said, explained why the President felt it necessary to write Gardner a long letter also expressing his regrets.

Dulles (and all the top State Department officials) gave me the impression on that visit that the newly appointed Ambassador, Earl E. T. Smith, would get very different instructions than Gardner had been getting.

Poor Cuba was getting still another businessman, a

complete novice to diplomacy and to Latin America, whose only known qualification for the appointment was that he was finance chairman of the Republican Party State Committee in Florida in 1955 and had helped to raise funds in the 1956 campaign. He was a wealthy sportsman and broker.

Everyone at the State Department realized that if ever a post required an experienced career officer, Havana in 1957 was the place. They had a candidate, and the White House agreed, but alas for Cuba and for the United States, Freeman (Doc) Matthews, then Ambassador to Sweden, could not accept for personal reasons. It is on such quirks of Fate that history turns.

The fact that I was supposed to have briefed Earl Smith before he went to Cuba came up somewhat sensationally in 1960, and especially in the Senate Subcommittee hearing which I have already mentioned. Arthur Gardner, who apparently did not approve of his successor, first testified that "he [meaning me] briefed Earl Smith."

Smith, whose testimony was altogether more responsible than Gardner's, was asked about this by J. G. Sourwine, the Subcommittee's counsel. Here are the passages that concern this so-called briefing (Pages 682-3 of the hearings put out by the Subcommittee):

MR. SOURWINE. Is it true, sir, that you were instructed to get a briefing on your new job as Ambassador to Cuba from Herbert Matthews of *The New York Times?*

MR. SMITH. Yes, that is correct.

MR. SOURWINE. Who gave you these instructions?

MR. SMITH.   William Wieland, Director of the Caribbean Division and Mexico.

MR. SOURWINE. Did you, sir, in fact see Matthews?

MR. SMITH.   Yes, I did.

MR. SOURWINE. And did he brief you on the Cuban situation?

MR. SMITH.   Yes, he did.

MR. SOURWINE. Could you give us the highlights of what he told you? . . .'

MR. SMITH.   We talked for 2½ hours on the Cuban situation, a complete review of his feelings regarding Cuba, Batista, Castro, the situation in Cuba, and what he thought would happen.

MR. SOURWINE. What did he think would happen?

MR. SMITH.   He did not believe that the Batista government could last, and that the fall of the Batista government would come relatively soon.

MR. SOURWINE. Specifically what did he say about Castro?

MR. SMITH.   In February, 1957, Herbert L. Matthews wrote three articles on Fidel Castro, which appeared on the front pages of *The New York Times,* in which he eulogized Fidel Castro and portrayed him as a political Robin Hood, and I would say that he repeated these views to me in our conversation. . . .

MR. SOURWINE. What did Mr. Matthews tell you about Batista?

MR. SMITH.   Mr. Matthews had a very poor view of Batista, considered him a rightist, ruthless dictator whom he believed to be corrupt. Mr. Matthews informed me that he had very knowledgeable views of Cuba and Latin American nations, and had seen the same things take place in Spain. He believed that it would be in the best interest of Cuba and the best interest of the world in general when Batista was removed from office.

Allowing for a sour note or two, this was accurate testimony. It was correct information and good advice that I gave to Earl Smith, and it was a pity that neither he nor the State Department based their policies on it. We would not, in January, 1959, when the revolution triumphed have had a hostile, suspicious group of revolutionary leaders and an embittered Cuban nation against us.

In one respect, which Smith did not mention, I thought he was taking my advice. I told him that Havana was not Cuba and that the atmosphere in the rest of the country was very different, and I suggested that he travel around and see things for himself.

One of the first things the Ambassador did was to go to Santiago de Cuba, the only city where we had a consulate, and to our mining interests in Moa Bay as well as Guantánamo Naval Base. In Santiago, a large group of middle-class women demonstrated against Batista and were brutally treated in front of Smith by the Cuban police. Smith was shocked and said publicly: "Any sort of excessive police action is abhorrent to me."

President Batista and his associates were very angry and protested to Washington. I had immediately moved in with an editorial praising Smith highly for what he had done and said. Secretary Dulles strongly defended the Ambassador in a press conference, and we praised Dulles for that. Later I got warm thanks from both Smith and Dulles for my help.

This was the last gesture Smith made on behalf of the Cuban people and against the Batista regime. On later trips I was to hear bitter criticism from Cubans of Earl Smith for what was considered his support of Batista.

Smith's basic mistake—and there is none worse in diplomacy—was to keep on backing a losing horse, and even in the homestretch, with the winning horse way out in front, to try to nullify the victory. He had for months been calling Fidel Castro a "ruffian" and a "bandit" and this was known to all Cubans for whom Fidel, at that time, was a great hero. There are no doubt millions of Americans who would say today that Earl Smith was right. This is a matter of opinion, but what is not merely an opinion is that a United States Ambassador with any sense of diplomacy does not insult the man and the movement who are taking power in the country where the envoy serves.

Thanks to Smith and, I would say, clumsy work at the State Department, the United States started out in January, 1959, with an unnecessarily resentful and suspicious Cuban Government in power.

It was, and is, a great injustice to two devoted and competent United States officials to blame them, as Gardner, Smith, Senators Eastland and Dodd, ex-Ambassador Hill of Mexico, Ed Pawley, the tycoon, and many columnists have done for the defeat of Batista and the triumph of Castro. I refer to Assistant Secretary of State Roy R. Rubottom and William Wieland, who is mentioned above.

In the first place, they could not have prevented this outcome. In the second place, their policies in 1957 and 1958 favored Batista and hampered Castro. It is an astonishing distortion of history to say the opposite. It is equally a distortion of the facts to say that they were getting or taking any advice from me about Cuba. In fact, we argued frequently about the Department's policies.

There was no excuse for the charges made against Rubottom and Wieland, or for the way they have been treated. This is typical of the McCarthyism that events like this bring out in the United States.

The first time the American people were outraged against Fidel Castro was when he and his troops kidnaped forty-five Americans and three Canadians at the end of June, 1958. It was a typically daring and provocative piece of work that showed a contempt for American opinion and American power which was more prophetic than anyone realized at the time. It was Fidel's way of registering a protest against American favoritism for General Batista and a demonstration that he controlled the eastern end of the island.

The incident was also prophetic in showing that there was nothing the United States could do about it. This is a fact of the modern world, as Egypt and Africa generally have been demonstrating. The Soviet Union could do something about Hungary in 1956 and get away with it, because this fitted the methods and aims of totalitarian communism. For the United States to treat Cuba as Russia treated Hungary would mean the end of our democracy, our freedom, our civilization, our way of life.

The dilemma is a serious one, and there are always those who want to resort to force. At the time of the kid-

so The U.S. Resorts To Covert Actions using the CIA. (I.E. Bay of Pigs, Guatamalia)

73

napings, some high officers at the Pentagon and some Senators wanted to send American Marines in to rescue the kidnaped men. Wiser counsels prevailed.

It was Raul Castro, Fidel's younger brother, who engineered and carried out the kidnapings. This twisted, enigmatic character has played an important but always subordinate role in the Revolution. He is four years younger than Fidel and without any of his popular appeal. Sharp of visage and of character, without warmth, a disciplinarian, a good administrator, a hater of the United States, an admirer of communism and the Sino-Soviet bloc —Raul has long been seen as the evil genius of the Cuban Revolution.

Because, in his student days, he went on one of those junkets behind the Iron Curtain for a few months, Raul was labeled a Communist almost from the beginning. He has always denied this, and neither the CIA nor the American Embassy ever found proof that he was a Communist. No one could deny that for all practical purposes he might just as well have been a Communist, and yet there was a Cabinet meeting late in 1959 in which Raul, furious with the Cuban Reds, shouted that if they got in the way of the Revolution he would cut their throats. Two of the Cabinet Ministers present told me that.

There was no excuse for the kidnapings, and for the first time I found myself impelled to write sharply critical editorials about the Revolution. This caused some heartburnings among my Cuban friends who neither then, nor in the future, could find any attitude acceptable that was not 100 per cent for what they believed.

It was typical of the Cubans that they could not understand the anger and resentment of the Americans over the kidnapings. Fortunately, none of the captured Americans or Canadians was harmed. On the contrary, some of them found it a stimulating adventure which aroused sympathy for the rebel cause.

This was typical of the romantic, youthful aura that surrounded the rebels in those months of struggle. Communism and the hard realities of making a social revolution in a hostile world were many months away.

The guerrillas spread out from the Sierra Maestra in the summer of 1958. Raul Castro's "Second Front" was at that time in the Sierra del Cristal on the northern side of Oriente Province.

There was still another "Second Front" in the Sierra de Escambray in the center of the island on the south coast of Las Villas Province. This was where the *Directorio Revolucionario,* organized by the university students' Federation, had been operating since the previous November. It was not linked to the 26th of July Movement but had the same objectives. Although smaller than the Sierra Maestra operation, and rent by quarrels, it was of some nuisance value.

One thinks of it now because several of its leaders made minor history. Eloy Gutiérrez Menoyo, the nearest thing to their military commander, is now an exile in the United States. Fauré Chomón, whom I had interviewed in Havana with the other students just after seeing Fidel, is now Ambassador to Moscow.

The most interesting figure in the Sierra de Escambray

75

was the tough, uneducated young American, William A. Morgan, who could hardly speak Spanish when he arrived. He wrote me several times, once to complain of other groups in the Sierra, and once to grumble against Che Guevara, who refused to see Morgan's command.

The interesting thing about Morgan, which entitled him to a passing fame as a child of our times, was that he had ideals. On February 24, 1958, he wrote and sent me a "credo" headed "Why am I Here." Considering that Morgan's American citizenship was taken away from him, and considering also the contemptuous way the American press treated him, one owes him the tribute of quoting a few sentences:

"I cannot say I have always been a good citizen," he wrote, "but being here I can appreciate the way of life that is ours from birth. And here I can realize the dedication to justice and liberty it takes for men to live and fight as these men do whose only possible pay or reward is a free country. . . .

"Over the years we as Americans have found that dictators and communist (sic) are bad people with whom to do business yet here is a dictator who has been supported by the communist and he would fall from power tomorrow if it were not for the American aid. And I ask myself why do we support those who would destroy in other lands the ideals which we hold so dear?"

Morgan was consistent. He went on fighting for liberty and against communism until he was stood against a wall in the dry moat of La Cabaña fortress on March 11,

1961, and shot. So far as I am concerned, William Morgan was a good American.

Fidel Castro's insurrection was written off as lost by virtually all American journalists when a general strike was attempted on April 9, 1958, and failed miserably. The entire Cuban trade-union leadership, in the pay of Batista, refused to support it. So did the Communists. It was badly organized and badly led. "The days of Fidel Castro," said the first sentence of a despatch to *The Times* from Havana on April 16, "are numbered, according to informed sources."

General Batista evidently thought so, and soon afterwards mobilized his greatest—and what was to be his last—offensive in Oriente Province to crush the rebels. Here was the proof that the rebellion was won by Fidel Castro and his guerrilla forces aided—and he needed it— by the civic resistance. But for Fidel the insurrection would have been crushed in the spring of 1958.

The general strike failed; the civic resistance in Havana did not rise, but the guerrillas in Oriente Province went on fighting. Their strength grew, although the combatant elements were always very small. They fought off the Government offensive of May–June, 1958.

At this point, everyone in close touch with Cuban developments could have known that Fidel Castro was going to win and General Fulgencio Batista was going to lose. This is where the State Department, the Pentagon, the CIA, and Ambassador Smith made their great mistakes. There was no evidence that they realized the game was up until October, a month after Fidel began his final offensive with three columns that fanned out from the Sierra Maestra, led by Raul Castro, Camilo Cienfuegos and Che Guevara. (Incidentally, October, 1958, was the month the Cuban Communists jumped on the bandwagon.)

From the beginning there had been a bewildering, contradictory and amateurish array of future solutions, programs and demands of and by Fidel to newsmen who visited him in the Sierra Maestra. Each one got a different version of the Cuban future depending, so far as I could tell, on what would pop into Fidel's mind on the particular occasion, or what he had happened to read on the previous day.

Meanwhile, his representatives and the Cuban exile organizations in the United States, Costa Rica and Venezuela were getting out an equally confusing collection of programs.

The charge that Fidel "betrayed" the Revolution is based on the fact that he always, in those years, promised democracy, elections, a free press and other civic rights as well as his social revolution. Fidel never had any original political ideas and he knew nothing about economics, government or administration. This was always obvious. He could not be pinned down in any given month, let alone any year, to a consistent policy. Those who think he is going to retain his present admiration for the Communists may get a surprise in 1962 or 1963, although that is unlikely now.

Yet a certain consistency does run like a pattern through all Fidel's pronouncements and speeches, from his famous

self-defense after the 1953 Moncada Barracks attack—
"History Will Absolve Me"—to his latest speeches. The
Cuban social revolution is always there, and it was made.

In mid-February, 1957, when I went up to see Fidel,
the underground publication of the 26th of July Movement, *Revolución*, published what I believe was the first
program.

"The Revolution," it wrote, "is the struggle of the
Cuban nation to achieve its historic aims and realize its
complete integration. This integration consists in the complete unity of the following elements: political sovereignty, economic independence and a particular or
differentiated culture.

"The Revolution is not exactly a war or an isolated
episode. It is a continuous historic process, which offers
distinct moments or stages. The conspiracies of the previous century, the War of '68, of '95, the uprising of the
1930's and, today, the struggle against the Batista terror,
are parts of the same and unique Revolution.

"The Revolution is struggling for a total transformation
of Cuban life, for profound modifications in the system
of property and for a change in institutions. . . .

"In accordance with its goals, and as a consequence of
the historic, geographic and sociological reality of Cuba,
the Revolution is democratic, nationalist and socialist."

This, in every respect except one, is the Revolution that
Fidel Castro has made in the year 1961. The democracy
he spoke of then was liberal democracy; the democracy
he has now is totalitarian democracy.

Note the use of the word "socialist," which Fidel also

employed in talking to me in the Sierra Maestra in 1957. Yet a tremendous hullabaloo was made on May 1, 1961, when Fidel, Che and others referred to the Cuban Revolution as "Socialist." It was agreed in the United States that the Russian Communists call themselves Socialists; the Cubans call themselves Socialists; therefore the Cubans are now Communists. To be sure, this bit of logical nonsense, put out by the State Department and the American press, had a practical basis from the fact that the Cubans were praising the Communist system to the skies, trying to copy it in innumerable ways, and going in that direction.

I am simply arguing that Fidel Castro always called his revolution Socialist, and he then meant Socialist—not Communist.

The way things are going he will have a state indistinguishable from communism, and then, perhaps, he will call it Communist. He is not afraid to say what he thinks, and Che Guevara even less so. Whatever else these young revolutionaries may be, they are not hypocrites.

Writing to *The New York Times* from Havana on March 22, 1958, during a trip, I said one of those things which in 1960 and 1961 so infuriated Americans, who have their own decided opinions about Fidel Castro.

"The key factor in this dramatic year [since my interview] has proved to be the courage, dynamism and leadership of Fidel Castro, the most remarkable and romantic figure to arise in Cuban history since José Martí, the hero of the wars of independence."

Exactly! If anyone had courage, dynamism and leadership it was Fidel Castro. And those who doubt the romantic appeal of Fidel to millions of Cubans and many, many more millions all over Latin America, do not know what is happening. To be accused, as I am now, of building up Fidel Castro as a "Robin Hood" is sheer nonsense. To think that *The New York Times* and not the Cuban people were behind him is even more nonsensical.

It is often forgotten in these months when I have been made an exclusive scapegoat, that a great many other American journalists were writing the same things I wrote. Andrew St. George, who became the outstanding news photographer of the Cuban Revolution, wrote an article for *Coronet*, published in February, 1958, which was typical. St. George had spent weeks in the Sierra Maestra with Fidel.

"The world has known few revolutionary leaders like Fidel Castro," he said. "In Cuba, thousands of staid, solid middle-class citizens work for him at the risk of their lives. One newspaper recently estimated that 90 per cent of the Cuban population supports Castro. The Government of Cuba's dictator Fulgencio Batista has often claimed that the revolutionists are crypto-Communists; yet when newly appointed U.S. Ambassador Earl E.T. Smith was asked, on the occasion of his first press conference in Havana last summer, whether the U.S. State Department had seen any proof of Castro's alleged Communist connections, Ambassador Smith answered firmly that the United States had no such evidence."

(Incidentally, even in this late summer of 1961, the United States has no such evidence.)

Another unfair accusation against *The Times* was that we wanted a revolution and not a peaceful solution of the Cuban crisis. I challenge anyone to study the editorials we printed in 1957 and 1958, which I would with few exceptions have written as I still do, and find substance for such a charge. The contrary is true. We did call attention to the arrests, tortures and killings of the Batista regime (which very few other newspapers in the country did); we pointed to the corruption, and we wrote of the folly of the State Department and Ambassador Smith supporting so-called elections which were obviously farces that would not be accepted by the Cuban people.

Add these up and one can argue that *The Times* certainly helped to overthrow General Batista. We also helped, in a similar way, to overthrow General Juan Perón of Argentina, General Gustavo Rojas Pinilla of Colombia, General Manuel Odría of Peru and General Marcos Pérez Jiménez of Venezuela. Argentines, Colombians, Peruvians and Venezuelans were and still are very grateful to me and to *The New York Times* for the role we played. We are not criticized for it; we are praised.

So were we in the case of Cuba, deliriously, and by Cubans who now bitterly attack us because neither Fidel Castro nor the Revolution turned out the way they—or anybody—expected.

Much was made of the fact in after months and years that on March 14, 1958, the United States canceled an arms shipment to Cuba and thus, in effect, instituted an embargo against Batista. At first, the State Department pointed to this as evidence that it was not favoring

Batista. Later, critics of the State Department indignantly brought this up to argue that the United States sabotaged Batista. Both points of view were greatly exaggerated.

Batista by that time did not need any more American arms and from the viewpoint of military power he had far more than he needed to crush the rebellion and repress civic violence. It was not a lack of arms that weakened or defeated him. In fact, the British sold him jet planes and he bought other arms in Europe. On the other hand, it is true that the American embargo was a moral and political setback for him.

The embargo was an acknowledgment of the fact that something like a civil war was occurring in Cuba. To soften the blow, the United States encouraged a proposed Presidential election in Cuba called for June 1, 1958, which would have been an utter farce in behalf of General Batista. When the election was postponed until November 1, we incredibly still encouraged it. The United States has an absolute fetish about elections—anywhere, everywhere, whatever the circumstances. A Batista who holds a farcical election with chosen and bought candidates deserves praise; a Castro who scoffs at the only sort of elections Cuba has known, and dispenses with them, is condemned for the wrong reasons. He is wrong to think that mass demonstrations and his brand of totalitarian democracy are a true substitute for genuine elections. He is right to say that a great majority of the Cuban people are utterly disillusioned with what they know of as elections and are not interested in them. Aside from that is the fact that Fidel could not have held elections without putting a halt to his revolution.

This is getting a bit ahead of our story, but the purpose is to contribute some understanding of why the Cubans were so anti-American when the Revolution started. A good witness to the way they felt in the spring of 1958 is Jules Dubois, Latin American correspondent of the Chicago *Tribune,* whose fierce opposition to Fidel Castro starting a few months after the insurrection triumphed absolves him from any calculated sympathy.

"Our Embassy and State Department are in the doghouse with the Cuban people again," Dubois wrote on March 21, 1958.

"Cuban public opinion, although throttled by the most severe censorship ever exercised by Batista, is outspoken against the United States. The people, from the leaders of the civic, religious, professional and social institutions who demanded that Batista resign, to the students, accuse the United States of pursuing a policy to support a dictator and lose the friendship of a nation.

"[Ambassador Earl E. T.] Smith is being branded as worse than his predecessor, Arthur Gardner. . . . Opponents of Batista insist that Smith has been captured by Batista's friends and business associates just as Gardner had been.

"They add that he has accepted the Batista propaganda that Fidel Castro and his top rebel leaders are Communists. Batista has been shouting this line to the world ever since Castro landed here from Mexico in December, 1956."

Our high military officers sometimes show an admiration for the worst type of foreign officials and a callousness toward the political objectives of the United States Government that are harmful, and Cuba was no exception. On September 5, 1957, there had been an uprising which mainly affected the south-coast port of Cienfuegos. The Cuban Air Force, using planes acquired from the United States, bombed and strafed Cienfuegos with a ferocity that resulted in the killing and wounding of many innocent citizens, women and children included. The Cuban officer who ordered the bombing was Colonel (later General) Carlos Tabernilla Palmeros. In November, 1957, the United States Army gave Colonel Tabernilla the Legion of Merit at a banquet where he was praised highly.

That same month General Lemuel C. Shepherd, Chairman of the Inter-American Defense Board, stopped in Cuba on an official visit and in a ceremony at the Presidential Palace responded to General Batista's toast as follows:

"In my name and that of the IADB, I thank you for this cordial welcome. We thank you especially for what you have just said, since it comes not only from a great President but also from a great soldier."

These words were splashed by the Batista-subsidized press (virtually all Cuban newspapers) in the largest type and broadcast by all stations. At the same time, an important arms shipment for Batista was made from a New Jersey port, but United States customs agents arrested thirty-one Cubans at Piney Point in the Florida Keys as they were loading the yacht "Philomar III," with arms, medical supplies and uniforms for Fidel Castro; and a federal court ordered investigation into all activities of Cuban exiles.

For some reason, a myth has grown up that the United States Government winked and connived at the Castro exiles' attempts to get arms, materials and money in the United States to fight Batista during the insurrection. As a matter of fact, a relatively small proportion of the arms —perhaps 40 per cent—got through and of that amount not a great deal reached Fidel in the Sierra Maestra. To compare this with the massive CIA help for the Cuban exiles in 1960–61 is ridiculous.

Three American military missions—Army, Navy and Air Force—went on instructing Cubans in arts that the Cubans used against their fellow Cubans. These Americans were still at it when the 26th of July Movement took over Havana and Fidel sarcastically remarked that if they could teach Batista's armed forces no better than they had been able to, he would gladly do without them.

Americans should keep in mind when they contemplate Latin American anti-Yankeeism, that tributes, honors and decorations by the dozens have gone over the years to Latin American dictators and their officers from high-ranking officers of the United States Armed Forces and from high officials. The most famous of all was President Eisenhower's decoration of Venezuela's brutal dictator, General Pérez Jiménez with the Legion of Merit in 1954. There was also the unforgettable day in 1955 when United States Secretary of the Navy, Charles S. Thomas, in a ceremony in Buenos Aires publicly compared General Perón to George Washington.

To give the State Department credit, there is almost always moaning and groaning when these things happen, particularly as they get blamed for American policy even when reactionary, ignorant and simple-minded Senators and military officers—or for that matter—the press, are to blame.

The end of the Batista regime approached with the United States in the doghouse and the American public blissfully ignorant of that fact, or even of the fact that Batista was doomed.

No one could know the exact day the break would come since it was within General Batista's power to hang on for some weeks longer.

I had a vacation coming to me and it was an obvious hunch for my wife and me to go to Havana on December 27, 1958, to watch things happen. Not being superstitious, I do not subscribe to the theory that newspapermen are endowed at birth with a sixth sense, but it seemed to work that way.

As a vacation, it ended on New Year's Eve. Ruby Hart Phillips, our Havana correspondent, Ted Scott of the Havana *Post*, my wife Nancie and I and some friends had the traditional dinner—paper hats, horns, champagne and what not—at the Havana Riviera Hotel. The son of Jake Arvey, the Chicago politician, was at our table with his wife. Arvey casually remarked, as if it were hardly worth saying, that earlier that evening, from the window of their house overlooking Camp Columbia Airfield, he had seen

87

a number of cars with women, children and luggage streaming toward the airfield. We four—the newspaper people—made hasty excuses. We knew what was about to happen, although it took until 4 A.M. to confirm that Batista had fled.

I could not repress a sense of personal triumph. In 1945, ending a book I wrote called *The Education of a Correspondent,* I said:

I have done my part at the wars in the past ten years, and often I thought I would write *Finis.* But it is not for a man to sign off. That seems a little like suicide. . . . A newspaperman is the soldier of fortune, the Ulysses of this [Tennyson's] poem who yearns

. . . in desire
To follow knowledge, like a sinking star
Beyond the utmost bound of human thought.

. . . One always has that urge to learn more of the world and of the virtues and vices of humanity. The way I feel now I do not ever want to roam any more . . . I have paid my price to history, and it is for the younger men to take up the burden, while I sit back and say that we did things better in my time, for "there were giants in those days."
But if there is another war?

It had been fifteen years since I had heard what Ernest Hemingway called "shots fired in anger," but I heard them those first few days in Havana before the 26th of July boys could get in and restore order, and they were like the sound of trumpets to an old war horse.

It had been my triumph, along with others. I will not yield it to my critics or to history. But what had been won? What had been lost?

CHAPTER THREE

The Revolution

IT WAS EXTRAORDINARILY difficult to convince the American people that Cuba was having a revolution—a real revolution, not a changing of the guard, not a shuffling of leaders, not just the outs getting in, but a social revolution in the direct line of the French Revolution of 1789.

This was the first great failure of the American press, radio and television in their coverage of the Cuban Revolution. I am not saying that anybody could have known what kind of social revolution it was going to be or just how it would turn out—not even Fidel Castro had any idea of that.

What he knew, and what anyone in close touch with him and his associates knew, was that the whole fabric of Cuban society was going to be overturned.

"The unique factor about the events in Cuba," I wrote on January 10, 1959, two days after the triumphant Fidel Castro reached Havana, "is that there has been a real revolution. While dictators have been eliminated recently in Nicaragua, Argentina, Peru, Colombia and Venezuela, in none of these countries have there been such profound changes as those that promise to be seen in Cuba in coming months."

I then went on to describe the sort of democratic social revolution all of us—Cubans included—hoped for and expected in those delirious days. I would include Fidel Castro among those hopefuls, for he had not yet begun to grapple with the task of making a social revolution.

On July 15, 1959, on my third visit of the year to Cuba, I began a despatch from Havana with these words:

"Half a year after the revolt against the Batista regime, Cuba is in the midst of the first great social revolution in Latin America since the Mexican Revolution of 1910."

That this still needed to be said in July, 1959 and that it was news to American readers shows how slow the United States was to grasp the essence of what was happening. True, there had already been the charges that Cuba was in the midst of a Communist revolution, but this was not true and it merely distorted the picture.

The Cuban Revolution has had a profound effect in the hemisphere because it was a Cuban and Latin American phenomenon. The fact that it became communistic has weakened its effectiveness. The revolution is not to be explained away so easily.

It seems to me that I have spent a great deal of my time in the last two and a half years describing what a complicated phenomenon the Cuban Revolution is. The ones who were sure they knew exactly what it was all about and what was happening were at best naïve and at worst fools, simpletons or knaves. Those who harped on the Communist line later said: "I told you so." They helped to make their guess come true. For a year and a half—certainly in 1959—nobody could know.

In March, 1961, I gave the annual Lectures in History —three of them—for City College of New York on the subject of Cuba and Latin America.

"These are lectures in history for your History Department, so keep in mind some truisms," I said to begin with. "History-in-the-making is even less of a science than the academic history of the past. We are dealing with human beings, not imaginary recreations of what we think happened; with complex and conflicting forces that have their roots in other years and in different traditions, racial characteristics, customs, religion, philosophy of life, economic and political systems.

"No mind can grasp all the forces at play in a given situation even if you can get hold of all the facts—which you cannot. Clausewitz wrote of the fog of war; there is also a fog of history through which we journalists grope our way as best we can. At least we are in the midst of what is happening.

"Despite the handicaps, I am going to try, in these lectures, to look at the Cuban revolution and its consequences in the hemisphere as history, with the detachment that the historian needs. Cuba has been drowned in emotions and ignorance in the United States during the last few years. There has been a woeful lack of understanding."

The fact that Cuba was ripe for revolution was recognized in no less authoritative a document than the now famous "White Paper" on Cuba put out by the State Department on April 3, 1961. It was supposed to have been written by Arthur Schlesinger, Jr., one of the professorial advisers at the White House.

"The character of the Batista regime in Cuba made a violent popular reaction almost inevitable," the document says. "The rapacity of the leadership, the corruption of the Government, the brutality of the police, the regime's indifference to the needs of the people for education, medical care, housing, for social justice and economic opportunity—all these, in Cuba as elsewhere, constituted an open invitation to revolution."

Boiled down, what we were seeing in Cuba was a revolt against a small, corrupt, wealthy ruling class whom the United States had put in power and helped to keep in power. I am not saying, of course, that we deliberately chose or wanted venal politicians, corrupt businessmen and an atmosphere darkened by gambling, narcotics and prostitution. Nor was there any excuse for the Cubans who were so dishonest and selfish. I do say, and history will bear me out in this, that we accepted, condoned, worked with and helped this ruling class to stay in power.

We did so for business reasons, for strategic reasons, and in the name of stability. We built up the already existing sugar economy to an overwhelming role, and for most of this century dominated the industry. Even in 1958 we still controlled 35 to 40 per cent of the sugar production and dictated Cuba's relative prosperity or the lack of it through our sugar import quotas.

We live in a world where nationalism is the most important of all political emotions. It takes a destructive, xenophobic and often revolutionary form. Therefore, of course, the Communists profit by nationalism and we suffer. In Latin America, nationalism inevitably becomes anti-Yankeeism.

In Cuba we had also given the Cubans many good reasons to be our friends and to work with us, and it was and always will be to their advantage to do so. But we also gave them many reasons to resent us. A lot of chickens came home to roost.

In the White Paper on Cuba, for the first time in more than two years, Washington conceded that Americans had to take some blame for what was happening in Cuba. The self-righteousness of American officialdom, press and business community with regard to Cuba played a great role in creating the disastrous misunderstandings between us and the Cubans in the crucial first years of 1959. This does not excuse the stubborn, passionate self-righteousness on the Cuban side, but two wrongs do not make a right, and every element of the situation placed the burden of understanding more heavily on our shoulders than on those of a people exploding with long-pent-up emotions. At any rate, we did say in the White Paper:

"The people of Cuba remain our brothers. We acknowledge past omissions and errors in our relationship with them."

A social revolution was narrowly averted in Cuba in

1933, as stated before, when another brutal and predatory dictator, Gerardo Machado, was gently eased out by our diplomacy. The situation was ripe for revolution at that time, too, and it was a time when we had the power, through the Platt Amendment to the Cuban Constitution, to influence the Cuban situation decisively.

As it happened, our influence was directed toward holding together the existing fabric of Cuban government, business and society. This, again, was to protect our investments, to maintain stability and for the usual strategic reasons. Then, as now, we used as an excuse for undermining and overthrowing the chosen government of President Ramón Grau San Martín the accusation that he had "communistic tendencies." Considering Grau's later record, this was ludicrous, but it worked in 1933.

So Cuba had twenty-six more years of corruption, inefficiency and profitable business, this time, under the domination of Fulgencio Batista. The General ended with seven years of straightforward military dictatorship that were in the worst Latin American tradition, during which time he had the friendship or the benevolence of the United States.

In 1959, nothing could or would prevent a social revolution because in addition to all the other factors that made Cuba ripe for such an upheaval, a man of destiny had come on the scene, one of those extraordinary creatures who make history through some qualities that they possess. In a real sense, this was Fidel Castro's revolution. It was he who gave expression and drive to all the social and nationalistic pressures that had merely been threatening revolutions in Cuba and in other Latin American countries. Even though he had needed the island-wide civic resistance to soften up and weaken General Batista, it was Fidel Castro around whom the nation rallied for those two bitter years of insurrectionary struggle, and it was his small but effective guerrilla columns that delivered the decisive blows.

The defeat and dissolution of the Army meant that Cuba, unlike Argentina, Peru, Colombia and Venezuela, could have a revolution of a profound social, political and economic type. This really was what Fidel Castro had planned and what he and his followers fought for from the beginning, although curiously enough it was not realized by most Cubans, and still less so by Americans. I am not talking here of the fact that the revolution turned out to be different than anybody—Fidel Castro included—expected at the time.

The point being made is that Fidel Castro was out to make a radical, social revolution that was necessarily Leftist, since it was directed against the former ruling classes of big landowners, big businessmen and bankers, high military officers and politicians, all of whom were the beneficiaries of a corrupt oligarchical system. Fidel was bound to come into conflict with the United States because American property and businesses were going to suffer, and because in any event his nationalistic revolution had as a major objective breaking United States domination of the Cuban economy.

Under the circumstances it was understandable for Castro to accept help from the then small and unimportant Cuban Communist movement, even though it had done nothing to help him and had, in fact, supported Batista. As the internal conflict and the conflict with the United States intensified, the Communists were first tolerated, then used and then needed. The economic struggle with the United States meant that Cuba would either have to come to terms with the United States or would have to turn to the Soviet Union for help.

I doubt that historians will ever be able to agree on whether the Castro regime embraced communism willingly or was forced into a shotgun wedding. My own belief is that Fidel Castro did not originally want to become tied up with the Communists and dependent on them. I believe he was trapped in 1959-60 by his revolutionary aims and the massive pressures against him from the United States policies and the attitude of the American people. Then he persuaded himself that it was the best thing that could happen, after all.

After an event happens, it takes on an inevitability and one feels that it had to happen. Historians—and journalists—build a neat pattern to explain just how a course of events progressed naturally and inescapably to its conclusion. Those who live close to the events, who are a part of them, who know that the forces and pressures involved at any given time in any particular circumstance are enormously complex, that those who are making the history are driven by emotions, consumed with doubts and fears, unable to understand how their opponents feel, unable to grasp all the complicated factors at work—those who understand and see this know there is no inevitability.

There is a special reason why the Cuban Revolution, of all contemporary events, was incalculable. This was, as I said above, because it was given its original form and direction and was dominated at all times—even within possible limits today—by Fidel Castro. If ever there was an incalculable creature on earth, it was Fidel.

He took over quickly. Looking back, it would seem incredible that he ever expected to do anything else. Knowing him, I would say that every fiber in his body cried out for leadership, but I would also say that he could have fooled himself into believing that he did not have to take command of the revolution. He came to Havana untrained in the arts of politics, economics and administration. He had no idea what it meant to carry out a social revolution in actual fact and not in romantic, unsystematic theory. There was no communism whatever in the revolution at the time, and Fidel was, in those days, instinctively and emotionally anti-Communist.

Latin American history has been dominated for the past 150 years by a phenomenon known as "personalism." The *caudillo*, the dictator, the strong president, the individual—these have been the rulers. The instinct of the Latin American, his loyalty and trust and obedience have gone to men, more than to parties, more, even, than to the nation.

In Cuba democracy had been growing until Batista made his garrison revolt in March, 1952, but it was still a feeble growth. Fidel Castro was a hero to 90 to 95 per cent of the Cubans, and to an emotional, worshipful degree that had to be seen to be realized. It was in vain

97

that he set up the well-meaning but weak and little-known lawyer, José Miró Cardona, as Premier. Everyone went to Fidel with everything, however big or small. If ever a man was drafted as leader, it was Fidel Castro. One might add that, if ever a man was willing to be drafted, it was also Fidel Castro.

Leadership satisfied his ambitions, but it also conformed to the necessities of the moment and to the ideas that he and his associates developed at the time. In fact, back in December, 1957, Fidel had written to the Cuban exiles in Miami that "anarchy is the worst enemy of a revolutionary process."

Modern social revolutions, ever since the French started them, in 1789, have followed certain roughly similar patterns. The parallels between the French and the Cuban Revolutions are, in fact, striking.

"When you undertake to run a revolution," Mirabeau said early in the French Revolution, "the difficulty is not to make it go; it is to hold it in check." And to quote another Frenchman, it was Chateaubriand who pointed out that "the patricians begin a revolution; the plebeians finish it." As we would say today, "the middle-class intellectuals begin social revolutions; the demagogues (of the Left or the Right) finish them."

Those who had fought in or supported the civic resistance against Batista in the cities were like the Girondins of the French Revolution.

"The Girondins," wrote the English historian, H. A. L. Fisher in *A History of Europe,* "were the last apostles of the liberal idea. They believed in liberty, local and personal. They had a vision of France settling down to a blameless and brilliant existence under a Republican Constitution, the finest in the world."

However, it was the fanatical, tyrannical, violent Jacobins who got the upper hand, and when Robespierre and the other Jacobin leaders were guillotined in their turn in 1794, and the Girondins tried to make a comeback, not they, but Napoleon Bonaparte came to power. The unhappy lesson of all modern social revolutions is that the moderate, the liberal, the democratic elements have to wait until the revolution has spent its force.

"The clue to an understanding of revolutions," to cite Fisher again, "is that they are worked by small fanatical minorities." And as Albert Camus pointed out in *The Rebel:* "All modern revolutions have ended in a reinforcement of the State."

The Castro revolution has conformed to type. In a haphazard, opportunistic way, almost as if it were responding to compulsive forces, it quickly built up a centralized structure of which Fidel Castro became absolute master.

What Fidel, Che Guevara, Raul Castro and the others did, was to use the technique first evolved in this century by Lenin (and later also used by the Fascists, the Nazis, Franco in Spain, some Latin American *caudillos*). Power is seized by a determined minority through control of the army, police and means of communication. It is used to make the revolution, not (or not at first) to create a power élite or the super-mechanism of the party or state. That comes later. Walt Whitman Rostow, incidentally, says that "transitional societies" are peculiarly vulnerable to such a seizure of power—and Cuba in 1959 could be described as a nation in which the foundations of transition toward a "take-off" had been laid.

In any event, modern social revolutions of the type exemplified by the French Revolution all have totalitarian characteristics while they are taking place. This is no excuse for totalitarianism; it is a simple statement of fact. There are other types of social revolutions—Uruguay and Costa Rica are examples in Latin America—but such a peaceful, essentially evolutionary method of change was not possible in Cuba in 1959.

In the case of the Fascists and Communists, the totalitarianism is doctrinal and it becomes relatively static, at which time it ceases to be revolutionary. The Soviet Union is not a revolutionary country today nor, for instance, was Fascist Italy in the 1930's. There is nothing static about the Cuban Revolution, although it is on the way to becoming a type of Communist regime.

I think in these days we can dismiss the Fascist revolutions. There are fascistoid regimes, such as Spain's and Portugal's, but with the defeat of the Axis in the Second World War we put an end for the time being to the true Fascist regimes and there is no evidence that doctrinal fascism can make a comeback anywhere. Elements of fascism are a permanent part of the contemporary world and we even see them in the United States in the John Birch Society and the types of people and organizations which support the recrudescence of McCarthyism in all its forms.

The post-war social revolutions are nationalistic and

Leftist, and at best, neutralist. None has been truly Communist except China's and Yugoslavia's, plus those satellites of the solid Soviet bloc forced into communism by military pressures. Many of the new African nations and Egypt, Iraq and Indonesia are examples of the nationalistic, neutralist type of revolution.

Leon Trotsky somewhere wrote of "the innate inability of the Anglo-Saxon political genius to understand a revolutionary situation." How true that was! Americans could not even see the Cuban revolution for a long time, and when they did they could not understand it. This was not true of Latin Americans, nor even of Europeans. We should not forget that even Thomas Jefferson disapproved of the French Revolution. Andrew Jackson would probably have understood the Cuban phenomenon better. So would Franklin D. Roosevelt. Certainly not Dwight D. Eisenhower.

A social revolution destroys the existing political, economic and social fabric of a nation and transfers power and the control of the economy to a small group of men who are necessarily extremists. They thereupon create a new structure on the ruins of the old. If the work of destruction is done thoroughly (and this is the case in Cuba) it is never possible to turn the clock back, to restore the *ancien régime*.

In order to understand a social revolution, you must put yourself in the place of those making the revolution and recognize that revolutions have their own logic. You must not—and this was a cardinal error in American thinking—interpret what is happening by your own yardsticks. In our case this meant trying to interpret what was happening in Cuba in terms of our own stable, moderate, efficient, orderly, mature, democratic way of life. These had no relevance to Cuba. In any circumstances, it is not possible to apply criteria of normalcy to a revolutionary situation. Democracy, elections and free enterprise are simply not possible while a revolution of this type is being made, not because it is Communist but because a system like ours requires peace, stability and slow evolution, not sudden revolution. Criticize the Cubans, if you will, for having a revolution, or for making their revolution the way they are doing. Ask them to have democratic elections, but don't ask unless you realize you are asking them to give up their revolution.

It should not be necessary to say (although apparently it is) that to explain and describe a social revolution like Cuba's is not to praise or excuse it. I do not believe in quarreling with history. The failure to understand what happened in Cuba in 1959 was, to me, the inexcusable thing. No one can say how much difference this may have made, but a failure to understand would, in any circumstances, have been fatal.

Social revolutions of the Cuban type inevitably have a class character. The "revolt" is against the existing ruling class already described and which in Cuba, as elsewhere in Latin America, was a small group of landowners, businessmen, bankers, high military officers and the politicians who came from these elements. These are middle- and upper-class groups. Those whom the revolution aims to favor are the masses—in Latin America mainly the peasants, but also the urban proletariat of the mushrooming slums.

To make such a revolution, you need new men whose first qualification must be loyalty to the revolution and its leader. There was astonishment and ridicule when Premier Fidel Castro appointed Che Guevara as President of the National Bank of Cuba in November, 1959, to succeed one of the most competent and internationally respected economists in Cuba, Felipe Pazos. Yet, it was a logical move at that stage. Che knew nothing about banking, but Fidel needed a revolutionary, and there are no revolutionary bankers.

The old ruling class, as I said, was displaced and dispossessed. Anyway, it was thoroughly discredited, for it had permitted and profited by all the abuses and failings that made Cuba ripe for revolution. The replacements were naturally, for the most part, young men. This meant they had no experience in business, public administration or the professions. There were no millionaires, no generals, no politicians and few technicians.

Obviously, one was not to expect efficiency or organization. The disorganization in Cuba was, in fact, appalling.

Yet, a revolution sets great forces in motion. It is like a cataclysm of nature. A nation is alive; it is the composite of the men and women who live in it—and few nations are as vividly alive as Cuba. The country had been geared to a certain pace, a certain way of life, a whole complex machinery of economy, government and social relations.

The revolution upset all this. It gathered momentum

fast. A revolution is a process, not an event. The dynamism was such that those who lost touch with Cuba for even a few months did not really know what was happening. Yet the momentum of civic life does not stop. Everything keeps going but unevenly, clumsily, uncontrollably. Everybody tries to carry on as before, to do his work, hold his job, his property or his business. The complicated bureaucracy of government has to continue as best it can.

All the time, the powerful forces unleashed by the revolution are beating on this structure with the fury of a tropical storm—and it crumbles. The new leaders are not only inexperienced and unrealistic; they are concerned far more with social and political objectives than with the economy. They have to be tough, hard, contemptuous of the sufferings of the few, intolerant—one is tempted to say, fanatical. Your dedicated idealist in the revolutionary field is like that. Revolutions are not made by weak or timid men. The new leaders play to win and in the process break many hearts, commit many injustices to individuals or groups.

A revolutionary leader has to be an extraordinary character with extraordinary qualities of courage, leadership, ability, intelligence, popular appeal. In Latin America, with its invariable, inescapable feature of "personalism," the revolution will be made by one man, in the past a general, in Cuba a charismatic leader.

What makes the phenomenon a revolution in the true sense of the word is bringing about a complete change—social, economic and political. What makes it a Leftist revolution in modern terms can be expressed in very old words from the "Magnificat" of Luke: "He hath put down the mighty from their seats, and exalted them of low degree."

Within this general framework, revolutions take their particular, national form. This was—and still is—a Cuban revolution. Even granting that it has become more and more communistic; even supposing it goes on to become a Communist revolution, it would still be a Cuban revolution; it would have to be interpreted in Cuban and Latin American terms. At the very most, it would be a bastard child of Moscow and Peiping, and a very unruly one—in fact, a juvenile delinquent from their point of view.

Chancellor Jaime Benitez of the University of Puerto Rico tries to explain the dichotomy by making a distinction between "the two Castros, the two revolutions," "the one reaching for social reforms through liberalism and freedom," the other "a haphazard, totalitarian, propaganda operation, run in mobocratic fashion; complete with government by marathon television spectaculars, by artificial crises, organized hysteria, calculated bloodletting and deliberate vulgarization. It is a corruption of the Cuban Revolution that has not yet destroyed it."

For Dr. Benitez, the revolution is not based on Marxist principles—"really it is much less scientific and profound." This was the opinion that Ambassador Adlai Stevenson found prevalent in South America during his trip in June, 1961. He said Latin America made a distinction between the Cuban Revolution and communism, a distinction that the United States Government (quite wrongly, in my opinion) stopped making in March, 1960.

On our part, we were failing to understand, over-simplifying, not grasping the fact that the Cuban Revolution, for all its startling newness, had profound roots in Cuban and Latin American history. It came out of the past, not out of Moscow.

Latin America has been notorious—even a little ridiculous—for its political instability, its innumerable so-called revolutions. Yet there has, on the whole, been social stability—almost immobility—for 450 years. The same ruling classes are still in control—those I have mentioned before. They were, at first, the aristocratic, hereditary landowners and the military officers and *caudillos* who came out of that element, and then, also, the business and banking interests when they developed. The political leaders came out of these same groups. Taken together, they make a small privileged, often corrupt, relatively (sometimes fantastically) wealthy, exclusive ruling class. Through the military establishments, whose generals and colonels belong to this class, they hold the decisive power in nearly all the Latin American countries.

As a general rule, the masses (at first rural workers and then also the urban proletariat) have lived in real or at best, relative, poverty, ignorance and disease. We all know, surely, in the year 1961, that this state of affairs is no longer acceptable. Those masses now know that their misery is not the will of God or Allah or destiny, but is due to the selfishness, inefficiency and corruption of their rulers. This is not a Latin American phenomenon; it is world-wide.

The revolutionary pressures one sees and hears about in Latin America are essentially a demand for social justice —a higher standard of living, a better distribution of wealth, what President Kennedy in an address at the White House in March, 1961, gave as "homes, work and land, health and schools." This idea is also at the basis of Pope John XXIII's Encyclical of July 21, 1961.

Who is going to satisfy these demands, or, to be more realistic, give the promise of satisfying them? This is where the cold war comes into the Western Hemisphere, and it was brought in by the Cuban revolution. Until that upheaval we had an ideological monopoly in the Western Hemisphere. The Latin American nations had only one road to take—the long, slow, uphill but sure way to our capitalistic, free-enterprise, democratic system. We said, in effect: "First you have your economic development; then you can make your social changes. Evolution, not revolution."

But this post-war world is revolutionary. Not our part of it, to be sure, not our affluent society with its fantastically high standard of living, its peaceful, stable, mature, democratic way of life. The rest of the world— what sociologists are calling the southern half of the world—underdeveloped, backward, inexperienced, uncommitted, clutching wildly for the better things of life— this world is now hearing another siren's song.

There were two streams of political thought that came out of the eighteenth century. We, the British, the Northern Europeans, the Anglo-Saxon Commonwealth nations and a few others, are products of a liberal democratic stream. The Communists, the Fascists, the authoritarians of different varieties, are products of another stream, the one J. L. Talmon calls "totalitarian democracy." It has been flowing in eastern Europe and Asia, and seeping into Latin America. It says, in effect: "First you make your social change (in other words, first have your revolution) and then have economic development."

This is what Russia did and what China is doing. It is what Cuba is trying to do. It is the revolutionary road— radical, Leftist, socialistic, communistic.

It may be that a third road is beginning to open up (in Africa and Asia, as well as in the Western Hemisphere). In Latin America it might be hewed by the Brazil of President Janio Quadros—not a free-enterprise, capitalistic system like ours, nor the totalitarian-socialistic type of the Soviet bloc, which Cuba is embracing. It would be socialistic in the sense of a very high degree of government planning and control, but it would be capitalistic in the considerable field left to private enterprise and the orthodox methods of banking, credit and financial operations generally.

Most important of all, it would be politically neutral and independent—in the case of Brazil, essentially democratic. It would not try to copy the United States or the Soviet Union. It would not be dependent on either. Insofar as it resembles any contemporary form, it would be a social democratic (hence socialistic) welfare state with an exceptionally strong executive. It would be intensely nationalistic, and hence would be no country's satellite.

The evolution of such a type of government is possible in Brazil, and perhaps in a few other rich and developed Latin American nations like Mexico, Argentina and Chile. Whether there is time, opportunity, leadership and United States, as well as local, wisdom are the great questions. In this year 1961, as in 1959 and 1960, we have been seeing a polarization of thoughts and aims in Latin America, brought about by the Cuban Revolution. There was only one way before 1959 because of our overwhelming power, wealth and influence. It was our way.

Fidel Castro and his associates were the first in the history of Latin America to come along and say: "There must be another way. The old way brought us social imbalance, corruption, political inefficiency and subservience to a foreign power—the Yankees. Let us break with the past and find new ground." If the Cuban Revolution fails it will be because they do not find "new" ground; because they do not make a *Cuban* Revolution. They will have moved into the different, but neither original nor especially Latin American, ground of totalitarian communism *à la Moscou.*

I am saying: "if." I am not saying they have yet failed to make a Cuban Revolution. It is too soon to say; the Revolution is too dynamic, too dominated by individuals who are under no orders and no discipline, and, above all, it is under the supreme direction of one of the most original and incalculable characters of the twentieth century —Fidel Castro.

In its idealism—and there has been and still is genuine idealism behind it—the Cuban Revolution is an expression of the aspirations and the needs of the masses of the people in Latin America. It is a result of the forces that have been at work in Cuba and in Latin America—not for years, but for generations. The causes of the Cuban Revolution and of the revolutionary pressures in the hemisphere go back centuries before Marx and Lenin or the birth of Fidel Castro. This means that if we succeed in destroying, or helping to destroy, the Castro regime, we and Cuba would be facing the same pressures, the same ideals and aspirations and demands for social justice.

What we would also be facing in Cuba (and this is something that Americans do not seem to want to recognize) is a revolution that has triumphed, a revolution that has been made. Not all the Cuban exiles, even if they had succeeded in their invasion of April, 1961, not the Central Intelligence Agency, not even the American Marines if we were so mad as to use them, could put this Cuban Humpty-Dumpty, whom we once nursed so carefully, together again.

A detailed attempt to analyze what has and what has not been done in Cuba by the Castro regime would be out of place in this book, aside from the fact that the dynamism of the Revolution is such that events quickly overpass the descriptions of a given period. The Cuban Revolution is a process, as I remarked before, not a set piece that one can photograph. It must be felt, understood, watched for its trends and calculated on the basis of the complicated Cuban and international forces at work, as well as the individual factors, with special attention paid to the overwhelming personality of the revolutionary leader, Fidel Castro.

However, certain broad features of the process need underlining if only because American press, radio and television coverage, official propaganda and the wishful thinking of Cuban exiles have tended to give a mistaken impression. The Cuban economy is not going to collapse. There was a possibility of this in 1959 and especially in 1960 after we cut off the sugar quota imports, but so long as the Communist bloc continues to help, the Castro regime can carry on and, in fact, the general trend this year is, if anything, slightly upward.

American press coverage has generally concentrated on the bad or weak features of the Revolution, of which there have been many. As a result, the fact that the regime was making good progress in some directions and doing some very good things was overlooked. José M. Bosch, Cuba's leading businessman, told me in 1960 that before the Revolution Cuba was going downhill fast economically and would have been ruined in five or six years. To be sure, Señor Bosch and other Cuban industrialists are convinced that the country is now going downhill even faster.

This depends on what one means by downhill and who is going down. It must never be forgotten that economics is a secondary factor in a social revolution. Most foreign observers have agreed that the Cuban agrarian reform is working fairly well, but even if it were not, the important thing is that there is an agrarian reform. This is what made such a great impact around Latin America where the need for land reforms is basic.

Anyway, the Cuban peasants—say 40 per cent of the population—and many city dwellers, were living at not much better than a subsistence level before the Revolution. Whatever the Revolution did, it could not take them lower. In truth, it has bettered their lot. Even if the agrarian reform creates a Communist-type State system the peasant did not have freedom and democracy before, does not know what they mean and cannot be expected to care.

He does know that for the first time in Cuban history a government cares for him, wants to help him and is helping him. He is now part of a cooperative or state-run farm; he is getting new and decent homes, schools for his children, hospitals, roads. For the first time proper attention is being paid to public health in such matters as digging wells and providing shoes for poor children.

In the United States one hears, or reads, almost nothing about one of the most extraordinary features of the Cuban Revolution—its civic honesty. This is the first honest Government that Cuba has seen since Columbus discovered the island.

Professor Harry Stark of the University of Miami, in his book, *Social and Economic Frontiers in Latin America*, issued in the summer of 1961, paid tribute to the unaccustomed honesty of Cuba today:

Public corruption was entirely eradicated, especially that which had always been rampant in the national lottery. The augmented proceeds from these lotteries were employed to build low cost housing. . . . Military personnel was forbidden to drink alcoholic beverages in public places. Smuggling and customs house corruptions were ended. Tax collections became more efficient and rigorous. Public begging was suppressed. Many new public works projects were started. . . . Noteworthy is the fact that all of this was accomplished with the maintenance of a high quality performance, with strict honesty, and with unbelievable speed.

Let it be conceded in all fairness that the accomplishments of the revolutionary government received almost no news coverage or recognition, and certainly no praise, in the United States.

Whether the public works were of high quality or not, one thing was certain—all the money assigned to a project went into it. Under all preceding Cuban Administrations (and the relatively democratic regimes of Grau San Martín and Prio Socarrás were among the worst) from 40 to 60 per cent of the public monies went into the pockets of government officials and businessmen. General Batista's regular cut, as I mentioned before, was 35 per cent, without counting what others took.

Integration is another feature of the Cuban scene somewhat neglected by Americans. We must not forget that the so-called "image" of the United States throughout Latin America is gravely damaged by the continuance of segregation here. We do not get credit for the progress being made toward integration; we do get the worst kind of publicity from such incidents as the brutal beating by whites of the "Freedom Riders" in Alabama in the spring of 1961.

Negro slaves were imported to Cuba in the first half

of the nineteenth century, mainly to work on the sugar plantations. The aboriginal Indians had died off or been killed off long before. By 1943 a census listed about one quarter of the population as Negro or mulatto. There were no "Jim Crow" laws in Cuba and much intermarriage in the lower levels of society. However, there definitely was a "color line" in society, army, industry, the professions and politics. The ruling classes in Cuba right up to 1959 were overwhelmingly white. The upper-class society was almost wholly white. They had strict color bars in their clubs. Batista, who was of mixed blood, was embarrassed when this was sometimes pointed out.

In revolutionary Cuba there are no color bars. The chief of the Army, for instance, Juan Almeida (who was with Fidel when I went up to the Sierra Maestra in February, 1957) is a Negro. There were no Negro high officers before under the Republic.

It would not have been necessary to call attention to these features of the Cuban Revolution if they had been fairly reported to the American people. I do not mean at all to give the impression that Cuba is now a paradise, that all is well, that the Revolution is a shining success.

Far from it! Terrible mistakes have been made; some very bad things have been, and are being, done. I was one of the first in the United States in 1959 to point to the absolute power that Fidel Castro had assumed. As I wrote for Stanford University's Hispanic American Report in August, 1960: "The regime is a dictatorship, without freedom, under the control of one man. Law is an arbitrary concept." I brought sorrow to my Cuban admirers when I told an audience of alumni at Columbia University in June, 1961, that Cuba was then and had been for some time "a totalitarian police state."

I do virtually all the editorials on Latin America that appear in *The New York Times,* including those on Cuba. For nearly two years now these editorials have been uniformly critical, although they have not paralleled the emotional and sometimes misinformed interpretation of most United States newspapers, and they have not seen the Cuban Revolution in the same terms as those of the exiles in Miami. Being "pegged" to news items from Havana and Washington, they did not do justice to the good features of the Revolution, either, but it has taken courage on the part of *The New York Times* to keep its editorials on Cuba within the bounds of the true situation.

That situation was especially open to criticism in the drift of the Castro regime toward and into the communistic camp. This is the feature of the Cuban Revolution that has dominated American thinking and emotions, as well as the policies toward Cuba of the Eisenhower and Kennedy Administrations. It has not at all played a similar role in Latin American thinking, as Adlai Stevenson found on his trip to South America in June, 1961, nor has Canada or the rest of the world accepted the American thesis.

The problem that future historians will have to face lies in the fact that the Castro regime was not communistic in its early stages but gradually moved deeper and deeper into the Communist camp, and if this trend continues we will have a Cuban variety of communism.

I do not believe myself that there will be any problem for these historians on the question of whether Fidel Castro, Che Guevara, Raul Castro and some other top leaders were, themselves, Communists. They always denied that they were and there is no evidence to date that the top three—Fidel, Che and Raul—ever were Communists in the sense of being members of any Communist party. Not even the United States White Paper was able to claim this. It surely should be obvious (although apparently it is not) that if the CIA or the FBI or the American Embassy in Havana or the State Department was ever able to unearth proof that any of these men were Communists, they would have proclaimed it triumphantly to the world. The argument that they might just as well be Communists is another matter, but this is quite different from saying that they were, or are, Communists.

New evidence may change the picture, but on the evidence available and on my personal knowledge of Fidel Castro, I have always said and I still say that he was not and is not a Communist.

The Publisher of *The New York Times,* Arthur Hays Sulzberger, was, like many others, puzzled by my insistence and asked me for an explanation after a trip I made to Cuba in August, 1960. This was my reply:

I have your note asking what my definition of a Communist is. I have a very simple and straightforward one—and I consider it the only exact one.

A Communist is a man—or woman—who 1) either belongs

openly to the Communist party or 2) is a crypto-Communist. In either case the person takes his orders from his party or movement, is responsible to it and is an agent of Moscow.

In my opinion it is most important to make this distinction. Take the Cubans. It may make no difference whatever *today* and in practice for the time being, whether they are Reds or simply doing as the Reds do. In the long run it can make all the difference in the world, because, if they are not under Communist discipline, taking orders from the party and Moscow, they can change. They can even turn on the Reds and destroy them.

The terms communism and Communist are much too loosely used in the American press and by Americans generally. I believe that the precise definition I have give above is the only one we should use in *The Times*—and as a matter of fact, I think it is.

The problem, from the beginning, was that Fidel Castro was making a radical, Leftist, nationalistic revolution that inevitably brought conflict with the United States. The old cry: "Our enemy is on the Right! No enemies to the Left!" heard in the West since the French Revolution was now being heard in Cuba.

The Batista dictatorship had laid the foundation for the Communists. In Cuba all the old-line political parties had been thoroughly discredited or broken up into fragments. The 26th of July Movement was a congeries of men, parties and classes, split down the middle by a dividing line between the Sierra Maestra group, who were out for a very radical social revolution, and the civic resistance, which wanted to make social reforms but in a democratic, evolutionary way.

This left only the Cuban Communists, trained, organized and ready. Their party kept on functioning from the Batista era. It was—and is—called the *Partido Socialista Popular* (Popular Socialist Party). It had not helped Fidel Castro—on the contrary—but it was naturally ready to help now and, being tolerated, became the only political party operating in Cuba. This did not mean that it even remotely had the sort of power Communist parties have in Communist countries, especially for the first year and a half, but American thinking with regard to communism is over-simplified and blinded by emotions, and this simple and obvious distinction was not made.

As a result, the Cuban Communists were given an importance all out of proportion to the reality. Some of us kept warning from the beginning that this played right into their hands. It was exactly what they needed to build them up and to attract adherents. The psychology of Fidel Castro and the other young revolutionaries was such that the more they were attacked for being Communists, or the dupes of Communists, the more difficult it became to oppose communism if they wanted to. For Fidel, especially, to turn against the Reds would have seemed like truckling to the United States, yielding to American attacks, and he would rather have his throat cut than do that.

In Cuba, nothing was more helpful to the Reds than the fact that the American press, radio and television, Congress and many American diplomats and businessmen conceded victory to the Communists long before they had won it. We surrendered before we had begun to lose.

The first, and probably most damaging, major attack in this field came from Stuart Novins of the Columbia Broadcasting System on May 3, 1959. The material had been gathered in March and April. The theme was that "this Cuban island is today a totalitarian dictatorship and is rapidly becoming a Communist beachhead in the Caribbean."

It was nothing of the sort at that time. Because it became more or less that, one gets the appearance of accuracy and prescience. Yet, anyone studying the text of the telecast then and now, knowing the facts or even using common sense, will see that the arguments Novins was using to "prove" his thesis were feeble to the point of ludicrousness. This was true of all the commentators and correspondents who harped on this theme from the beginning and who now say: "We told you so."

The historian will not have such an easy time of it and there is no validity, today, in saying: "What's the difference?" It might have made a lot of difference if there had been more understanding in the formative stages of the Cuban Revolution. This is aside from the desirability of keeping the record straight.

As I remarked earlier, it will never be possible to figure out the extent to which the young Cuban leaders wanted Communism and the extent to which they were forced into reliance on Communism. Those who were closest to Fidel Castro in 1959 could feel assured that neither he certainly, nor, with some doubts, any of the men in positions of control were Communists, and that they had a

Cuban revolution, not a Communist revolution. This will surely be the verdict of history.

However, it was always obvious that there were many Communists at secondary and lower levels. They naturally supported the revolutionary government from the beginning. Fidel, on his part, was making a revolution in which he had to attack the conservative, propertied, business classes on the Right. He asked why he should gratuitously attack the Communists on his Left when they were supporting him and when, as he confidently believed, they were weak and unimportant? He wanted to unite all the forces of the Left.

This was the position for many months, until he and his top advisers became convinced that the answer to their revolutionary problems lay in the methods of totalitarian communism. I would place the final decision on this, so far as Fidel was concerned, in the late summer or early autumn of 1960. So far as Che Guevara and Raul Castro were concerned, it would have come sooner and they undoubtedly influenced Fidel.

His early calculations were logical and understandable. He did not want a Communist revolution and I know what a low opinion he had of the Cuban Reds. He was not underestimating them personally, with the possible exception of Rafael Rodríguez, but he was underestimating the efficiency, skill and experience that lay in the Communist technique.

I suppose I was one of the first to warn him and all the young leaders of that danger, for I began in January, 1959, and was hard at it the last time I saw Fidel, which was in August, 1960. The most effective argument, I thought, was to impress upon them all that they could have a Cuban revolution, or a Communist revolution, but not both. I pointed out that the Reds were not working for Cuba or for Fidel and that their revolution was not his revolution. I was myself underestimating the danger, because I believed that the young revolutionaries recognized these threats and would fight against them in the showdown. I now think it is possible that they can have a communistic type of revolution that is also Cuban and Latin American.

The argument that the Cuban Reds had helped Batista, not the 26th of July Movement, was beside the point, in the same way that there was no use pointing out how the trade-union leaders had supported Batista. Fidel needed the urban workers and he thought he needed the Reds. The Communists really were useful to him in 1959. That was safe so long as he did not become dependent on them.

Fidel and I always spoke frankly to each other and he took criticism from me that no one else would have dared to utter. He knew that I was sympathetic, understanding and a friend, and since I was old enough to be his father, he respected my age. He is a normally poor listener, but he used to listen to me—and to my wife when we were both in Havana.

I mention this simply to bolster my argument that Fidel Castro had no desire or intention to go the Communist way until events, pressures, perhaps necessity, drove him that way. It was not a previously calculated or an inevitable development.

121

Historians will have to ask themselves how much the American attitude and policies helped to force Fidel Castro in this direction. If this was what he wanted all along, there was nothing the United States could have done to prevent it. If he did not, as many of us believe, then the position taken almost from the beginning by the American press, radio, television, Congress, Pentagon, State Department, the business world and so forth, helped to build up communism and drive Cuba irresistibly into the Communist corner.

There were forces at work in this Cuban drama beyond the control of the Castro regime or of Washington. The leader of any revolution conjures up a storm, and it soon becomes a question whether he is directing it or being driven by it.

The revolutionary chief who wants to sail between the Scylla of the United States and the Charybdis of the Soviet bloc, as Premier Castro did, has an infinitely harder task than President Nasser of the United Arab Republic in a similar situation. Nasser did not have an internal situation like Cuba's; his choice was not so limited; his Communist party was of no account, and his social revolution was not nearly so drastic. In the pinch, he did not become completely dependent on the Soviet bloc, economically, as Fidel Castro has been forced to do.

Here in the United States, since the Second World War, there has been a tendency to equate revolution with communism. We were saying, in effect: the Communists are revolutionaries, the Cubans are revolutionaries; therefore the Cubans are Communists. They were, with secondary exceptions, nothing of the sort, but the belief persisted.

Fidel Castro never realized the intensity of American fears, distrust and dislike of communism. No Latin American understands this, because the cold war has never affected the area directly. Moreover, the Cubans forget that the United States has kept its enemies away from the Western Hemisphere since 1815. Unlike the Europeans, we are not psychologically adjusted to having formidable enemies across a river or a boundary line. The mere threat of communism on our doorstep in Cuba was enough to set up a powerful reaction in the United States.

Americans do not realize it, but their attitude toward communism is just about unique in the world. Europeans, whose danger from communism is greater than ours, consider us positively hysterical on the subject. It is little short of idiotic that we should think communism is a great internal menace in the United States. McCarthyism had the abnormality of a disease, just as its contemporary equivalent of John Birchism has.

The shadow of Guatemala hung over Cuba from the beginning. The Guatemalans, in 1944, had overthrown a typical Latin American dictator, General Jorge Ubico. The major economic role in Guatemala was played by the United Fruit Company and bananas. The young revolutionaries were liberal, radical, nationalistic but not, in those early stages, pro-Communist. They were simply tolerant of the Reds.

The Communists worked cleverly; the Americans stupidly. We put ourselves in the position of opposing social reforms, leaving the field to the Reds. As in Cuba, our diplomacy was appallingly amateurish and reactionary. The Communists gathered strength; we registered alarm. The Central Intelligence Agency set to work. We realize now the extent to which Secretary John Foster and his brother, Allen Dulles, used to work together.

Here, too, a hostile and ill-informed American press helped to create an emotional public opinion. This, in turn, worked on Congress and, ultimately, on the State Department. Other factors were, of course, at work in Guatemala, but the American attitude would, by itself, have had the effect of strengthening the Guatemalan Reds and making a United States reaction inevitable.

We intervened by helping an obscure Guatemalan Colonel, Carlos Castillo Armas, to overthrow the Arbenz regime. It was easy because the Guatemalan Army had not been subverted by communism, as some of us were trying to make the American public and State Department understand. That wise statesman, José Figueres, ex-President of Costa Rica, felt sure the Guatemalans could have handled the problem by themselves if we had been more sensible.

Instead we mobilized all our efforts and propaganda, pistol-packing American Ambassador included, and arranged to throw President Jácobo Arbenz and the Communists out. (Let it be said in passing that Guatemala's social and economic problems are yet to be solved; it is one of the many countries where the United States fears an attempted Fidelista revolution.)

It should have been crystal clear that Cuba was no

Guatemala, that the Cubans were not Guatemalans and that Fidel Castro was not Jácobo Arbenz. If the CIA was looking at anything crystal it was a crystal ball.

Fidel Castro and the others knew that elements in the United States would want to repeat the Guatemalan experience. Although its effect on our Latin American relations and the Latin attitude toward us remain very bad, the event was rated as a triumph for Allen Dulles and the CIA, and our newspapers still treat it as such.

A number of writers have tried with varying success to analyze the process whereby Cuba went deeply into the Communist camp. The Communists have a technique for such situations and it was applied skillfully. They work from the bottom up through key features like education, trade unions, police, the army.

The three top leaders, as I said before, were not Communists, but two of them—Che Guevara and Raul Castro —were pro-Communist. Fidel, I believe, was instinctively and by conviction anti-Communist for a long time. The main factor, with him, was that he did not care much what the Communists did. The business of keeping the Revolution and the country going was so fantastically burdensome that he at first put the Communist problem in a minor category.

I had seen something like this happen in Spain during the Civil War. Premier Juan Negrín was no Communist and had no intention of allowing the Reds to get control of the key points of governmental power, but aside from that he did not care what they did. Because the Soviet Union was the only country helping the Spanish Loyalists, the Reds became more and more powerful internally. This, also, is what has happened in Cuba (and Che Guevara warned me early that it could happen).

For the purposes of this book, the basic facts to keep in mind are simple enough. This was, essentially, a revolution without a doctrine. At the beginning there was a vague philosophical content labeled "Humanism," but it was not original or precise enough for formulation as a system. In these matters, as Vilfredo Pareto, the Italian sociologist, pointed out a long time ago, you first have the concrete fact and then the abstraction. In the case of Cuba, the concrete facts, as they were performed opportunistically from day to day, led into the abstraction of Marxism (a special form of it) and the methods of totalitarianism, communistic style.

The Cuban Revolution has been taking form day by day under fierce pressures and with a desperate sense of haste. It could not invent any new philosophy. Anyway, Fidel Castro never was an original political thinker. Moreover, it was a revolution without a party and that, too, was a reason why the Communists were able to move in so effectively. In theory, Fidel could have developed the 26th of July Movement into a one-party system such as Mexico has with her Institutional Revolutionary Party (PRI) but, as I pointed out before, Fidel knew—or thought—that middle- and upper-class elements in the 26th of July Movement would not go for the radical social revolution he had in mind. This left the field clear for the Communist party. A forthcoming merger of the two groups was announced by Fidel on July 26, 1961. The "United

Party of Cuba's Socialist Revolution" is a creature of the Communist wing, not of the 26th of July Movement.

In this matter of communism, as in everything else connected with the Cuban Revolution, one must avoid over-simplifying. The factors and pressures that drove the Castro regime into the Communist camp were enormously complicated. Besides the features mentioned, there was the whole complex of relations with the United States, the historic factors, the economic problems, the pressures of the cold war and by no means least, the character of the young men making the Cuban Revolution.

I say they had no intention or desire of making a Communist revolution. For all of 1959, Cubans put a supplementary stamp on their letters to the United States with these words in English:

Our Revolution is NOT COMMUNIST
Our Revolution is HUMANIST

The Cubans only want the right to an education,
the right to work, the right to eat without fear,
the right to PEACE, JUSTICE, FREEDOM

At the trial of Major Huber Matos, commander of the Camaguey garrison, for treason in December, 1959, Premier Castro protested:

"Ours is not a Communist revolution. Ours is, I admit, a radical revolution—probably the most radical in Cuban history." He also said that his regime was "neither scientifically nor theoretically communistic." He had said the same things, even more strongly, during his trip to the United States in April, 1959—and he meant them.

A year later, Fidel was talking differently, but these were honest statements at the time they were made. It was, in fact, nearly a year later that Che Cuevara made a sensational—and often misquoted—statement on Marxism.

"On the question of whether we are Marxists or consider ourselves to be Marxists," he said in a speech, "I can tell you the following. If a man falls out of a tree a number of times, he makes certain deductions, draws certain conclusions, and on the basis of these, he may be considered a Newtonian.

"In precisely this way, we have made certain discoveries about the underlying conditions that relate to our situation. If these principles that we have deduced are Marxist principles, then in this sense it is possible to call us Marxists."

Che is no doctrinaire. I have never met anyone who more strikingly embodies the characteristics of the rebel than the Argentine, Ernesto Guevara. He instinctively rebels against society, country, Church and every other institution. It never was necessary to interpret his ideas and actions in terms of communism. His life, his character and the events in which he participated all put him on the Communist side, but if circumstances change he will have no emotional or intellectual problem whatever in becoming anti-Communist. He called himself, in an interview with Laura Bergquist of *Look* magazine, published on November 8, 1960, a "pragmatic revolutionary."

So far as I could see, his one and only loyalty—sincere

and overriding—was his admiration and affection for Fidel Castro. This dates back to their first association in Mexico when the landing was being planned. Che is far and away the most intelligent of the men around Fidel, and he has the un-Cuban characteristic of being well organized in his work. He is unquestionably the most influential person in Cuba aside from Fidel Castro, but it must never be forgotten that his power and influence on events are delegated by Fidel. He has gained his position because of his abilities and persuasiveness, and because his ideas conform to Fidel's.

Raul Castro likewise gets his power and influence from Fidel and would be nothing without his older brother. He is unattractive and unpopular, but a first-rate administrator. Both these young men are intensely anti-Yankee, for different reasons, and both were pro-Communist from early student days. The fact that Raul attended a World Youth Festival organized by the Communists in Prague, when he was twenty-one, and that he spent a few months behind the Iron Curtain at the time, has been taken by Americans, naïvely, as "proof" that he was Communist. As with other matters, one can argue that Raul Castro might as well have been Communist, but this is another argument.

At the Huber Matos trial, during his testimony, Raul Castro said "[if] at any time the Communists place themselves against the Revolution, we will fight the Communists." Of course, the Reds would not and did not.

What was more to the point was a statement Che Guevara made to some Australian journalists in Havana on July 13, 1960. While Cuba is grateful to the Soviet Union, he said, any attempt by the Russians to establish a Communist satellite in Cuba "would be resisted to the last drop of blood."

This should not be doubted, although, of course, the contention that Cuba is a Communist satellite lies at the heart of the United States policies toward the Castro regime. I would deny it in the sense that the Castro Government takes no orders from Moscow, often, in fact, disconcerts Moscow by its policies, and because I feel sure that the young Cuban revolutionaries did not fight, as they saw it, against "Yankee imperialism" just to fall under the yoke of Russian imperialism.

On the other hand, the way events and our policies developed, the Castro regime became dependent on the Soviet bloc, especially after we cut off their sugar import quota in July, 1960. At the same time the Cuban leaders convinced themselves that something similar to the Communist methods—something they called "Socialism"—provided the answers to their problems.

"Every day my admiration for Lenin grows," Fidel Castro told K. S. Karol in an interview that appeared in the English weekly, the *New Statesman*, on May 19, 1961. "The more I know about his work and his life and above all the more I understand the revolution, the more I admire Lenin. Only now can I grasp the difficulties Lenin had to overcome and the magnitude of the heritage he bequeathed humanity. . . . It's not the same thing to talk about revolution in theory—and actually to carry one out oneself."

So, by 1961, Cuba had become (to coin a word) communistoid. It was not communism as Moscow and Peiping understood it, but it was communism as Washington understood it. It was not socialism as understood and practiced in Great Britain and Western Europe, but it was a form of socialism.

It had borrowed its ideas and methods from Iron Curtain Europe, but it remained a Cuban and Latin American revolution. Above all, it remained Fidel Castro's revolution.

CHAPTER FOUR

Fidel Castro

No ONE CAN know the Cuban Revolution who does not know Fidel Castro. I had a unique opportunity to get to know him, to have his confidence, respect, friendship, even his ear—all of which, obviously, made no difference to what he did or what he believed. I wish I could say that I influenced the Cuban Revolution; it would have been a very different revolution if I had been able to.

Not that I tried, especially, but it was impossible not to argue or to say and write what I believed. Many people thought that Fidel would listen to me, and only to me. He would listen—and then do what he always had it in his mind to do at that particular time.

One of the minor aberrations of the first weeks of the Revolution in January, 1959, was an attempt—not by me —to get me named United States Ambassador to Cuba. Among the Havana newspapers that picked up the idea was *El País,* run by Guillermo Martínez Marques, ex-

President of the Inter-American Press Association. On January 13, 1959, the Havana *Post* ran a front-page story:

> Jules Dubois, Chicago *Tribune* correspondent currently in Cuba, went on record yesterday as endorsing Herbert Matthews, editorial writer of *The New York Times* as United States Ambassador to Cuba to fill the spot vacated by Earl E. T. Smith.
>
> Dubois, President of the Committee on Freedom of the Press of the IAPA, sent his recommendation in a cable to Vice President Nixon and several other high Washington officials.
>
> Others receiving a copy of the Dubois cable included Press Secretary Hagerty and Senators Morse and Aiken.
>
> Commenting on the recommendation Matthews said: "It is the gesture of a friend but I don't think it possible or convenient."

In fact, it was impossible and would have been quite wrong, although I take a sardonic pleasure now in looking back on the episode. Actually, it is important for an envoy to be uncommitted. Considering how involved I had become, I am sure I would not have been a desirable candidate.

There was a point, however, in seeking an ambassador who understood what had happened and who had the respect and friendship of Fidel Castro. I have often thought that Cuban-American relations could have taken a different turn if we had had such an envoy in the first six months or more of 1959. But diplomacy is not like that any more.

In any event, the important factor then, and later— never sufficiently grasped in the United States—was the overwhelming role that Fidel Castro played. It really was his revolution, as I stated before. He has been driven by the force of events outside his control, but he has also, himself, been the major driving force of the revolution inside Cuba. It was within his power to give the revolution, to a considerable extent, the direction, the pace, the tone and the intensity that it has taken.

In the United States he was underrated, ridiculed and misunderstood, and we have paid a heavy price for this folly. One of the things for which I can genuinely claim credit in this Cuban affair is to have recognized from the beginning, up in the jungles of the Sierra Maestra on February 17, 1957, that this was a man of remarkable qualities. A week after he reached Havana in triumph I wrote for *The Times's* "News of the Week" section:

"Whatever one wants to think, everybody here seems agreed that Dr. Castro is one of the most extraordinary figures ever to appear on the Latin American scene. He is by any standards a man of destiny."

This was the period, just before the executions of the "war criminals" began, when the American press was praising and romanticizing Fidel Castro as if he were a knight in shining armor who had come to Havana on a white horse and who was going to make democracy, bring social justice but otherwise let things go on as before. Some of this rosy aura still hung around Fidel when he came to the United States in April, 1959, at the invitation of the American Society of Newspaper Editors. That, his efforts to please and his terrific personality brought him a truly friendly reception.

So, Americans have been saying ever since: "We

praised and welcomed him at first; we wanted to be friends, but look at the way he treated us!"

In reality, Americans were welcoming a figure who did not exist, expecting what could not and would not happen, and then blaming Fidel Castro for their own blindness and ignorance. All of us have much reason to feel reproachful and critical about many of the things Fidel has done. The revolution has not gone the way we hoped, but with knowledge and understanding, one could always realize why things happened the way they did, what forces were operating to make developments understandable, and how that incredible young man must have felt and thought to act the way he did.

"All the world's a stage" and we have to take these leading characters as they come on, watch them, applaud or hiss until the curtain goes down.

> Then, a soldier,
> Full of strange oaths, and bearded like the pard,
> Jealous in honor, sudden and quick in quarrel, ...

Fidel Castro was born with some of the wild qualities that we ascribe to jungle animals like lions and tigers. His rebelliousness, essentially, is not *against;* it is an expression of independence, freedom, pride and power—the power to be alone, at the top, and to meet all challengers with a ruthlessness and cruelty that is amoral, almost impersonal. In this one respect, I thought Fidel to be like Batista.

I mentioned before how the manager of the United Fruit Company's vast sugar plantation in Oriente Province, adjacent to the property owned by Angel Castro, Fidel's father, told me of remembering Fidel as a child—wild, husky, unruly, one of a healthy brood that swarmed over the farm lands.

The father, Angel, was an immigrant from Galicia, Spain, who started as a pick-and-shovel worker on the United Fruit plantation. By hard work, thrift and shrewdness he acquired property of his own and it was on his sugar plantation that the sixth of his nine children, Fidel, was born on August 13, 1926. The family prospered, so much so that he was able to send his children to the best schools and when he died in 1956, each child is believed to have inherited more than $80,000.

Fidel attended the Jesuit preparatory school of Belén, in Havana, where his teacher, with remarkable prescience, predicted greatness for him in his graduation report.

A picture of him at that time was given to Eric Sevareid in Rio de Janeiro and published in a column in the New York *Post* on May 15, 1961. It was one of those flashes that illuminate a whole character and is reprinted here, with permission:

The other night I sat in a Brazilian patio with a Cuban lawyer who had gone to school with Castro. He told me the story of 16-year-old Fidel and the mountain:

"So the professor said to me, you go and talk Fidel out of this crazy notion to climb the mountain. So I went to Fidel and in 30 minutes he had talked me into joining his expedition. So two of us rode the train with Fidel three, four hours. We got off at a village. 'Where is the mountain, Fidel?' we asked him. 'This way,' he said, 'Just follow me.' So we walk, we walk all night. In the morning there is no mountain.

"We walk all day. At night there is still no mountain and we have to sleep. 'How do we sleep here in the jungle?' we ask Fidel. 'We have all these tents,' said Fidel. We struggle with the tents and say, 'Fidel, how do we make the tents work?' And he shrugs his shoulders and says, 'How do I know about tents?' So we lie on the ground with the canvas over us like blankets. In the morning we have no food and Fidel says, 'We find food some way, I guess.' So we eat some fruit on the way, but we are very hungry. We walk all day again and sleep the same way but we find the mountain."

"Did you climb it?" I asked.

"Of course we climb it. You cannot stop Fidel, you cannot argue with Fidel. But the thing was when we get down, we find there is a smooth road right from the railroad to the foot of the mountain. This Fidel, he gets where he is going, but I tell you, he never knows how, he don't care how; to make plans is a bore to Fidel. He just goes, goes and you got to go with him, or too bad."

Fidel entered Havana University in 1945, at the age of nineteen, in the Faculty of Law. Put charitably, he was a wild young man, but his enemies never put it charitably. During an interview with President Batista in June, 1957, I asked the General if he ever considered coming to terms with Fidel Castro.

"Mr. Matthews," General Batista replied, "do you seriously believe that after all the crimes this man, Castro, has committed, beginning in his student days when he killed two men, and continuing in Mexico, as well as Cuba, the Government should forget his acts and enter into political deals with him? It is difficult to believe that anyone, save a few of Castro's admirers, would expect the Government to sit down with this criminal and work out an arrangement which would grant him special privileges because of his past crimes."

Fidel is also accused of having been a Communist since his student days, with special reference to the fact that he and a fellow student were in Bogota in April, 1948, during the great uprising known as the *Bogotazo*. This was during the Ninth Inter-American Conference when Secretary of State George C. Marshall headed the American delegation. At the hearings of the Eastland-Dodd Senate Internal Security Subcommittee the *Bogotazo* kept being brought up, especially by our ex-Ambassadors. It was sarcastically or reproachfully wondered how I could have written so favorably of Fidel Castro knowing, as they said, that he always had been a Red.

Of course, I knew nothing of the sort, but I did know what there really was to be known of these episodes in Fidel's youth, having naturally checked on them as early and as often as I could.

At Havana University Fidel was a close friend of Emilio Tro, one of the founders of the *Unión Insurrecional Revolucionaria* (UIR), a terrorist organization. During Castro's association with the UIR he was arrested several times in connection with political murders allegedly perpetrated by the group, but he was never held or convicted of any crime. Tro was killed in September, 1947, during a factional dispute within the UIR and soon afterward Fidel left the organization. There is no evidence, as Batista put it, that "he killed two men" or killed anybody. He was in Havana at this period and the police would hardly have let him get away with murder.

Incidentally, 1947 was also the year in which the twenty-year-old Fidel took part in the abortive Cayo Confites plot against Generalissimo Trujillo of the Dominican Republic. The Cuban Government broke the expedition up before it got away from the Cuban coast and Fidel had to swim to freedom.

I saw an intelligence report of this period which described Fidel as "a typical example of a young Cuban of good background who, because of lack of parental control or real education, may soon become a full-fledged gangster." This was a period of Cuban history, during the presidency of Prio Socarrás, when gangsterism flourished. Actually, Fidel never was the gangster type.

The *Bogotazo* came in April, 1948. I have a photostatic copy, from the files of the Cuban National Police, of a document dated March 15, 1948, on the stationery of the University Student Federation (FEU). It is headed (in my translation): "First Steps of the Latin American Movement Against the European Colonization of This Continent." The text lists seven points of a resolution launching an "anti-imperialist struggle" and deciding to send three student delegations to a number of Latin American countries to prepare for an Inter-American Congress the following October.

"To carry out this project," reads Point Six, "preparatory sessions will be held beginning the first week of April, with the object of preparing our theme, as well as other aspects connected with the organization of said Congress. The sessions referred to will take place in Bogota and with that in mind the Student Federation of

Cuba will arrange an agreement in Colombia whereby that city [Bogota] shall be the seat of the preliminary negotiations."

It was noted in the final point that the preparatory student meeting would coincide with the Inter-American Conference and thus have a Latin American audience. The two Cuban students chosen were Fidel Castro, who was President of the Law School student body, and Rafael del Pino (whom Fidel was to have sentenced to thirty years in prison as a counter-revolutionary in 1960). I see little reason to doubt that there was some Communist inspiration behind the Movement and the proposed Congress, since there usually was in such cases, but this did not make the two youths Reds. They indignantly denied being Communists, or having any connection with Communists, on their return to Havana, and no proof was ever adduced to the contrary.

The charges that Fidel knew there was going to be an uprising and that he helped to prepare it are quite simply absurd. The Colombian Government employed Scotland Yard to make an investigation of the *Bogotazo*. The report of the mission, which was headed by Sir Norman Smith, for some reason was not published until April 11, 1961—thirteen years after the event. It brought out the fact that the assassination of the Liberal Party leader, Jorge Eliécer Gaitán, at one twenty in the afternoon of April 9, 1948, was done by a lunatic, Juan Roa Sierra, who had no connection with any of the three political parties —Liberal, Conservative or Communist.

It was this incident that sparked the uprising for which

the Communists were blamed by Secretary of State Marshall and almost everybody else. What happened was that the Reds took advantage of the mob fury aroused by the assassination of a popular figure during a period of political tension between the Liberals and Conservatives. (The Government of the time was Conservative.)

Fidel had a boyish crush on Gaitán, and Sir Norman's report brought out the remarkable coincidence that Castro and del Pino had an appointment with Gaitán for one o'clock on the afternoon of April 9. It was never kept, of course, Gaitán being still out in the street taking part in a demonstration when he was killed.

Jules Dubois of the Chicago *Tribune* was in Bogota for the conference and hence was an eyewitness to the dramatic events of the next few days. The account he gives in his book, *Fidel Castro*, absolves the two Cuban students of any role in organizing the uprising that followed or of any connection with the Communists in Bogota.

Sir Norman Smith's report bears out this interpretation. Castro and del Pino reached Bogota in the last days of March, he wrote, and put up at the Hotel Claridge. (The report continually refers to them as *"los dos Cubanos"*— the two Cubans.) They had made a nuisance of themselves at a cultural meeting in the *Teatro de Colón* on the night of April 3 by showering leaflets containing propaganda against the United States from the balcony of the theater into the orchestra. When the police checked on them the next day they found that the two youths did not have proper Colombian visas in their passports, although they had registered on the day they entered the country. They were told to report to the Police Headquarters on April 5, which they neglected to do. When their hotel room was searched, more propaganda leaflets were found. The young men were located the next day, April 6, and taken to the Prefecture of Security where they were admonished and told to stop their hostile acts.

(Let us note in passing that already in 1948, at the age of 21, Fidel Castro was anti-Yankee and agitating against "Yankee imperialism.")

During the *Bogotazo* he and his companion, Rafael del Pino, got hold of arms and were seen by the police shooting—at whom or what was never ascertained. Sir Norman Smith's report says they returned to their hotel on the night of April 9 "bringing a large quantity of arms and staying there for many hours, talking on the phone, in English, with various people." This must have been del Pino, who had American as well as Cuban citizenship. Fidel spoke no English at the time and still has no fluency in the language.

The two youths stayed at the Hotel Claridge until the thirteenth, when they took refuge in the Cuban Embassy. Evidently, the Colombian police were after them. The head of the Cuban delegation to the Inter-American Conference was the well-known lawyer-diplomat, Guillermo Belt, who not only gave them refuge but arranged for them to fly back to Havana in a cargo plane that had brought pedigreed cattle to Bogota. Belt was to regret this act of kindness later.

In spite of his wildness, Fidel stayed at the University

of Havana and studied enough to get degrees in Law, International Law and Social Sciences. Hence his right to be called "Dr. Castro."

After graduation in 1950, he began a law practice and specialized in defending men and women whom he considered to be the victims of social injustice. He joined the *Partido del Pueblo Cubano*, better known as the *Ortodoxo* party, then headed by his hero, Eddy Chibás. Fidel was standing for election to the House of Representatives from Havana Province as an *Ortodoxo* candidate when General Batista staged his successful garrison revolt. He tried in vain to take legal action against Batista and then, typically, turned to action.

This was when he organized and led the mad attack with about 165 young men, nearly all university students and the two girls, Haydée Santamaría and Melba Hernandez, on July 26, 1953. About this oft-told story it is only necessary to keep a few facts in mind for our purposes.

Of the hundred-odd men in Castro's force killed by Batista's soldiers, only ten were killed in the attack. The others were slaughtered in cold blood after surrendering, some after torture. Abel Santamaría's eyes were torn out and brought to his sister, Haydée, to get her to talk—which she did not do.

Fidel escaped to the Sierra Maestra where he was not saved by the Archbishop of Santiago de Cuba, Monseñor Enrique Pérez Serantes, as the persistent myth has it. Orders were out to kill Fidel on sight but the young

Lieutenant, Pedro Sarría, who captured Fidel, disobeyed orders and brought him in alive.

After eleven weeks, incommunicado, Fidel was put on trial alone before the *Tribunal de Urgencia* in a room of the *Hospital Civil*, on October 16, 1953. The public was excluded except for a few reporters who could publish nothing, because of the censorship, but who took down Fidel's long and impassioned self-defense stenographically, word for word. One of the journalists gave a copy of the speech to "a group of Cuban intellectuals united by common sympathies and admiration" who first published it in June, 1954. It is the now famous exposition of his revolutionary ideas, as well as his defense, known for its concluding words: "History will absolve me."

Fidel, Raul Castro and some other survivors were sentenced to fifteen years' imprisonment and sent to the Isle of Pines. In May, 1955, lulled by internal apathy, following a farcical presidential election, General Batista gave an amnesty to all political prisoners, Fidel Castro included. By a curious process of reasoning, the fact that Fidel's life was spared by Batista, along with some others, is put forward by many American commentators who ought to know better as evidence that Batista was more civilized and merciful than Fidel Castro, who executed Batistianos and some counter-revolutionaries. The slaughter of the captured students in the 26th of July attack, and the fact that in the two years of the insurrection Batista had thousands of Cubans killed, often after torture, is conveniently forgotten.

Fidel went right on with his revolutionary activities but

soon had to flee to Mexico. In October, 1955, he went to the United States on an organizational and fund-raising tour for his 26th of July Movement. After Fidel had made some speeches in New York and Florida, the Cuban Government protested and the United States immigration authorities cut short Fidel's stay and canceled his visa for future visits.

The amount of funds and arms he received from the United States during his insurrection in the Sierra Maestra has always been exaggerated. American authorities, quite properly, did their best to prevent the shipment of arms, and generally succeeded.

It was from Mexico, in November, 1956, that Fidel Castro made the almost disastrous "invasion" landing of December 2, which took him into the Sierra Maestra.

A revealing picture of the Fidel Castro of his Mexican period was drawn for the Mexico City magazine, *Humanismo*, in the January-February issue of 1958. It was written by Teresa Casuso, who was a member of the Cuban Embassy staff in 1956. She later became a delegate for the Castro Government at the United Nations, but broke with Fidel in 1960 and afterwards wrote some very different and harsher judgments about her former hero and his revolution. The first article was about *Mi Amigo Fidel Castro.*

"If Fidel were preparing a voyage to Mars," Teresa Casuso wrote, "and you did not want to go to Mars, keep away from him. Because, otherwise, you would soon find yourself on the way to Mars. And what is more, you might get there. . . .

"I have seen him in love. . . . He is the perfect lover. . . . He is so masculine with women that he makes them feel beautiful and satisfied in his company, even just as a friend. . . . He has the physical resistance of a Titan. . . . Physically, as well as mentally, he is very healthy and athletic. He swims like a champion; his only vice is to smoke cigars; he doesn't drink alcohol. Although he likes women very much and very normally, he is hopeless in a party. And he does not even know how to dance!"

"Fidel," Teresa concludes, "is like a dormant volcano."

The volcano exploded, much to the dismay of Teresa Casuso and a great many other admirers. As is the habit with volcanoes, it was uncontrollable.

In those two years in the Sierra Maestra, at least, Fidel Castro showed a patience and self-discipline that no one believed he possessed. The insurrection, with its triumphant entry into Havana on January 8, 1959, was nothing less than an epic. Whatever else history does to him, that much can never be taken away.

My wife and I caught up with him in Camaguey on his wildly joyous progress from Oriente Province. On the night of January 12 we saw him again at Camp Columbia and I sent this interview to *The Times* the next day:

The only word that adequately describes Fidel Castro's condition at the moment is groggy. Uninterrupted work and public adulation over four grueling days has made him punch drunk. Last evening, talking intimately to him, one got a sense that for the first time he is appalled by the weight of the burden now placed on his shoulders. It seemed as if he had just realized that his life from now on is not going to be his and that he must live constantly in a goldfish bowl.

"I haven't had a minute to myself" he complained "They won't leave me alone. Thousands of things are brought to me that I do not know about. When I tried to get away from the crowd by going from one place to another in a tank, people climbed into and on the tank with me before I knew it.

"I am one of those people who live in the present. It isn't in my temperament to plan what I am going to do after I finish the task in front of me. . . ."

As the writer was taking his leave Dr. Castro introduced four young bearded soldiers from Las Villas Province who had been waiting.

"You see," he said in despair, "these are my comrades in arms whom I've been trying to see—and they have been waiting for me for thirty-two hours. How can this continue?"

At the end, as we stood up, Fidel asked what I thought of what had been happening. I said it was wonderful and a great event.

"Back in February, 1957, when I saw you," I said, "I wrote a lot of good things about you and the 26th of July Movement."

"I did not disappoint you?" he interrupted.

"No," I replied "and that was the greatest satisfaction of all for me."

It was, indeed, a great satisfaction, although I have had some disappointments, as well as satisfactions, since.

Germán Arciniegas, Colombia's noted historian, journalist and diplomat, in an interview with *El Tiempo* of Bogota, printed on February 2, 1960, gave expression to one widely held point of view about me and Fidel Castro in Latin America.

"Before leaving our country" [to take up his post as Ambassador to Rome], *El Tiempo* wrote, "Germán Arciniegas told us that he had received a letter from Herbert Matthews of *The New York Times*. The great journalist of that newspaper was the first to interview Fidel Castro in the Sierra Maestra. He gave so much publicity to the heroic struggle that many people called the conflict against the Batista dictatorship 'Herbert Matthews' revolution.'

"Matthews, in his letter to Arciniegas was still defending Fidel Castro—the Fidel Castro of today.

"Arciniegas, in talking to us, made this comment: 'It is the case of a father who does not want to recognize the errors of his son.'"

As a matter of fact, I can see plenty of errors, and the last time I saw Fidel in Havana he conceded that he and his associates had made many mistakes.

As I was saying from the beginning, no one knows the Cuban Revolution who does not know Fidel Castro. Yet his is a character of such complexity, such contradictions, such emotionalism, such irrationality, such unpredictability that no one can really know him.

The men who make history have to be extraordinary men. The man in the street, the journalist, the opponent, are tempted to dismiss such men in their lives by applying comforting labels such as paranoiac, megalomaniac, manic-depressive or—in our day, depending on the political complexion—Communist or Fascist.

This is a waste of time with Fidel Castro. He is not certifiably insane; he is certainly not a Fascist, and it is most unlikely that he was, or is today, a Communist. He is himself, and he fits no category, although one can get some vague help from the knowledge that he is a Galician Spaniard by blood, a Cuban by birth and upbringing and a creature—a very wild creature—of our times.

He will be written about as long as historians write about hemispheric affairs. No single person has made such a mark on Latin American history since the Wars of Independence 150 years ago. Yet there will be no unanimous analysis of his character, not 100 or 200 or 500 years from now.

I would not for one second compare him with Queen Elizabeth I or Napoleon in importance, but Elizabeth was an example of a towering figure working in the fiercest light of publicity in her day and she is, and always will be, an enigma to history. She was to her closest associates. So will Fidel Castro be. Historians still argue whether Napoleon was motivated by greed for power and glory, or really had the ideals of the French Revolution at heart. In the same way, historians are going to argue whether Fidel Castro wanted to carry the Cuban Revolution into the Communist camp, or was forced to do so by American policies and attitudes and the compulsion of events beyond his control.

One of the baffling facts about the Cuban Revolution, therefore, is this fact—that it is Fidel Castro's revolution, and he is an emotional, incalculable force. One may be sure they are as puzzled about him in Moscow and Peiping as they are in Washington.

Several versions of what Nikita Khrushchev said to John Kennedy about Fidel Castro at the Vienna meeting in June, 1961, have been circulated. One highly reliable source in Washington told *The Times* that the Russian Premier said he had little use for Castro and considered him "romantic and unreliable." All accounts agreed that Khrushchev clearly indicated he could not and did not trust Fidel.

The best story I heard, because it seemed so apt, was told to me by a Latin American statesman. Khrushchev is supposed to have said to President Kennedy: "Fidel Castro is not a Communist, but *you* are going to make him one."

Fidel's very instability, his emotionalism, his irresponsibility, his volatile character—his defects, in short— were our opportunities if we had known how to make use of them, or had had the wisdom to do so. Each year since 1957 there has been a different Fidel Castro to deal with, yet each year—each day, in fact—he is treated as if the ideas he holds then and the policies he is following will not or cannot change.

One hears a great deal nowadays about the charismatic leader, a term invented by the sociologist, Max Weber. No doubt the term is abused and used too loosely, but I have always felt that Fidel Castro is a perfect example of the charismatic leader, one whose authority rests upon a popular belief in qualities like heroism, sanctity, self-sacrifice, even in superhuman, miraculous powers. He is the object of hero worship and, in turn, he demands blind obedience of all. There is a primitive, irrational quality in charisma.

For Theodore Draper, who has written acutely but not always understandingly of the Cuban Revolution, Fidel

Castro is one of "the greatest pseudo-Messiahs of the century." Yet it was on this basis of his charisma that Fidel Castro got absolute power in Cuba. Of course, he has been losing worshipers with the passage of time, as he knew he would (he told me and my wife that as early as March, 1959) and he has acquired other, more material and effective instruments of power, but he was born with the qualities that have made him one who has had a greater effect on the Western Hemisphere than any other single figure in Latin American history.

Obviously, he has an extraordinary magnetism. When he went to Caracas, Venezuela, a few weeks after his triumph, the tremendous popular emotions aroused frightened the Venezuelan Government.

I remember saying to him back in February, 1959, a month after he came to power, that men with this remarkable gift can do a lot of good, like Gandhi, or a lot of harm, like Hitler.

"How can such a gift, as you call it," he said wonderingly, "be dangerous in the hands of one who lives only for the people, who has no strength except in popular support?"

This conviction of the righteousness of everything he does is basic to his character. He is always certain that he is doing good, that he is morally, as well as practically, right. In the case of the attempted exchange of tractors for Cuban prisoners in June, 1961, there was not the slightest understanding on his part of our sense of moral shock. As Jaime Benítez of the University of Puerto Rico puts it, "moral coventry does not much affect those who do not see morality in the same terms."

Fidel, as I remarked before, fits the description a contemporary Frenchman gave of Robespierre: "You may laugh at him now, but that man will go far; he believes every word he says."

But let no one underestimate the true and fine characteristics that go with the weak ones. Fidel's idealism is genuine. So is his passionate desire to do what is best for Cuba and the Cuban people. If he fails it will not be because he is an evil man, as Hitler was, or because he is a Communist playing a double game; it will be because of mistakes, misjudgments, amateurishness, emotionalism, fanaticism.

Those of us who were in touch with him and were watching him from the beginning had to ask ourselves if Lord Acton's famous dictum—that all power tends to corrupt and absolute power corrupts absolutely—would apply to Fidel.

Alas, it has! Acton, of course, was not thinking of material corruption. For anyone who knows Fidel Castro that is unthinkable. Acton meant a spiritual corruption.

> The Strongest Poison ever known
> Came from Caesar's Laurel Crown.

as William Blake wrote.

One sees it in the case of Fidel in the way he became more and more autocratic. He was power hungry, and the appetite grew by what it fed on. All his life he had to be Number One—the captain of his basketball team at school or the *Jefe Maximo* (the Chief Leader) of Cuba.

He takes no advice. He brooks no opposition. Anyone who gets in his way is broken with complete ruthlessness. He is too dedicated and fanatical a revolutionary to feel gratitude or loyalty to people whose loyalty to him weakens, whatever they did for him in the past.

Two spectacular examples of this occurred in 1959 with the brutal elimination of the man whom Fidel, himself, had chosen for President, Judge Manuel Urrutia Leo, and the imprisonment of Major Huber Matos, Commander of the Camaguey garrison, who had been one of Fidel's most trusted guerrilla leaders during most of the Sierra Maestra period.

Urrutia had shown what was considered to have been incompetence and a lack of sympathy for the revolution. He was also too openly anti-Communist to suit the Premier. Fidel's move was positively Machiavellian. On July 17 he suddenly resigned and that night made a nation-wide television and radio speech accusing the President of near treason. Urrutia, shocked and in tears, resigned—an example of a child of the revolution being devoured by its creator.

The case of Huber Matos was even more revealing, and is considered by some students of the Cuban Revolution as a watershed. In my own opinion it was a logical, although reprehensible, development, and perhaps even inevitable.

Matos, like many other officers and members of the former civic resistance, had watched the growing strength of communism in the Army with alarm. He tried to argue the matter out with Fidel, but Fidel would not listen or even see him. So, on October 19 Huber Matos presented his resignation. The next day he was arrested, charged with "treason," and in December was tried, convicted and sentenced to thirty years in prison, with Fidel Castro himself as the bitterest accuser.

Put thus baldly, it was an utterly shocking business— but a revolution is not a tea party, and a great deal happens in revolutions that is shocking. Matos had won over many other officers in the Camaguey garrison to his point of view. Had he had his way, the defections would have been very serious. It was a dangerous moment for Fidel and the Revolution, and he struck hard and definitively. From that time on everyone was on notice that Castro was not going to let anybody oppose him and the revolution he was making. In this respect, one might say that the Huber Matos case did represent a watershed in the Cuban Revolution.

At all periods since my Sierra Maestra interview with Fidel Castro, I have been approached by Cubans at critical and dramatic moments for my intervention, and this was no exception. I was never in a position to intervene and I never tried, but I always answer letters, and to one Cuban who wrote me at the time I said that the case "involves the very delicate and essentially subjective problem of what is or is not treachery during a revolution."

By the logic of the Revolution, Huber Matos was a traitor. Those who condemned the outrageous way he was treated, had to condemn the Revolution.

There were many similiar cases the first year. Ex-President José Figueres of Costa Rica had sent arms to Castro in the Sierra Maestra (the first time by Huber Matos, incidentally) and had in many ways given invaluable support to Fidel. Yet when he went to Havana in April, 1959, Fidel Castro did not meet him, did not receive him and, after "Pepe" Figueres had made a speech arguing for friendly relations with the United States and warning against communism, Fidel called him "a bad friend of Cuba, a bad revolutionary."

Governor Luis Muñoz Marín of Puerto Rico was another valuable and influential friend of the young rebels who has been treated in a most outrageous way by Fidel Castro. He and his Government are under daily attacks of the worst sort—a "stooge" of the United States, a "tyrant." Cuban policies are to back the infinitesimal Puerto Rican independence movement in the most vociferous way.

President Romulo Betancourt of Venezuela was still another case in point. All these men are too wise, too experienced and too generous not to understand the reasons behind Castro's insults. From the beginning he attacked all friends of the United States, democratic or dictatorial, in the hemisphere, and soon he was attacking every single government, since all of them naturally feared Castro revolutions in their countries and were anti-Fidelista.

There was always method in Fidel Castro's madness, as everyone who knew him would have realized. One of Fidel's early ephemeral supporters in the United States was Congressman Adam Clayton Powell of New York. Powell evidently thought at first that he could get something out of the Revolution, but he was quickly disabused. "Fidel has just gone to hell," he told a friend on returning to Washington from Havana in March, 1959. "He is on benzedrine, still keeps on his twenty-one and twenty-two hour days, but the problem is to find him! He disappears completely for two days at a time. He has taken up with a very pretty widow; spends a lot of time with her.

"I'm scared of Castro. He's like a madman. His old friend Rufo Lopez Fresquet [Minister of the Treasury] cried while listening to that crazy speech ordering those aviators retried. 'He's been destroyed,' Lopez Fresquet kept saying, over and over."

That "crazy speech" was one of the first evidences that Fidel Castro had no conception of what was normally considered justice, and also that he was utterly ruthless. Forty-three airmen from the Batista Air Force had been acquitted by a military court in Santiago de Cuba at the beginning of March. Fidel called the acquittal "a grave error," and ordered the men retried by a new tribunal with the clear understanding that the airmen were to be sentenced to prison—as they were.

If Fidel had taken up with "a very pretty widow" at the period, as is quite possible, that would not have lasted any length of time. Fidel Castro has no intimate friends. He loves women, not any one woman.

He was married on October 12, 1948, to a pretty young girl from Oriente Province, Mirtha Díaz Balart, sister of a college mate of Fidel's, Rafael Lincoln Díaz Balart. Both the brother and the father, Rafael, Sr., were Batistianos.

They opposed the marriage. A son, Fidelito, was born on September 1, 1949.

Fidel, it need hardly be said, was not much of a husband. Mirtha divorced him while he was a prisoner in the Isle of Pines in 1955, and married Emilio Núñez Blanco, son of Dr. Emilio Núñez Portuondo, Chief of the Cuban delegation to the United Nations. In December, 1956, Fidelito, then living with two sisters of Fidel in Mexico City, was seized by Cuban agents, acting under direct orders from President Batista, and spirited away to his mother in Cuba. He later spent a year at a school in Queens, New York. After Batista fled, Fidelito shared his father's triumph, but Fidel has let him grow up quietly out of the public eye.

The one woman who has really meant a great deal in Fidel's life is the faithful Celia Sánchez, and it would be difficult to say just what she does mean. Celia is the daughter of a physician of Pilón, near Manzanillo in Oriente Province at the foot of the Sierra Maestra. She was in the 26th of July Movement when Castro and the eighty-one men landed in the Granma on December 2. In fact, Celia had been waiting for Fidel up in the mountains since November 29—and she has been by his side ever since.

It is true that he sleeps in four or five different places in Havana, partly for safety's sake, but most nights he is in Celia's apartment. She is a brave, simple, gentle, pious creature—even though she fought courageously in some skirmishes in the Sierra. Celia is a bit older than Fidel, very feminine but not sexy, with a fine, delicate, appealing but not beautiful face. She is devoted to Fidel, utterly loyal, and watching them together one gets the impression that her feelings are more maternal than anything else, but this is her secret and Fidel's.

In the United States, and by embittered Cuban exiles, Celia Sánchez is labeled as a Communist. To anyone knowing her this seems utterly absurd; there never was a creature less political or less interested in politics than Celia Sánchez.

So far as she was concerned, Fidel could do no wrong. Devotion and loyalty were qualities that Fidel Castro has not only craved, but demanded. With him, it is all or nothing, for or against. There is no compromise, no middle ground.

He often acts like a man with a sentence of death against him—assassination. It would have been easy to assassinate him, presuming the one who did it was prepared to die. However, his Cuban opponents—and evidently the American Central Intelligence Agency—always realized that matters would be worse, in Cuba and so far as the United States was concerned, if Fidel were killed. As Dr. Benitez put it: "There are times when a live demagogue is infinitely preferable to a dead martyr."

The image of Fidel would be more potent throughout Latin America dead than alive. This is aside from the fact that he, alone, holds the fabric of Cuban society together and without him it would break down into chaos, anarchy and a blood bath fearful to contemplate.

The American image of Fidel Castro, incidentally, has no relation to the Cuban or Latin American one. Ours was

created at the time of the executions of the "war criminals," which began in mid-January, 1959. Since then,
Fidel has been a brutal, bearded monster to Americans,
with an early addition of the greatest of all political sins
to Americans—the Communist taint. Once a public image
is created, it becomes indestructible—good or bad. The
good image of Dwight D. Eisenhower has never been
diminished in the United States, although many of us
feel he turned out to be a poor President. An image of
that type becomes a myth. The potency of such a myth
was pointed out brilliantly early in the century by the
Frenchman, Georges Sorel. It operates in Fidel Castro's
favor within Cuba and against him in the United States,
but they are two different myths, two images.

The reality might resemble neither picture. Fidel, for
instance, works at demoniac speed. One would think
from what one reads about him in the United States that
he spends most of his time fighting guerrillas, preparing
for—and repelling—invasions, raving against the United
States on television or before mass meetings. Actually, he
works eighteen or twenty hours a day at running his
revolution, and most of all with the agrarian reform.

It is true that he does seem to be burning himself up.
One continually wonders whether any human being can
live long at such a fever heat, well or ill, working so hard,
sleeping so little, consumed with emotions, burning the
candle at both ends with a fierce flame.

Such men cannot change or be changed. Professor C.
Wright Mills of Columbia University used a clever phrase
in describing Fidel's personality—"he does not know

limits." It has also been said of him, and with a good deal of truth, that he does not count the cost of his actions.

The well-known joke has for a long time been applied to Fidel about St. Peter hastily summoning a psychiatrist up to Heaven where God is pacing up and down muttering: "We've got to throw the Old Testament out of the Bible. We must change the Ten Commandments. Those Psalms have to be rewritten."—"You see," St. Peter says to the psychiatrist, "He thinks He is Fidel Castro."

Theodore Draper, in an impressive article for the English magazine, *Encounter,* reprinted in June, 1961, by the American weekly, the *New Leader,* draws a picture of an almost humble, self-reproachful Fidel Castro. It is drawn largely from an interview Fidel gave to the correspondent of the Italian Communist newspaper, *L'Unità,* in February, 1961. In it Fidel confesses to a sense of ideological inferiority with regard to the Communists. However, the uneasy and intelligent Draper adds: "I cannot suppress the feeling that the new, self-critical Fidel is totally out of character."

Indeed he is! If there is anything inconceivable about Fidel, it is a genuine sense of humility. That he never possessed and never will.

The average or normal or ordinary person, and also older, experienced men, figure out what they would do in a given situation or what ought to be done, and then expect Fidel Castro to do it. But characters like Fidel are not normal and do not think along customary lines or act as other people do. Fidel's actions are unpredictable, especially as he does not confide completely in anybody. His motives are not always clear.

He is impetuous and, as I said, highly emotional, the reverse of a cold and calculating thinker. In this, incidentally, he is *muy español*—very Spanish. He relies on intuition, instinct, flare, guided—if at all—by a very considerable intelligence. It is extraordinary that his intelligence should be so underrated in the United States, as if any man could have accomplished what he accomplished and be transforming the whole Western Hemisphere and still be unintelligent.

He has genius, of course. As the French would say, he is an original. There is nothing of Hamlet in his character. And there is no use trying to outguess him, as he probably does not know himself what he is going to do next. He has been called a deceiver, a liar, a traitor to his own revolution by opponents who quote what he said at one time, and point to the fact that he is doing the opposite.

The most effective expression of the "betrayal" thesis, as a matter of fact, came in the United States White Paper of early April, 1961, in which the theoretical American groundwork for the coming invasion was laid.

The charge made is that "the leaders of the revolutionary regime betrayed their own revolution, delivered that revolution into the hands of powers alien to the hemisphere. . . ."

The key passage of the White Paper reads as follows:

The positive programs initiated in the first months of the Castro régime—the schools built, the medical clinics established, the new housing, the early projects of land reform, the

opening up of beaches and resorts to the people, the elimination of graft in government—were impressive in their conception; no future Cuban government can expect to turn its back
on such objectives. But so far as the expressed political aims
of the revolution were concerned, the record of the Castro
régime has been a record of the steady and consistent betrayal
of Dr. Castro's pre-revolutionary promises; and the result has
been to corrupt the social achievements and make them the
means, not of liberation, but of bondage.

Presumably, one must put aside for the purposes of this
argument the fact that an overwhelming majority—perhaps as much as 75 or 80 per cent of the Cuban people—
support Castro and his revolution, and hence do not think
that they have been betrayed. For the rest, I would say
that the changes in Fidel's policies are better explained
by two facts—the first, that he thought he could do certain things and then found that they were not possible,
or were contradictory to other aims, and the second, that
he had no concept of the true meaning of freedom and
democracy and was never to have one.

I confess that, like so many Cubans, I did not at first
realize that Fidel had this complete blind spot in his
mentality. He still does not realize it himself. It took a
gradual unfolding of Cuban developments to make it
clear that so long as Fidel Castro remains in power there
will not and cannot be democracy and freedom in Cuba.

I am convinced that he really thought, while he was
in the Sierra Maestra, that he could have democracy, a
free press, elections, private enterprise and the like, and
still have a radical social revolution that would free Cuba

of American economic domination. He found that he could have democracy or revolution, but not both. He found that he could not be independent of the United States without becoming dependent on the Soviet bloc.

Like the Sorcerer's Apprentice, he conjured up forces beyond his control. I am sure that he feels he has been true to the basic ideals he always had for a social revolution, and that his deviations were responses he had to make to men and circumstances seeking to thwart him, or beyond his control.

A leading Cuban banker who worked with the revolution in 1959 said it was like operating in a fourth dimension; it made sense, but only within a special revolutionary system of logic.

Fidel Castro's dictatorship was never organized or institutionalized, like Generalissimo Franco's, in Spain, for instance, unless his new united Socialist party provides such institutionalization. It has been a straightforward exercise of personal power in behalf of the revolution. This is different from the classic Latin American military *caudillo* of the Batista, Perón, Somoza, Trujillo, Pérez Jiménez type. They were dictators for themselves and for a small clique of the traditional ruling classes, all of whom enriched themselves by corrupt practices or who supported the dictatorship in the name of law, order, stability and anticommunism. Those dictators worked to hold things down. They were conservatives and Right-wingers. Fidel Castro is Leftist, radical, dynamic.

I said of him a long time ago—you don't take him or leave him. Being where he is, with the power he has and will have as long as he lives, and his character being what it is, you take him. We are going to have to live with Fidel Castro and all he stands for while he is alive, and with his ghost when he is dead.

If there is one thing I have been harping upon incessantly for more than two and a half years now, it is the warning that this is a very formidable young man, that he cannot be intimidated, not even by the United States, or, if it comes to that, by Russia, and that he will not back down or surrender. On the contrary, he has had a firm conviction that the only hope for Cuba was to hit back twice as hard for every blow he received.

And he is tough—very tough. He showed that right at the beginning when he executed some 550 Batistiano "war criminals" in the face of loud American protests. These protests were well intentioned and based on a proper Anglo-Saxon conception of the right of all accused to a fair trial, whatever the circumstances; they were wrong in their complete failure to understand why Fidel Castro carried out the executions and how virtually all Cubans at that time approved of what he did.

The American press is to be blamed for this failure to understand and explain—but of that, more in another chapter.

The executions began in mid-January and ended May 15, 1959, when Castro ordered revolutionary war-crimes trials ended. American Congressmen and American news commentators went on writing as if the executions never stopped. The fact is that in almost a year and a half thereafter only five Cubans were executed.

Executions were resumed for "counter-revolutionary" crimes, but it is doubtful that as many as 100 more were shot by the summer of 1961. By revolutionary standards, this has not been a sanguinary affair. When the Reign of Terror ended in France on July 28, 1794, there had been 2,600 victims in Paris alone. In the street rioting in Caracas, Venezuela, that followed the overthrow of the dictator, General Pérez Jiménez, in January, 1958, some 2,000 were believed to have lost their lives at the hands of wild mobs. There were no bloodthirsty mobs in Cuba, thanks to Fidel Castro. Batista not only killed his thousands in the two years of the Castro insurrection, but torture was commonly used. In Castro's revolution, there has been police brutality, very bad prison conditions, a species of police terror, delation—all inexcusable—but there has been no torture.

These facts are not given to excuse Fidel Castro, but to throw light on his character, to give some idea of its complexity and of that quality within him which "does not know limits." This man is a born fighter. His courage is boundless; it has a mad, rash quality. He has done things to us Americans and said things that would have seemed incredible if one did not know that he is capable of anything. He certainly has done many things simply to shock and defy us.

There are lots of other characteristics that could be noted. He is a poor administrator and a worse economist. He is politically astute, but the world's worst statesman; a demagogue, but with a genuine, paternalistic love of people. Yet I do not believe for one moment that he trusts people, not even his beloved *guajiros*—the peasants.

His use of television (so frighteningly reminiscent of George Orwell's "Big Brother") is effective because of his magnetic personality and because he is a naturally gifted orator of the first order. After a trip to Cuba in June, 1959, when Fidel's oratory was at its highest and longest, I coined the phrase: "government by television."

The length of his speeches—running as long as five or six hours in the early months and still taking a normal two or three hours—aroused amusement and ridicule in the United States. It so happened that Cubans listened to Fidel from beginning to end, and anyone taking the trouble to read the text of his speeches would find that they are effective, clearly reasoned, interesting and well organized. Obviously, he always knows in a general way what points he wants to make and how he is going to make them. Then he cuts loose with his natural oratorical gifts, his fervor and passion, his vivid gestures and all the paraphernalia of his extraordinary personality.

He has a unique oratorical style, so much so that anyone reading a passage taken at random from any of his speeches would know that the speaker was Fidel Castro.

Here is the briefest example, taken from his speech to the tremendous mass rally on labor day, May 1, 1961, a few weeks after the invasion had failed. Allowances, of course, have to be made for the translation; Fidel's florid style better suits a Latin language than English.

Besides, given certain circumstances, it is impossible to crush a revolution. . . . The blood that was spilled there was the blood of workmen and peasants; the blood that was spilled there was the blood of humble sons of the people, not the blood of big landowners, not the blood of millionaires, not the blood of gamblers, not the blood of thieves, not the blood of criminals, not the blood of exploiters. . . .

It was blood spilled in defense of an ideal. . . . Not the ideal of the mercenary who sells his soul for gold to an imperial power, but the ideal of the worker who does not want to go on being exploited, the ideal of the peasant who does not want once more to lose his land, the ideal of the youth who does not want once more to lose his teacher, the ideal of the Negro who does not want once more to face discrimination, . . .

and so forth and so on for an interminable sentence of hundreds of words that is still balanced, hypnotic in its repetitive rhythm, and rounded out with fine phrases: "because the Revolution is his life, because he has identified his life with it and his future and his hope."

Part of the reason for this incessant oratory was the necessity of keeping the enthusiasm of the Cuban people at fever pitch. This is partly the reason for the virulent anti-Yankeeism. In some ways one of the most important and one of the features of the revolution least understood in the United States centers around the character of the Cuban people.

There are few things in the world more difficult to make than a social revolution. And of all the places to make one, I would say that Cuba is the most difficult. In speaking to the American Society of Newspaper Editors in April, 1960, I said: "The Cuban people have many wonderful qualities; they are a superb race, but they are very individualistic. They are a violent people, as their history shows. They have a curious and terrible history of spies, informers and traitors who may be one in millions, but if you follow their long and brave struggle against the Spaniards, you will see it dotted with the treachery of individuals. . . . They are a fanatical people, politically speaking. They never stick with any party or any man. They are always against the government that is in power, whatever government it is."

There are many other characteristics, good and bad, that could be added—pride, sensitivity, passion, courage, cynicism, intelligence, lack of restraint, lack of discipline, warmth, volatility.

I could go on for a long time, but for those who know the Spanish race, I will end with a reminder that the Cubans are Spanish-Americans. A wonderful people, but not the type to sustain a social revolution.

Fidel Castro knew this. He knows his people and he knew he was going to have to make his revolution against fierce and growing opposition. This explains many of his actions.

The older I have got in this game of watching and recording history, the more clearly I see how much derives from the human factors, how little one can trust to appearances, to surfaces, to patterns, even to logic. Without the human factors there is no understanding of the Cuban Revolution.

Take the simple fact that this is a revolt of youth, not the "youth" of the forties which we are now talking about in the United States, but youths in their twenties and early thirties. Some of us older folk have all along toyed with the idea that this is mainly what is wrong with the Cuban Revolution. Youth is idealistic, Utopian, radical, and, in Latin America, extremely nationalistic. It is also inevitably amateurish and inexperienced. Youth sows its wild oats, does rash things, cares little for wealth and property, is impatient, impetuous, callous of the suffering of the older generation.

It is well to keep youth in mind whenever one thinks about Latin America. The population in that area is growing at the fastest rate in the world. Forty per cent of Latin Americans are under fifteen years of age. The median age in the United States is about 29.5 years; the average age of the Latin American is 21.5 years. The youth are moving in to take over, and the first of his generation to do so is Fidel Castro. I do not deny that this is a frightening thought.

Che Guevara, in his manual for guerrilla fighters, *La Guerra de Guerrillas,* holds that Danton's slogan is the right one for a revolution: *"De l'audace, de l'audace, toujours de l'audace."*

These are the *enfants terrible* of the Western world. The small group who originally got up into the Sierra Maestra, and those who gathered around Fidel Castro at the beginning, were all fanatical, dedicated, intelligent and loyal young men and women. Not a one of them has defected, although a few quit the Government, and they are today the leaders of the revolution.

The excesses one sees are in part explicable by the rashness and inexperience of youth and in part by the fact that the manner of coming to power after the long, lone guerrilla struggle in the mountains went to their heads. Nothing seemed impossible. They are now, for instance, confidently embarked on a conflict in which they expect to defeat the United States. This is what might be called the David and Goliath complex.

We would be naïve and shortsighted not to recognize that these young men and women in Cuba have high ideals, however mistaken we may think they are in trying to achieve them. The young men and women being recruited for work and government jobs in Cuba are generally inexperienced, but they are enthusiastic, honest, patriotic and hard-working. Many are now Communists and these have their special objectives, but they also want the revolution to succeed. They are chosen first for the quality of loyalty.

These young Cubans share a distrust and even contempt for what free enterprise and elections meant to the Cuban people. They have a profound scepticism of existing interests, a suspiciousness of advice from interested quarters, an approach that is more theoretical than practical, a disdain for orthodoxy, an indifference to individual suffering or injustice if it is done for what they consider the good of Cuba. The original group was puritanical to such a degree that it set out in the beginning to abolish gambling, narcotics and prostitution—in vain, for the most part.

Fidel Castro was so old-fashioned when he first reached Havana he argued that interest on money was a sin. In many respects, these young Cubans started with ideas that belonged in the pre-Marxist, pre-scientific ages of

Socialism. The acceptance of Marxist Socialism was a development that came with their practical experience of government.

In order to complete the record, I should, perhaps, repeat here that in my opinion Fidel Castro never was and is not now a Communist. Let us dismiss this aspect by quoting the Deputy Director of the U.S. Central Intelligence Agency, General C. P. Cabell, who testified to the Senate Internal Security Committee on November 5, 1959, that his organization believed that Castro was not a member of the Communist party, and did not consider himself to be a Communist.

The young not only dream of Utopias; they believe in them, so these young men set out to make Jerusalem in Cuba's "green and pleasant land." Never in the history of the Western Hemisphere have young men held such power and so gloried in it. They are having a wonderful time creating a brave, new world, but creation, like birth, is painful and messy.

Even now, in this fall of 1961, Fidel Castro is only thirty-five years old. John Kennedy is ancient by comparison. We who watch Fidel and his companions would do well to ponder that these young men and women could be riding the wave of the future in Latin America. Think, when you see Fidel Castro in the newsreels, and hear his hoarse, impassioned voice, that you may be seeing and hearing a prophet. Should we say a prophet of doom?

I spent the whole day of his thirty-fourth birthday with him, August 13, 1960. He was then recovering from an illness that led to the wildest sort of speculation by American correspondents and the American press. Had they been in contact with him or with his close associates they would have known that all he had was virus pneumonia, followed by a typically nasty reaction to the antibiotics pumped into him.

The morning after his birthday I wrote out for myself an account of the day we spent together which, I believe, will give an idea of what sort of a person Fidel Castro is. I am reproducing these notes here exactly as written; not a word has been changed or taken out.

Stepping out of the elevator a little past midnight at the Banco Nacional I walked into him, literally, as he was standing right in front with his back turned. He was cordial but disconcerted, he said, to meet me so casually when he had wanted to come and see me at the Hotel Nacional. After chatting a little, he said he had to go home because the doctors insisted he must have seven or eight hours sleep but we made an appointment for the coming day. "I don't like just to sit and talk. We will go out into the country toward Pinar del Rio. I'm more interested in chickens, sugar and agrarian reform than in the OAS."

"Major Fajardo, his Negro military aide who has taken the place of Yanes (they said that Yanes, aside from being forgivably a terrific ladies man had been using INRA money for his private purse—Fidel forgives a lot in his associates, said Núñez Jiménez who told me this, but not dishonesty), came for me a little before ten and took me to Celia Sánchez's apartment, 1007 11th in Vedado, a shabby little apartment house with the usual sloppy rebel soldiers on guard at the entrance, up one narrow flight. The apartment was furnished from their house at Pilón, Celia's blonde, younger sister who does not remotely look like her, told me. Celia came in, dressed in a flossy, floor-length, light-blue organdy gown with blue ribbons at the waist and neck. The room was uncomfortable, untidy, without the slightest taste, with chromos on the walls. It must look like thousands of middle-class, middle-income homes in Cuba. This is where Fidel sleeps most of the time when he is in Havana.

While waiting briefly for Fidel we talked about the Sierra. She said she had gone up on Nov. 29th, [1956] the day before Fidel was supposed to land, and waited for him. She knows and remembers everyone who had been there and promised to make me a list and give me her recollections. I discovered from her the important fact that she kept every single document of the whole two years in the Sierra—his orders, even to patrols, his proclamations, declarations, texts of his *Radio Rebelde* talks, the letters he received, the messages, the negotiations with the civic resistance—everything. They are carefully sorted and wrapped in nylon and are at Cojimar. As historic archives of the Revolution they are obviously invaluable.

Fidel looked rested but his nervousness or restlessness was shown when he made a few phone calls and paced up and down the short length of the cord incessantly while he talked instead of sitting or standing still. The informality of his life again struck me.

We drove off very soon and the first thing he did again was to apologize to me for the way we had met, which he clearly thought was disrespectful and must have looked as if he had been trying to avoid me, whereas he assured me he had told everybody how much he wanted to see me.

It was obvious from the whole day's experience that his heart and soul—and the heart of the Revolution—is unquestionably in the Agrarian Reform. The day was, in fact, a process of seeing the reform in operation with discussions and arguments in the car and at the end, in Pinar del Rio, on

174

every topic of importance—the U.S., the OAS, communism, defections, economics, the Church.

I asked him what about this business of the cooperatives paying in chits up to 80 per cent which I had read and heard about often. He had been making a eulogy of cooperatives and was to do so several times during the day. He is convinced that the *guajiros* prefer it that way—it gives them security, a community life (they are very sociable, he said), wages, profits, incentives and is more efficient for productivity, especially in commodities like sugar, cattle, chickens, dairies. Not tobacco which requires special care and skill on small farms—he has left the industry alone thus far but from what he said about "problems" I suspect that something is going to be done. On the question of chits he laughed and said that is typical counter-revolutionary propaganda. "Why should we give chits instead of money when there is nothing to be gained by doing so?" He said he wanted to show me a *tienda del pueblo* of the INRA which has now taken the place of all private grocery and butcher stores and where goods are sold at obviously reasonable prices. A little later on we came upon a little one and dropped in. There Fidel, asking the manager about chits, seemed a little surprised and disconcerted when the manager said, Yes, many people bring them here, and he took a batch out of the cash register. As it happened, Fidel was right, although it seemed curious that he had not acquainted himself with the process. The chits were not payment for work, they were loans by the cooperative concerned to workers in advance of wages, but since the wages are paid twice a month and since the worker does not have to borrow if he need not, the process is simply a convenience. Whatever is borrowed is deducted from the next wage and no one is allowed to run over, so that the old, bad system of lifelong indebtedness does not apply.

Fidel earlier had made the point that everything about the agrarian reform from the beginning had been done by him, under his orders and every payment, every check, every policy is his. There was no reason to doubt this, although he did not seem acquainted with every detail. The choice of a very radical type of reform instead of the one made by Humberto Sorí Marín in the beginning was known to be Fidel's and was typical, as we could see later, of the extreme radicalness of the Revolution in every field.

While driving along in the first hour we came upon one of those *playas*, or popular beaches, he had made for Habaneros —sports fields, pool, beach for bathing, club house, restaurant, soft-drink bar, rafts, row boats. It was crowded and when they saw Fidel and word got around there was a pandemonium of joy and enthusiasm. He was almost mobbed. Nothing could have been more spontaneous and it was obvious that he is still literally worshiped. An old Negress brought along a really ancient crone who held out her hands to Fidel. "My mother," the first one said. "You are 34 today and she is 98." Children galore were brought up to touch him or be patted on the head. What he had wanted to show me most of all, and the main reason for stopping there, was the menu, as he had been arguing that they are providing things cheaply for the people. It was true that the prices were very reasonable, especially the table d'hôte which provided meals from 70 cents to $1. The enthusiasm of the greeting he received was typical of the whole day, although at the farms and cooperatives, where he is evidently a familiar sight, there was a very friendly warmth and not the excitement caused when he stops somewhere unexpectedly.

In all we must have stopped at six or eight farms and cooperatives and a number of places where construction is taking place for farm houses, fertilizer manufacture, incubation, artificial insemination and the like. Certainly, so far as the Province of Pinar is concerned it is wrong to say that all the agrarian reform has done is to take over existing properties and make them cooperatives. Almost all the places I saw were either new creations or old latifundia in process of expansion and improvement. Fidel and Núñez, who joined us at a poultry farm at lunch and stayed with us, claimed that the same sort of expansion and new work is going on around all the island and that this was typical. If one could accept their statement, there is no question that the reform is making progress and will increase productivity although whether they are doing it well or wisely or efficiently is another thing. Certainly critics of the regime are convinced not, but after what I saw I must retain doubts that they really know everything that is happening. The extent to which the agrarian reform is the real heart of the Revolution was never impressed upon me so strongly as yesterday. It gives a focus and meaning to the Revolution as a Revolution that is so much more important than the political side or even the international, except as these can destroy the Revolution.

Many times during the day Fidel spoke to workers, asking about their problems and farms, and he heard some complaints —two especially were strong in their complaints, one who argued heatedly while we were eating lunch that he couldn't get the water he needed, another who said that his farm was too small for a family of nine (Núñez said: "Why don't you join a cooperative?"). On the whole the complaints were few and contentment the rule.

We shared a lunch with the workers at a poultry farm— broiled chicken, frijoles, rice and platanos fried, washed down with warm Hatuey Malta—no drinks when one is with Fidel. We sat on boxes at a board table surrounded by the men who wanted to listen or argue, and swarming with flies—but everything we ate was good and hot and plentiful. Fidel ate a large plate of rice and frijoles and then a whole chicken—not a little broiler either. This was between 1 and 2 and I was to see him again tackle a hearty meal at 6:30 so there is certainly nothing wrong with his appetite. Fajardo solicitously forced him to take his medicine at both meals—estreptodiacnil and charcoal.

Fidel's energy has not flagged. We were in and out of the car innumerable times, with him striding as always as if he had 7-league boots and not a second to lose. The title of a day like that could be: "Keeping up with Fidel." His enthusiasm at seeing thousands of chicks or ducklings, innumerable pigs, sows and piglets. He never tired of watching the sucklings at their meals—*que espectáculo precioso!*" His thrill at seeing a good field of grain or sugar cane or tobacco was obviously real and spontaneous, because he would continually interrupt what he was saying as we drove along to exclaim. He is a real countryman. He knew and asked about every breed of pig, or chicken or cow, and identified every growing field instantly. He would have made a good farmer.

His enthusiasm was more like someone 14 than 34. I was more impressed than ever with the fact that this is a revolt of youth. Driving back from the Campo de la Libertad airfield in a jeep with Núñez, he [Núñez] argued in all seriousness that nobody over 40 could really understand and work with the Revolution. The exceptions, like Roa and Dorticós (both in their forties) simply proved the rule. The radicalism, the demands that are made for discipline, faith, courage, loyalty, comradeship are quite possibly beyond the capacities and temperament of anyone who is not young. Fidel spoke with anger and reproach of the defections. Raul Chibás had given his word of honor as an officer, he said, that he would not try to go away and he had received every assurance of safety. Miró Cardona had been friendly with them all right up to the end and not given an inkling of his intention to defect or even argued about policies. Felipe Pazos he discussed simply as one who could not understand or sympathize with the Revolution, but Fidel was bitter at the idea that he was working against the Revolution.

The interesting thing in all this was that Fidel is convinced that in every case these men were persuaded to defect by the United States Embassy. He feels absolutely sure about that, and it is part of his conviction that the U.S. was out to over-throw him from the beginning. His feeling applies to many other defectors, as he feels the Embassy has been plotting constantly in every way it can against him.

"You ought to have heard the conversations with Ambassador Bonsal from the beginning," he said. "He lectured me, criticized us and our Revolution, complained, threatened. There was never the slightest understanding of the Revolution or sympathy with what we were trying to do. I can assure you I felt humiliated as a Cuban at the way I, the Prime Minister of Cuba, was being talked to. This was not the attitude of two equal and friendly nations of the OAS. This was an effort at dictation, direction and complaint. You ought, also, to hear how the Soviet representatives talk. They are friendly, respectful, sympathetic, understanding. They are not ordering us about, not making demands. They make us feel like a sovereign country. The United States Ambassador tries to make us feel as if we must do what the United States wants.

(Remember Roa telling me at lunch about the delivery of the notes of protest on the oil refinery seizures—the British Ambassador, so human and friendly, Bonsal "restraining his fury," grim-looking, stern, delivering his note with hardly a word and stomping out.)

(All this, with other things I heard, makes one wonder whether they are planning to break relations with the U.S. on the theory that they would be better off without an Embassy staff here since they are really convinced that the staff is plotting as hard as it can against them. Fidel, like Luis Buch [the President's Secretary] and others, feels strongly about the two FBI men they expelled. "Those photos that Friedemann had," he said, "from Goering and others were not souvenirs. They were inscribed to Friedemann and pre-dated the war.")

He went into a long harangue about how respectful the Revolution had been of all Church rights, how he had intervened in favor of the Church in cases like Villanueva University, how he had done everything he could to accommodate the Church. Then he asserted, like all of them, that the Church in Cuba had always been on the side, first of the Spaniards, then of the Cuban ruling classes, and that the people of Cuba never liked or respected their Church. "We are a religious people, but not a clerical one; Cubans, in fact, are anti-clerical." Here, too, he felt certain that the United States had intervened and that the Church was influenced by the Americans. They had provoked the demonstrations in front of the Churches. "No revolution could have been so patient, so considerate. We know what a bad effect a conflict with the Church will have on our international position and this is why the United States took their part. However, we have no doubts that the Cuban people are on our side and the Church cannot turn them against us." Like the others, he pointed out that a large majority of the clergy are Spanish, which in his eyes linked them to Franco and to the United States policy in favor of Franco. Of course, he said, there are many Cuban priests who understand the Revolution, and have been helpful. "If it is necessary to engage in a conflict with the Church we will do so, but I hope we do not have to. Nothing will be allowed to stop our Revolution."

Three or four of the farms we saw were for pigs, which indicates that they are going in for them in a big way. Fidel constantly referred to the fact that the best breeds, the best machinery, etc., come from the U.S. and that is where he wants to buy them and is buying them. "I'm going to get you the best breeding bulls there are," he told one farmer. When I asked where, perhaps Argentina, he said, No, there was hoof and mouth disease there; he would get them either in the U.S. or Canada. As I saw, there was much interest in incubation and artificial insemination. Fidel said that in the pre-revolutionary days Cuban agriculture was antiquated—although not in fields like sugar and the big cattle ranches.

About six o'clock we ended up at a house on the old garrison grounds of Pinar del Rio. This was obviously where he had gone when he was moved from Havana during his convalescence. We sat around talking and drinking Coca Cola. Fidel had smoked incessantly all day—cigarettes when he was not smoking cigars. Fajardo told him he had to take a rest, as the doctor ordered. Fidel complained. "Look, Matthews is older than I and he doesn't need to rest." The others pointed out that I had not been ill a week ago and Fidel had. They sat down to another copious meal which I did not join, having an appointment at eight for dinner in town.

Fidel was reminiscing during and before the meal about the Sierra and especially my trip up there. To meet me they had descended to the foothills and really put themselves in Batista territory where they knew patrols were working all the time. It was an even more dangerous business than I realized at the time, although I naturally was suspicious from the fact that we at all times had to talk in whispers. This was the first get-together in the Sierra of the 26th of July group and hence was more historic than I realized. After talking to me they quickly moved back up to the high Sierra and narrowly escaped ambushes and clashes. Fidel has promised to write out or dictate his part in the incident.

Núñez was going back in his INRA helicopter and offered to take me—an hour and a half instead of three hours in a car— so we left at seven. Fidel, typically, said there was so much more he wanted to talk about and so many other things he wanted to show me, especially the "pueblos." I had seen a number of the new little towns being put up to go with the cooperatives—houses, church, school, clinic, shops etc.—but none in the region we went through had been completed. He wanted to show me some finished ones. I said, the next time, when Nancie is with me.

It was a friendly day. What does one know of this Revolution who does not know Fidel?

"It was," as I wrote, "a friendly day," and neither I nor my wife has ever lost a sense of friendliness. I doubt we ever will, whatever he does and however critical we get. In ending the first of my three lectures on the Cuban Revolution at City College of New York in March, 1961, I said:

"I would not have anything I say here, or that I will say, interpreted as support of the Cuban Revolution in its present form.

"Yet, there is much that is good as well as much that is bad. All I do say to you of this Cuban Revolution is— open your eyes, open your minds, open your hearts. You need them all to understand the Cuban Revolution. If you understand, you will condemn and you will condone. You will accuse and you will sympathize. You will see that there is much that is evil and much that is good.

"And if you see all that, you can criticize as much as you want; you would be compelled to criticize. But if you understand, you will feel that for all its errors, its injustices and its cruelties, there is something idealistic in this Cuban Revolution which should be preserved.

"Those here in the United States who are trying to kill it, would destroy a lot of idealism, a lot of hope, a lot of life. The death of the Revolution as an ideal would leave a desolate Cuba, haunted by the ghosts of an ignoble, wicked past.

"But it would also be haunted by the ghosts of Fidel Castro and the young men who were with him, who destroyed this sinful past, who tried to build something better.

"I do not think, myself, that this Revolution can or will die. It has the vigor of a creeping vine—or you might think, of noxious weeds—but it has vigor."

From very early in the game, it had been my contention that the Cuban Revolution was shaking the Western Hemisphere the way the French Revolution shook Europe. In an editorial I did for *The Times*, printed on June 21, 1960, we said:

"What is happening in Cuba and because of Cuba is, without question, the most important, dynamic and fateful development in Latin America since the Wars of Independence 150 years ago."

CHAPTER FIVE

The Hemisphere

SOMETHING NEW, EXCITING, dangerous and infectious has come into the Western Hemisphere with the Cuban Revolution. Latin America has had hundreds of political and military revolutions in the last century and a half, and it has had two isolated social revolutions in Mexico and Bolivia, but it has never had anything like this.

"*Fidelismo* challenges the structure of the established Latin American universe," Professor K. H. Silvert, one of our leading Latin Americanists wrote in a paper for the American Universities Field Staff on January 29, 1961, "its distribution of economic, social and political power, its accommodation with the Church, its set of relationships between the person and the world—in short, its total self-conception."

A drastic social revolution, the massive pressures everywhere in Latin America for social justice, the cold war, and an extraordinary young man have given the Cuban

Revolution an importance unequaled by any event in the Western Hemisphere since the Wars of Independence. A new era began on January 1, 1959, when the Cuban insurrection triumphed. The excitement has been worldwide. Americans would be astonished, if they could see the interest in, and the sympathy for, the Cuban Revolution in Europe and the Middle East.

History never operates in a vacuum. It is often likened to the flowing of a river. At some time, the modern concept that a man has a right to a decent life whatever his color, wherever and to whomever he was born, was bound to approach the point of overflowing in Latin America. When that point was reached it only needed an upheaval and the man, to make it come to the flood.

This is what Fidel Castro and the Cuban Revolution have done, and if I may belabor the analogy, let me point out that rivers do not flow backward. The flood will subside, but we will all be sailing in a different place and toward an unknown shore.

There are so many more elements at hand now to make Latin American revolutions! They used to be done by handfuls of military officers backed by their garrisons or by a rabble. The mass of the population was unaffected and did not care. Now it is the poverty-stricken, ignorant masses in Latin America who provide the decisive weight, or at least, the decisive threat.

The social awakening of these masses is the significant, new feature of hemispheric life. The population explosion —the highest rate in the world—is bringing intolerable pressures. It demands of an underdeveloped, largely agricultural region that it raise production fast in order simply to stay in the same place. It drives peasants, literally by the millions, from their rural communities with their ancient, immutable, immemorial ways of life, into the slums of great cities, where they provide a wretched, bewildered ferment for the radicals and demagogues.

Everywhere there is a potentially revolutionary mass. Nowhere is there a mature, liberal, stable, democratic nation in our sense of these terms. By themselves, the masses might proliferate in apathetic misery, but this is the 1960's, and politics works in some ways almost as if it responded to physical laws. Where there is a revolutionary mass, there will be revolutionary leaders.

In modern times, revolutions are always led by the middle classes, and one of the striking features of social life in Latin America in recent decades has been the growth of the middle class. It is even becoming what some Latin Americanists are calling "the middle mass." This is the element that made the Cuban Revolution as it made the French, the Mexican, the Russian and other modern social revolutions. They get their ideas from totalitarian democracy or liberal democracy, from Marxism or the Enlightenment, but what is new today are the mass communications media which in Latin America convey these ideas to the peasants in once remote regions of the sierras, the jungles, the coastal lowlands, the valleys of the Andes and also to the illiterate, wretched urban proletariat of the mushrooming slum areas in the great cities.

Keep the broad outline of the Latin American picture

in mind. To be sure, every Latin American country is different from every other, and if I treat the region in this book as if it contained one nation, it is only because I am extracting general features. The needs, desires and hopes of a Cuban sugar worker, an Indian agricultural laborer in the Andes, a Brazilian squatter in the Amazon valley are the same. The cold war that has now entered the hemisphere is the same cold war we have been fighting everywhere else since 1945. Latin America is an under-developed region and all underdeveloped countries have similar problems.

There has been—and in most respects the situation is still unchanged in Latin America—the long background of feudalism, militarism, the small ruling classes, the social imbalances, the agrarian and mineral economies.

The dominant hemispheric power was—and is—the United States, with its Monroe Doctrine, its power and wealth, its democratic, capitalistic, free-enterprise system.

On this traditional structure has come the impact of the contemporary world, bringing demands for more effective governments, for industrialization, for social justice. With this goes the realization that poverty, ignorance and disease are not necessary. A popular assault is being made against economic oligarchy as well as political dictatorship.

So the people of Latin America—or their spokesmen in the middle class—ask: Who is to blame and who will satisfy our demands?

These are the challenges that have been given a form and a voice by Cuba. The blame in Cuba is put upon the

Cuban governing classes and upon the United States. The satisfaction is now being sought in a Leftist, non-democratic, socialistic-type system allied to communism.

We hoped and believed that our capitalistic, free-enterprise, democratic system could be developed in Latin America. The Cuban Revolution jarred us into a realization that we have not yet succeeded. As President Kennedy said to the Latin American diplomats in March of this year: "Our unfulfilled task is to demonstrate to the entire world that man's unsatisfied aspirations for economic progress and social justice can best be achieved by free men working within a framework of democratic institutions." It may be that we are deluding ourselves, and that we will, at best, have to settle for an intermediate, compromise solution, democratic enough, free enough, non-Communist if not anti-Communist, neutralist, independent.

This would be satisfactory, but can we get even that? This is one of the dangers that the Cuban Revolution represents for us and for the other countries of Latin America. There are revolutionary pressures; there may well be other revolutions. In present circumstances, these revolutions would try to copy Cuba; they would fight under the banner of *Fidelismo;* the Communists would be partners, agitators, perhaps leaders. The revolutions would be anti-Yankee.

What no Latin American country can do today, except the dictatorships, is to coast along, to carry on as in the past, to ignore the pressures for social reforms that the

Cuban Revolution and its leader, Fidel Castro, have dramatized.

The young men of Latin America, who are now coming to the fore, are tougher than their fathers, bolder, more nationalistic, more radical, more adventurous, more impatient, more demanding, more idealistic. They will not respond as easily to a mercenary approach, or to advice, or threats or pressures.

If they get corrupted, it will be by power, or the lure of power, and this goal of power is, unfortunately, more easily reached by the swift drama of revolution, than by the slow, plodding, unromantic way of evolution. We ask patience, economic orthodoxy, civic virtues, discipline, democratic elections, sacrifices by the privileged for the underprivileged.

"Priorities will depend not merely on need," President Kennedy said to Congress in explaining his new program for Latin America, "but on the demonstrated readiness of each government to make the institutional improvements which promise lasting social progress." The chances of getting voluntary acceptance of these sacrifices by the governing classes is, I am afraid, less than Congress, or perhaps even the White House, realizes.

And we ask Latin Americans to forget the past. We, with common-sense maturity and Anglo-Saxon phlegm, asked Fidel Castro and his fellow Cubans to forget what had happened before January 1, 1959, as we forgot what Germany, Italy and Japan had done to us when the Second World War ended.

But these were young and passionate men. In a sense,

one could say that Fidel Castro is taking revenge on behalf of generations of Cubans, and on behalf of all Latin Americans.

There is also a Messiah complex. Fidel has all along felt himself to be a crusader, if not a savior. He is out to achieve a "second liberation" of Latin America. The first was from Spain. This one is from "Yankee imperialism." Fidel sees himself as the champion, not only of the Cuban agricultural worker—the *guajiro*—but the Guatemalan and Peruvian Indians, the Puerto Rican workers, even the American Negroes.

One of the most striking and dismaying features of the Cuban Revolution was the way in which it quickly found itself in conflict with almost all the governments of Latin America. This was expected, and was natural in the case of the dictatorships of the Dominican Republic, Haiti, Nicaragua and Paraguay. It came as a surprise in the case of the democracies and such democratic leaders as President Romulo Betancourt of Venezuela, President Alberto Lleras Camargo of Columbia, ex-President José Figueres of Costa Rica and Governor Luis Muñoz Marín of Puerto Rico.

Ideologically, and because these were friendly governments and leaders, it seemed as if the Castro regime would have been on good terms with them. They had all helped the insurgent cause and wanted to help the new revolutionary regime. Instead, they were insulted, and found themselves struggling against internal oppositions which were greatly strengthened by the Fidelistas and their new-found allies, the Communists. In Argentina, *Fidelismo* and *Peronismo* were soon working together.

Of the so-called invasions from Cuba only one—the two small groups that entered the Dominican Republic in June, 1959—had Castro's official backing. The others were either the work of adventurers and mercenaries, like the landings in Panama in April and in Haiti in August, 1959, or groups that evaded Cuban vigilance. Washington made a great propaganda splash about Cuban "expeditions" and keeps on doing so, but no evidence was ever brought out to prove that Fidel backed or even desired any invasion except the Dominican one. In time, he even seems to have made a pact of mutual forbearance with the late Generalissimo Trujillo of the Dominican Republic.

The reasons why the Castro regime found itself at odds with all the Latin American governments before the year 1959 was out seemed logical enough. Fidel had decided early in the game that the United States was out to frustrate, and then to overthrow, his regime. He felt sure that we were working in every capital to isolate Cuba and he realized that this was a great danger to him. As far as he was concerned, the Organization of American States was a creature of the United States, and hence his enemy.

Moreover, he could see an obvious fact—that all the Latin American governments feared the example the Cubans had set. Even the democratic countries were controlled by the type of ruling class that he had destroyed in Cuba. These men did not want to see radical revolutions in their own countries.

Still another cause for conflict lay in the almost unanimous criticisms of the Latin American press. The newspapers and radio and television networks were for the most part controlled by the big business, banking and landowning interests for whom a radical revolution like Cuba's was anathema. Consequently, Cuba had a unanimously bad press, except for the Left-wing organs.

The powerful Inter-American Press Association, at first friendly, then tolerant, became hostile when Castro gradually repressed his own newspapers, radios, and television stations, and suppressed freedom of the press in Cuba. Fidel had found—or believed—that a free press would weaken his revolutionary program. This had happened in the Mexican Revolution. With all other freedoms going by the board, freedom of the press had to go, too.

We on *The New York Times* were as critical as anybody else on that score, although we did not show the same general sympathy for publishers and editors who had taken subsidies from General Batista, as was the case with all except *La Prensa*, the Havana *Times* and the weekly, *Bohemia*. These, too, were victimized in time by the regime. In any circumstances, there could be no excuse for suppressing freedom of the press, and we always condemned the Castro Government's policy in that field.

The logic of the Cuban Revolution was reprehensible, but it was clear. Everything and everybody against the Revolution represented the enemy, and was attacked. The ultimate in enmity became those who were friendly to, or who worked with, the United States. This was the real touchstone.

The Organization of American States is—or was before

the Cuban Revolution—the most successful of all the international organizations affiliated with the United Nations. It had been hammered out over nearly sixty years, between 1890 and 1948 when the Bogota Charter was drawn up. While it is true that the United States—the Colossus of the North—dominated the OAS as it did every feature of hemispheric life, it was an institution that gave authority and rights to every Latin American nation, however small. The doctrine of non-intervention was (or seemed to be) its greatest triumph.

Fidel Castro was soon attacking the OAS as an instrument of the United States. He also—verbally—repudiated such vital hemispheric treaties as the Rio Pact, which holds that an attack against one member is to be considered as an attack against all.

Fidel's position was open to the strongest criticism—until we backed the Cuban invasion of April, 1961, thus, ourselves, flagrantly violating the doctrine of non-intervention.

As a matter of fact, the OAS has not shown itself to be an instrument of United States policy, as we have never been able to get it, collectively, to support our policies toward the Castro regime. Nevertheless, Fidel goes on attacking it. There is, incidentally, no provision in the Bogota Charter for the suspension of the rights of membership or expulsion for any reason.

As a result of these conflicts and calculations, the Fidelistas cultivated the opposition in every Latin American country. In the nature of things, this meant the Left-wing, including the Communists, in each country. In

Argentina, what was left of Peronism was in the trade unions—the *descamisados,* or "shirtless ones," who gave General Perón his mass support. The military element of Peronism had joined the Government or become Right-wing.

The appeal of Fidelismo was swift and powerful. The Cuban Revolution, on its idealistic side, was a response to the very same problems plaguing every country of Latin America. Wherever there was poverty, misery, real or fancied oppression, social injustice, intellectual ferment, the lure of power, the emotions of anti-Yankeeism —and where would there not be these things?—the example of Cuba and the romantic, magnetic figure of Fidel Castro, cast their spell.

In chemical terms, it was like the process of catalysis. There was a crystallization of deep and powerful social forces, a polarization of political movements and ideologies, a ferment, a dynamism, a coming to life of hitherto dormant elements. It was as if the whole hemisphere were suddenly heaving and moving, responding to the natural forces of a storm—in this case a tropical hurricane.

The world of Latin America in this year, 1961, is very different from what it was on January 1, 1959, when Fidel Castro and his 26th of July Movement triumphed. And it will never be the same again.

The United States could not get the other Latin American countries, collectively, to follow its policies toward Cuba. For a variety of reasons, not all of them laudable, nations like Guatemala, El Salvador, Honduras, Panama, Peru and Paraguay followed our lead, but the major powers of Latin America—Brazil, Mexico, Chile, Argentina and Venezuela, in varying degrees and different ways —held back.

In all the countries, the governments had to contend with considerable support for the Castro revolution among intellectuals, students, opposition politicians, all the Communists and Left-wingers, and among peasants whose leaders were impressed by Cuba's agrarian reforms. Moreover, Fidel is doing things to, and taking up a posture toward, the United States that gives satisfaction to many among the new middle classes in Latin America. Uncle Sam, as they see it, is at last getting his due.

The potency of myths in politics can never be overlooked. There is a real Cuban Revolution, and there is an image—or a whole series of images—of it. The United States version is not accepted in Latin America, Canada or Europe.

"*Fidelismo* is an image with many faces," wrote the English weekly, *The Economist,* for April 22, 1961. "At its simplest it means to millions of Latin Americans that in a remote, but still a sister, country, a man as glamorous as any film star has given land to the poor, rooked the rich, and put the *gringos* in their place."

This has more relevance to the truth than the prevailing North American image of a hated and hateful Communist police state, where the people are enslaved and the nation is nothing more than a satellite of the Sino-Soviet bloc.

Fidel Castro and his Revolution are much better understood in Latin America than in the United States. He is a second-generation Spanish American of pure Spanish blood. His actions and words sometimes seem extreme to the point of madness to us, but the Spanish character *is* extremist. On the whole, Fidel's behavior, given the circumstances, is considered normal—or at least not especially abnormal—to millions of Latin Americans.

On the other hand, there is no doubt that the recklessness and distastefulness of many of Premier Castro's policies, and especially his links to communism, his repudiation of democracy and his attacks on the middle class, have alienated a lot of his support thoughout Latin America. The situation was well put by Tad Szulc in a despatch to *The New York Times* on January 8, 1961.

"Public opinion has been swayed against Cuba," he wrote, "by her ties with the Communist world, the clear emergence of dictatorial tactics by Dr. Castro's regime, the meddling in the affairs of many other republics, her conflict with the Roman Catholic Church and what is being increasingly seen here as a failure of the social and economic revolutionary experiment in terms of actually bettering the lot of the Cubans."

This was exaggerated, I believe, but largely true, except for the very last statement. There is no question that Fidel Castro has thrown away a degree of attractiveness and influence that might well have brought other revolutions in Latin America before this. As a purely Latin American phenomenon that seemed at first to carry the ideals of democracy and liberalism, as well as social reform, with it, the Cuban Revolution would have been irresistibly contagious.

Its historic role, as we see now, lay in another direction, in challenging the hemisphere to test the methods of socialistic totalitarianism as an answer to the political, economic and social ills which beset the region. As such, its potential effectiveness is all the greater (and the more dangerous to us) but the demands it makes are so drastic, and our response has been so violent, that other nations have thus far been unable—or unprepared—to follow the Cuban example.

The fact still remains that the pressures for social justice and economic development in Latin America have never been so powerful, and these are unsatisfied. The United States has finally been won over to a realization that the most pressing problem in Latin America is social development. This was recognized in a now famous speech by the then Under-Secretary of State Douglas Dillon to the conference of Economic Ministers of the OAS in Bogota, Colombia, in September, 1960. It is at the heart of President Kennedy's "Alliance for Progress" plan.

However, there does not yet seem to be a realization in the United States that satisfaction of social pressures has to be found in political, as well as economic responses. Unhappily for us, to achieve social justice, democratically, or by evolution, is infinitely harder than to do it by revolution. In fact, in an underdeveloped region like Latin America, revolution may prove to be the only way.

At least, the Cubans are trying to prove that it is the only way. It is up to us to prove that social development, in the circumstances faced by Latin American countries, can be achieved by our democratic, capitalistic, free-enterprise way. The alternative is to help slam a lid down —Rightist, militarist, conservative, dictatorial—on the revolutionary ferment, and then to sit on it.

There are democracies in Latin America—real democracies. Costa Rica, Uruguay, Chile, Mexico, Brazil, Venezuela in their different ways and degrees are all genuine democracies. Nevertheless, as I stated before, not one of them has produced a liberal democratic welfare state in our understanding and practice of those terms. In defending themselves against *Fidelismo* today, not even the democratic nations of Latin America have a maturity and a solidity that permits them to absorb the shock of these new and disturbing ideas. They are shaky structures.

The simple fact that what we call Latin America today was originally colonized by Spaniards and Portuguese, whereas the United States and Canada were colonized by the English and French, has made differences of a basic sort that we must never forget. Spain and Portugal went to the New World to exploit and convert. Their conquerors and settlers were religiously and intellectually intolerant, descendants of people who were not to know the Reformation or the Enlightenment, and who had no ideas, let alone desires, to implant democracy, civil liberties, or any of the arts of self-government.

It was an aristocratic, hierarchical, autocratic system that did not break down for centuries. Democracy and social mobility were slow growths until recent decades.

Cuba was the last of the Spanish colonies to become independent. The Spanish imprint remains exceptionally strong in Cuba, despite the great influence, attraction and power exercised by the United States in the twentieth century. Under the veneer of Americanization, under the subservience of the Cuban business and political elements, lay the ineradicable and dominating inheritances of Spain and Africa.

It stood to reason—or it should have—that faced with a crisis like the 1959 Revolution, Cubans would behave like Cubans and not like Anglo-Saxon Americans. It stands to reason that the rest of the hemisphere, having to face the Cuban Revolution and its effects, would react like Latin Americans and not like North Americans.

We should never have expected them to see eye to eye with us about the Cuban Revolution, or about communism, or about the whole complex of problems that have brought them into their present political and economic crisis. We see their problems in our way. We know how we would solve them—in fact we know the true and tried orthodox economic and financial solutions. We feel and believe that our political system is best of all—better than communism, better than any form of authoritarian government.

We ask the Latin Americans to be like us, to follow us, but they cannot do so, and in many respects they do not want to do so. Yet, in some ways there are no morally or practically valid arguments against what we propose.

Latin Americans should pay fair taxes. They should accept a just distribution of wealth. They ought to make land reforms, and make sacrifices for the education, health and a decent standard of living of the less privileged people in their countries. They should give the worker a fairer share for his labor and give him better conditions of life.

In these respects, we are not asking Latin Americans to do anything that we are not doing, or trying to do. We have a right to say that we will help only those who help themselves. What we cannot do is to compel any Latin American country to take our advice; what we cannot know is whether the ruling classes will want to go our way and will pay the price for doing so; whether there is still time, or whether the revolutionary forces at work will sweep them away.

This is where the example of Cuba works its potent spell. Successful or not, the Castro regime is seeking the answers to many of the evils that beset Latin America. It *is* redistributing wealth; it *is* making a land reform; it *is* concentrating on eliminating illiteracy, on raising the standards of health, on building homes, on diversifying agriculture, on industrialization—in short, on social justice and economic development.

But it is doing so by socialistic, totalitarian methods, not by democratic, capitalistic methods. This is where it challenges us, but it is also where it challenges the ruling classes in Latin America.

There could be no greater folly than to think of Cuba as an isolated phenomenon, or as merely an expression of communism at work. The ferment of modern political ideas is bubbling everywhere in Latin America, and Marxist ideas have their place in the brew. So have the liberal, democratic principles of the West.

The United States, after all, took revolutionary ideas to

Latin America. Our concepts of equality of opportunity, of the right of everyone to life, liberty and the pursuit of happiness, to a high standard of living, to social welfare, to education, to human rights—these and other ideas by which we live are very revolutionary, indeed. They did not, in the past, or, I am afraid, even now, appeal to the ruling classes of Latin America, who had such different concepts of life and society, but they are now beginning to have a mass appeal.

If there is a revolutionary ferment throughout Latin America—as there is—let us not forget our part in fomenting it. And let us not be so illogical as to say that *we* can have all the freedoms, a welfare state, a fair distribution of wealth and a high standard of living, and we would *like* to see Latin America enjoy these fine things but there must be stability, order and the status quo.

Revolutionary ideas have a tendency to express themselves in revolutions.

It is true that in some countries of Latin America the younger generation of businessmen, bankers and land-owners, have progressive, modern ideas. They have made a great advance beyond their parents, but they are still not in control and there are not enough of them. They are the hope of Latin America, but it is also the younger generations who are leading the revolutionary drive, who are attracted by radical ideas—often Marxist—who are a prey to xenophobic nationalism, who see the Cuban Revolution as an example to be followed, and are attracted by the romantic figure of Fidel Castro.

The governing classes in Latin America are not thinking

in terms of expropriation or a totalitarian economy that, in their case, would be Right-wing, which is to say Fascist or national-socialist. There is simply a failure, thus far, to accept the price that would have to be paid for industrialization and land reform. The ruling classes of Latin America are being called upon to make sacrifices of their wealth and privileges such as they never had to make in the past. They are called upon for a type of patriotism and civic virtue that was not necessary before and that was even outside of their ethics and their mores.

We should not underestimate how much we—and the social pressures of these revolutionary times—are demanding of the hereditary, traditional ruling classes of Latin America. The pessimism that most students of the Latin American scene feel nowadays is partly due to a realization of the magnitude of these demands.

On the economic side, the need for industrialization and, specifically, the infrastructure of roads, railroads, steel mills, petrochemical plants and other heavy industries, is obvious. The trouble is that the various countries have been relying too heavily on American and other foreign investors to provide this infrastructure when they could raise the capital themselves—or much of it—by adequate taxation and the proper use and distribution of their land.

Moreover, economic nationalism—the insistence on keeping the foreigners out of key industries like oil, power, railroads and public utilities, and even the nationalization of these industries—is a bedeviling factor. Too often, Latin Americans want to eat their cake and have it, a process that they might think the Cubans have pulled off success-fully. Revolutions defy the laws of orthodox economics, and in a sense they get away with it. From the point of view of law-abiding, orthodox economists and statesmen, it is highway robbery but, even so, the robbers benefit temporarily by the use of their loot.

There are plenty of enlightened leaders in Latin America and a great number among the ruling classes who see what needs to be done and who want to do it. They are willing to make sacrifices, to pay adequate taxes, to make social reforms, but there are many others among them who will not do so voluntarily. The instinct is still, and always, to pass the buck to us.

I think this is an inescapable conclusion for any student of Latin American affairs. We can help a country, for instance, to draw up an equitable income- and land-tax system; we cannot make it enforce the plan. In conquered Japan in 1946 we could impose a drastic agrarian reform— more drastic than the Cuban one; we cannot do that in any Latin American country.

In an article for *Harper's Magazine* for July, 1961, an American businessman and student of hemispheric affairs, Peter F. Drucker, listed some of the things that ought to be done.

"The traditional tools of foreign aid—money and trained men," he wrote, "will never do the job until Latin Americans face up to the rough things which they alone can do: collect taxes from the rich and clean out the sinecure jobs in the swollen government services; push through land reform and cheap mass housing; stop subsidizing the wrong crops; get rid of the pettifogging regulations that now separate the individual states of Brazil by mountains of red tape; enforce the factory and mining-inspection laws already on the statute books; and say 'no' to the blackmail of the generals who habitually threaten to overthrow a regime unless they get a few more unneeded jet planes, tanks or destroyers."

Simple? But this would require a transformation of the Latin American scene—in other words, a true "revolution." Can it be done peacefully? Can it be done our way?

"Latin America is in revolution," Adlai Stevenson said on his return from a trip there in April, 1960. "The dictators are being swept aside. . . . The whole continent is on the verge of great economic development, and they are going to build a new society under our methods of free enterprise, if possible, and if not, under socialism."

Fidel Castro and his associates say the answer is socialism. We say capitalism.

One of the most crucial questions of today's world is whether our capitalistic, free-enterprise system of economy is better suited to the underdeveloped south of the globe than the socialistic, totalitarian system. Let us not be too sure of ourselves or self-righteous about this. Moral factors are not going to be decisive. Victory will go to the side that persuades the masses, or that forces the masses, to accept its system and then proves it can provide the answers to their needs.

Our industrialists, economists and bankers, sitting in the midst of the proofs of their success, have nevertheless failed in Latin America. The trade, the investments, the aid, the technology, have not brought adequate standards of living to the masses in Latin America, have not benefited the people, have not distributed wealth, have not built national economies that give these countries a sense of sovereignty and independence.

This is not necessarily a fair criticism of American businessmen and the officials of the United States Treasury. They were certainly not evil men and, in fact, they have done an enormous amount of good. It so happens that in today's world their methods are not enough; they work too slowly; they benefit too few people at the top—or their benefits are not seeping downward to the masses fast enough.

They may take a righteous comfort, for instance, in pointing out that the miners in the American-owned copper industry of Chile earn the equivalent of $90 a week, while workers in Chilean-owned industries average $14 a week. It so happens that this sort of disparity in wage standards sets up dangerous social ferments.

The answer is obviously not for the American employers to reduce their wages to national levels, even if they could, nor is it possible for the low national wages to be raised to meet American standards. A widespread, massive attack has to be made on industry, agriculture and the social factors that foster disparities which are no longer endurable.

Can this be done by evolution—by our way? or can it only be done by revolution—the Cuban way?

Or is there an intermediate way? *Must* it be either free enterprise or statism? Our industrialists, our investors, our government officials are so blindly committed to the sys-

tem of free enterprise that we are finding ourselves somewhat out of tune with large sectors of Latin American
opinion.

The psychology of our world today drives political leaders toward the safeguarding of national resources, the
control of heavy industries and public utilities, and the
promotion of social reforms and, by this token, the yielding to liberal or Left-wing pressure groups. Governments
that respond to these pressures (Venezuela and Mexico
are recent examples) find the American investor turning
away.

In general, American private investments in Latin
America have fallen off in the last few years—in other
words, since the Cuban Revolution set up a chain reaction
of social pressures and fears to which governments and
investors responded in their different ways. The tragedy
is that every move by Latin American Governments, or
by their oppositions, to protect resources or stimulate economic growth through state action has been resented and
fought as *Fidelismo*—or even communism. The polarization of ideas and emotions is such that anything which
seeks to change the existing economic structure is condemned. Yet, if the economic structure is not changed
voluntarily and peacefully, there is going to have to be a
totalitarianism of the Right or Left. The American free-
enterprise investor will be left sitting forlornly like King
Canute while the tide sweeps in around him.

These facts are being recognized in Washington and
in many or most of the Latin American capitals. The
economic conferences of Bogota and Punta del Este, the

"Alliance for Progress" plan of the United States, like the previous "Operation Pan America" of Brazil, all point in the same direction. They are efforts to meet the demands for social justice as well as economic development by a combination of government aid and private enterprise.

Only a totalitarian system can long withstand a discontented people.

The falling off in United States private investments since 1959 is a factor working for the Cubans. It sets a vicious circle in motion: the Americans are getting to be afraid to invest because of the threat of revolutions, but the lack of American investments will intensify Latin America's already serious economic problems and hence intensify revolutionary pressures.

The Kennedy "Alliance for Progress" plan is an attempt to fill the gap. But it can only be a beginning and, being Government aid, it represents taxpayers' money. Can Latin Americans ask North Americans to pay taxes to aid them when their own moneyed, property-owning, salaried class won't pay income taxes in their own countries?

Many students of Latin American affairs believe that the answer to the worst economic and social evils of the region lies in taxation. The ruling classes—landowners, businessmen, financiers, high military officers, leaders in the well-paid professions (not teaching!)—do not pay a fraction of the income or land taxes that we and the European nations would consider fair and adequate.

Taxation is not progressive. We and the British, for instance, have created our welfare states, with their fair distribution of wealth by progressively higher taxation of incomes. Moreover, we and other states like us, have evolved taxation systems that cannot be evaded. We pay our taxes or we are punished. The evasion of taxation in Latin America is easy, and it is prevalent. Tax officials are nearly always underpaid and therefore susceptible to bribery, particularly in an atmosphere where tax evasion is normal.

This was, for instance, the state of affairs in Cuba before 1959. It is being corrected by the Revolution. If the necessity for paying taxes takes hold, Cuba will have gained something precious by the Revolution. This is one of the many ways in which the Cubans are at least trying to remedy social evils that they inherited. Even if they fail, the fact that they are trying at all is important. It is the sort of thing which is attracting attention and respect in other Latin American countries.

In some of these countries efforts are being made to reform the tax systems but they do not remotely strike deeply enough. The ruling classes will, after all, have to tax themselves and they have not yet reached a state of mind, a stage of maturity or a state of fear that will induce them to say: "We will abandon our special privileges, divide our lands, share our profits, pay just taxes."

Why should they do so if they do not, as they seem to think, have to do so? If you had asked these questions of the Cuban ruling classes five years ago you would have got a dusty answer. So they had a revolution!

The tragedy is that the Cuban Revolution in its present form has not been an answer, either, because it exacts such a high price for its reforms. It divides, destroys and levels down, and sends freedom and democracy away.

I believe any student of Latin American affairs would agree that the people of Latin America, or an overwhelming majority of them, do not want societies that are regimented, socialistic, dictatorial and combative. Still less would they want regimes that are Communist or allied with and riddled with communism.

The best that can be said for a social revolution is that it may in certain circumstances be the only answer to an unjust, corrupt and—from the nationalistic point of view— humiliating state of affairs. This was the case in Cuba.

I do not say that Cuba was ripe for *this* particular revolution in the form it has taken. Certainly, it was not the revolution for which the middle classes of the civic resistance fought—and one sees them all now in opposition. They wanted a political revolution, as was noted before, that would make drastic social reforms, but would keep the social changes within the framework of a democratic structure—that is to say elections, a legislature, an independent judiciary, the rule of law, a free press, habeas corpus and all the other civic freedoms. This is what Fidel Castro promised them.

I still believe that this was the type of revolution he thought he could make and that was why he promised these things. The great question to be asked about Cuba— and it would be the question to be asked if there were other similar revolutions in Latin America—is whether it is possible to make a drastic social revolution of an extreme, nationalistic type within a democratic structure.

Fidel Castro was soon convinced that he could not do so. Let me repeat that I am not making a moral judgment in saying that given the problems he faced, internally and externally, given the character of the Cuban people, and given the determination to make a radical, social revolution, Fidel came up with a logical answer. It may well be that there could have been a better answer.

At least the methods he has been using, the policies he has been following in Cuba and on the world stage, have in effect, given Cuba a social revolution, a place in the world out of all proportion to Cuba's size and resources, and the Cubans have set an example that other countries in the hemisphere may try to follow.

Fidel Castro is one of the half dozen most famous men in the world today. Fortunately for us there are no other Fidel Castros around, but there are revolutionary pressures. There is still only too much reason to believe that if there are other Latin American revolutions they will try to model themselves on Cuba. That is to say, they will be Leftist, pro-Communist, anti-Yankee and non-democratic.

One must always make that qualification—"try" to be like Cuba. The United States has made it clear that American power will be used to prevent any more Castro-type revolutions in Latin America. In so doing, will we not be lining ourselves up with the forces of reaction against social reforms? There is a real danger that the Latin American reaction to *Fidelismo* will be Right-wing, military oligarchies. The temptation for the United States to accept—or even to welcome them—will be great.

This is the dilemma that we and the ruling classes of

Latin America face today. The solution is to provide social reforms, or the hope of them, and thus forestall any more revolutions, or at least any serious ones. In that aim we should be helped by the fears that the Cuban Revolution has engendered.

"We call for social change by free men," as President Kennedy put it.

The magnitude of the problem is frightening. For our purposes it is simply necessary to note some general features.

The average per capita income of Latin America's 200,-000,000 people is a third that of Western Europe and a seventh that of the United States. The journal of the new Inter-American Development Bank, *Ecos de la América Latina*, says that at the present rate of economic growth it will take Latin America 252 years to reach a level one third of the present United States average per capita income.

There are not only appalling deficiencies in housing, education, health services and water supplies, but agri-tural production, upon which the region depends, is at a lower level today than it was twenty-five years ago. A report made for the Punta del Este Conference of the OAS in August, 1961, said this low productivity was the result of "an extremely unequal distribution of land ownership, obsolete production methods and often undesirable practices in the employment and compensation of agricultural labor." Put these polite phrases into their real terms of social and human misery and you can get some feeling of what is agitating essentially rural Latin America.

We had what might be called our agrarian reform in the United States after the War of Independence and finished it some time after the Homestead Act of 1862—let us say it took one hundred years. We could tell the Cuban and Peruvian and Colombian and Brazilian peasants that if they and their descendants would only wait a hundred years they will have a fine agrarian reform.

They won't listen—not today, not with Russia and China showing them how it can be done quickly—in their ruthless and costly way.

Chester Bowles, who was then a Representative from Connecticut, in an article on land reform in Latin America for the *Times* Magazine Section on November 22, 1959, pointed out that "1.5 per cent of the people, those with 15,000 acres or more each, own half of all the agricultural land in Latin America." President Kennedy has given comparable figures, and as he said: "The uneven distribution of land is one of the gravest social problems in many Latin American countries."

Former Secretary of State Herter, belatedly, but nevertheless admirably, announced United States support for agrarian reforms in Latin America in a speech to the Council of the Organization of American States on April 20, 1960. Land reform is also one of the key features of the programs announced at Bogota in September, 1960, and at Punta del Este in 1961.

The primary obstacle is the Latin American landowner, often an aristocrat who inherited his land, or a newly rich businessman who gets power and social status by owning land. Their aim, usually, is to grow cash crops like sugar, coffee and cotton and the methods are antiquated and inefficient.

As Mr. Bowles wrote: "Sweeping changes in Latin American land tenure are inevitable." But here, again, we and they face the dilemma: Shall it be by democratic evolution or by revolution?

In Cuba, with which we are especially concerned, 8 per cent of all landowners held more than 71.1 per cent of the land, according to the last inventory taken in 1946. It could hardly have improved during the Batista regime. Small holders (up to about 30 acres) owned 39 per cent of all the farms, but only 3.3 per cent of the cultivable land.

The *guajiro*, or peasant, was for the most part a laborer on land that belonged to the big Cuban and American landowners. On the sugar plantations, where the trade unions enforced good wages, the peasant had three or at best four months' work a year. For the most part he was unemployed the rest of the year.

The average peasant lived at a bare subsistence level, illiterate, ill-housed, diseased. Is it not ridiculous for Americans, and for the Cuban exiles in Miami, to come along now and pity these *guajiros*? Now, for the first time, they are being taken care of, given year-round work, new houses, schools for their children, new wells, roads, hospitals. What sense does it make to tell them that they are no longer free men living under a democratic regime because they have to work for cooperatives or State-owned farms?

The growth rate of production per head has practically halted in Latin America since 1955. Yet the population

is growing at the fastest rate in the world, ranging between 2.5 and 3 per cent. The report to the Montevideo
Conference mentioned above calls for an average yearly
rate of growth of real output of at least 5 per cent. In
present circumstances it looks as if there will have to be a
miracle.

I do not mean to give the impression that Latin America, or its economy, is stagnant. There are few areas in the
world in greater ferment or more dynamic in every sense
of the word. The point I want to make is that, generally
speaking, per capita economic growth has not kept pace
with population growth in recent years, and it has certainly not kept pace with the "revolution of rising expectations."

Moreover, the world prices of the commodities upon
which Latin American economy depends so heavily have
dropped, on the whole, in the last four years, while the
cost of imports has increased. Few of the countries have
escaped more or less severe inflation. Unemployment rates
are abnormally high in the cities.

A half or more of the population of Latin America are
not consumers at all in the sense of buying imports or
manufactured goods; they live on what they grow or make
or scrounge. To them, it makes little difference whether
the national economy is growing or declining and whether
American investments are going up or down.

President Kennedy put his finger on the nub of the
problem in his "Alliance for Progress" message to Congress last March when he said: "Economic growth without
social progress lets the great majority of the people remain

in poverty while a privileged few reap the benefits of rising abundance."

By and large, there is a profound discontent throughout the area, rooted in the economic state of affairs. It has dangerous revolutionary possibilities; and revolutionary ideas, as I keep saying, have a tendency to take the form of *Fidelismo*. One of the wisest young statesmen of Latin America, Foreign Minister Julio César Turbay of Colombia, has put it this way: "We will direct the evolution of our countries or our masses will direct their revolution."

The lines of direction are clear enough. On the economic side they are industrialization and increased agricultural output. On the political side they can be summed up as social justice for the masses—jobs for the urban workers, land to till, education, health, a fairer distribution of wealth, a higher standard of living.

How easy it is to formulate what is needed—and how hard to provide it! With variations, men and women have always wanted these things. What is new in history is that —allowing for some exaggeration—*all* men and women now demand these things, regardless of birth or color or race or where they were born. And they are demanding them impatiently.

The problem of providing enough economic and financial aid to satisfy the needs of Latin Americans is beyond our resources or those of the Soviet bloc. In theory we could do it by going on a war footing of controlled economy, austerity and sacrifices, which we are not going to do. Unfortunately for us, the Sino-Soviet bloc can force its people to make economic sacrifices for political gains.

We have, for instance, been seeing Communist China send rice to Cuba in 1961 at a time when her own people were starving.

In explaining his success in getting economic help from the Communist bloc on a trip at the end of 1960, Che Guevara said: "We could not make such a request on an economic basis; this was simply a political request." We did somewhat the same thing in Europe with the Marshall Plan. It required real sacrifices on the part of every American citizen—and it paid off. Yet we have been unwilling to meet a similar challenge in our own hemisphere. Latin America did not have any part in the Marshall Plan.

President Kennedy's "Alliance for Progress" plan is our substitute. It is also the American answer to Fidel Castro. The idea of offering $500,000,000 as a first installment of economic and social aid was originally put forward by Under-Secretary Dillon at Bogota for President Eisenhower in September, 1960. It was immediately labeled the "Castro Plan" by ironical Latin Americans. Certainly, they had Fidel Castro to thank.

The concept of devoting money, credit, goods and technical aid to a program concentrating on social development is splendid. The main objectives are land, education and housing—and they could not be better. The Punta del Este Conference in August, 1961, tried to give practical form to the goals.

We are concerned here primarily with the question of whether the United States, with the cooperation of the Latin American governments, can come up with satisfactory answers to the revolutionary pressures which are being given an example, a form and a direction by the Cuban Revolution. In this respect, as in other ways, the Cuban phenomenon is forcing us to go to the heart of the matter.

In its simplest expression, we must answer the question being asked in Latin America and everywhere in the underdeveloped world: Which way will bring us social justice sooner, your capitalistic, free-enterprise system, or the Communist socialistic, totalitarian system?

Nothing could be more dangerous than to fall back on the complacent, smug, self-righteous assurance that our form of capitalism is, of course, the best—and also morally right. However fervently we believe this, it is still a fact that we have not convinced the people of the underdeveloped nations and it is also a fact that the Communist bloc, especially the Soviet Union, is proving that its system works. Students of Russian affairs, in fact, tell us that the rate of economic growth in the Soviet Union is faster than ours.

Too many Americans are missing the point about the appeal of communism in Latin America. Our mood is one of anger and irritation with Cuba and a naïve belief that the danger lies in subversion by Marxist-Leninist ideology working from a Cuban base.

The true danger, and the true appeal of communism in Latin America is material and practical. China may be having agrarian troubles in recent years that are setting the country back, but taking the long range picture, both the Soviet Union and Red China have a remarkably effective argument in Latin America. (Incidentally, they are believed to be spending something like $100,000,000 in propaganda in Latin America alone, every year. This is more than we spend for similar purposes in the whole world.)

In essence, the Russians and Chinese say this: "Like you, we were underdeveloped, agrarian nations in which our peasants and workers were downtrodden and neglected. As you see (and we have invited many thousands from your lands to come and see) we have industrialized without foreign investments and we have bettered the lot of our workers and peasants. We give education and jobs to all our young people and positions of leadership to the best among them, regardless of birth, race, creed or color. You can do the same with our methods and our help."

As an example of how they can help, they are now pointing to Cuba. We know the price that two generations of Russians have had to pay for this material triumph and we can see the price that the Chinese people are in process of paying. Capital had to be formed somehow, and while it did not come from foreign investments it did come from the equivalent of slave labor and a temporary lowering of living standards of virtually everybody to a subsistence level.

In the United States, Canada and Western Europe—and for that matter among the ruling classes of Latin America—such a price is intolerable. There is not the slightest danger of such a way of life appealing to more than a tiny minority in a country like the United States, with all due respect to the McCarthyites, John Birchers, Unamericans and the like.

But we are now considering the situation in Latin America. One graphic way of approaching the problem was put to me by President Alberto Lleras Camargo of Colombia, as wise and liberal and democratic a statesman as is to be found in the hemisphere.

"Can I go out into the countryside," he asked me the last time I was in Bogota, "and go up to a peasant, standing in rags in front of his hovel, with his wife and children similarly ill-clothed, undernourished and no schools or hospitals for them to go to—can I say to this man: 'You are fortunate now; we have kicked out the dictator; you have freedom and democracy?'"

Naturally the peasant asks: "But will your democracy and freedom give me bread and clothes and a decent house, a school for my children, a hospital when we are ill?"

To be honest, the President and all of us have to say: "Yes, but you must be patient. These things take time."

The Communists have no scruples in promising speedy social justice that they know they will not be able to provide but, here again, we must not miss the point. The men who would lead this Colombian peasant and other millions like him in Latin America into social revolutions would not simply be cynical, greedy, power-hungry demagogues from the middle classes. They would be young men who have persuaded themselves that the totalitarian socialistic method is the best way for their countries.

This is what has happened in Cuba! In order to understand the situation—and it is a Latin American situation—

put yourselves in the place of the young Cubans who are making this Revolution.

As I keep saying, there is a stubborn tendency here to look at Cuba and Latin America in terms of our own stable, mature, democratic, capitalistic, free-enterprise system and way of life. These yardsticks do not fit; they do not apply; they will not work. When you use them you come up with the wrong answers. Cubans do not think the way we do, or feel the way we feel, or see the problems of the world, including communism, as we see them. The Cubans are not Anglo-Saxons, nor is Fidel Castro a John Kennedy gone wild.

Take capitalistic free enterprise, for instance. As so brilliantly defined and interpreted by American thinkers like Adolf Berle, who headed a Latin American task force for President Kennedy, our capitalism is, in truth, an efficient, democratic system that distributes wealth fairly and brings a high standard of living to a higher percentage of the population than any system ever devised.

So we say: "If it has done this for us, it can do the same for the nations and the masses in Latin America."

The young Cuban revolutionaries, looking at what capitalism and free enterprise meant to their country, with its rewards for the few, its corruption, its fantastically high unemployment rate, its subservience to the United States, said: "We have no faith in your capitalism; we do not want it."

It is vain for us to argue that they have had a parody, or a corrupt form of what modern capitalism can be; that their ruling classes and some American investors had betrayed the Cuba people. This was not an argument that could get a hearing. It was too late in Cuba.

In Latin America capitalism and free enterprise have not, as with us, operated to raise the general standard of living, to distribute wealth, to give the worker and farmer an ever greater share of the produce of their toil, to bring them leisure and the means to enjoy it. It has, on the whole, meant wealth, privilege and power to a few at the top and good profits for American investors. It has not greatly altered the traditionally hierarchical social system, with its exclusivity, its aristocracy of family and wealth, its color bars, its social immobility, its caste privileges. It has not brought what sociologists call pluralism—the melting pot, equality, fraternity.

The thinking is doubtless twisted, but is it not understandable for a Latin American to say: "We have been trying your capitalistic methods and things are getting worse; let us try the other method"?

We must recognize that the appeal of Marxism to Cuban revolutionaries like Fidel Castro, and more notably to his chief economic and financial adviser, Che Guevara, is great, and that it is not simply the result of anti-Yankee-ism, Soviet blandishments and orders, or a perverted desire to maintain power at all costs. There has been a genuine conversion to a belief that socialistic methods are best suited to solve the problems faced by revolutionary Cuba.

This is the sort of thinking we must fear in the rest of Latin America. President Eisenhower was in Santiago, Chile, early in 1960. While he was there, the University

Students' Federation of Chile wrote him an open letter which read, in part: "If the injustices of today are all that Christianity or democracy can offer this continent, no one should be surprised if the best children of these nations turn toward communism, seeking those elementary needs which they lack and which are the essentials to morality and civilization: food, shelter and education."

The answer prepared for President Eisenhower and later published was not convincing to these students. The leaders were invited to the United States and were impressed, but afterwards they went to Cuba and were impressed there, too.

But the impression was not made by communism in Cuba. It cannot be stressed too often or too much that the appeal of *Fidelismo* in Latin America is wider and deeper than the appeal of communism. In the United States, and in governing circles in Latin America, for that matter, there is a tendency to believe—or at least to say— that *Fidelismo* and *comunismo* are exactly synonymous.

We have not convinced the Latin Americans (or the Europeans for that matter) that the Cuban Revolution is simply a Communist revolution. Ambassador Adlai Stevenson learned that on his trip to South America in June, 1961. They know better. It is a paradox, but Latin Americans would continue to see this revolution as a Cuban and Latin American phenomenon even if it went on to call itself a Communist regime, as it now calls itself a Socialist regime.

For one thing, as I have said before, it would not be recognizable in Moscow or Peiping as communism. At the meeting of the eighty-one Communist parties of the world in the Kremlin in November, 1960, a new category was invented: "independent national democracies." Cuba was put in this grouping, and solidarity with her was pledged by "the Socialist countries, the entire international Communist movement, the proletariat of all the regions of the world," in Premier Khrushchev's words.

Whether this is semantics or not; whether we in the United States want to say there is no difference, the fact remains that in Latin America a distinction is made between *Fidelismo* and communism. If we are successful in pinning a purely Communist label on the Castro regime, we will have a much less difficult problem with which to deal, for this aspect of the Cuban Revolution weakens its appeal in other countries.

Meanwhile we must realize that the importance, the influence and the attraction of the Cuban Revolution in Latin America is not in its communistic coloration or its alliance with the Sino-Soviet bloc. The appeal lies in the fact that the Cubans are making a revolution which seeks to answer the problems that virtually all the Latin countries face.

Fidelismo attracts students and intellectuals, some industrial workers, the extreme nationalists with their anti-Yankeeism, the political oppositions of the Left and among these (as among all the other elements in varying degree) we find the Communists. Everywhere, as they did in Cuba, the Reds are getting on the Fidelista bandwagon. The non-Communist radicals are attracted by the Cuban Revolution, not by communism. Both *Fidelismo* and communism are providing the vehicle or means of expression for the social pressures that threaten to take a revolutionary form.

It has been utterly useless for Americans—government officials, businessmen and press commentators—to say to Fidel Castro and his associates: "We like your revolution and will support it, but you must give up the Communists and the support of the Sino-Soviet bloc."

If we had followed different policies in 1959 we may or may not have brought about that result. By 1960, and certainly in 1961, we were asking the impossible. That is to say, we were, in effect, asking Fidel Castro to give up his Revolution. President Kennedy goes on demanding the same thing, and perhaps it is good propaganda; perhaps it is a necessity. Let us not try to fool ourselves or anybody else. This is an oblique way of saying that we intend to destroy the Castro regime if we can.

Our position, as stated by President Kennedy is that "the United States would never permit the establishment of a regime dominated by international communism in the Western Hemisphere."

It remains to be seen whether we can make good on that threat in the long run, but one thing is certain—the answers to *Fidelismo* and communism in Latin America cannot be negative. They do not lie in the field of anti-communism or in maintaining the status quo at the cost of supporting Right-wing military dictatorships. This must be emphasized because our record in Latin America since the Second World War has been to oppose communism everywhere and at all costs, but not to oppose Right-wing, fascistoid, military dictatorships. In fact, we often went out of our way to favor the dictators.

The need for a new policy was recognized by President Kennedy. When he appointed Dean Rusk Secretary of State, he said:

"It is my hope that in the coming years the foreign policy of the United States will be identified in the minds of the people of the world as a policy that is not merely anti-Communist, but is rather for freedom, that seeks not merely to build strength in a power struggle, but is concerned with the struggle against hunger, disease and illiteracy."

This is a position more advanced, more sophisticated and more in tune with necessities than that held by a great majority in Congress during the Eisenhower Administration. However, the policy of using American aid to encourage social development in Latin America began with the Eisenhower Government.

If we had insisted on social reforms in Cuba sixty, fifty or thirty years ago (and we were in a position to do so) there would be no Cuban Revolution today.

But if we insist that social reform in Latin America must not bear the imprint of *Fidelismo* or communism, what then? The revolutionary pressures in Latin America do have these labels. In any event, they are radical, Leftist, nationalistic.

It is a sad acknowledgment to make—that we, with our wonderful Constitution and Bill of Rights, our freedom, our democracy, our equality, our fantastically high standard of living, should fear the undeniable and natural fact that Latin Americans now want, now demand what we have, what we helped to teach them to want.

When they set out to get these things, are we going to say it is communism? Or are we going to let the Communists be the champions of a social justice that we oppose because it is demanded, among others, by the Communists and the Fidelistas?

The Cubans are making a great play throughout the hemisphere of our supposed opposition to social reforms. Che Guevara put it crudely but effectively when he said: "By replying to the question of whether one is with Cuba or against her, one can tell if that person is for or against the people."

The dilemma that we face is not only baffling and painful; it is crucial. A friendly or neutral Latin America with which we can trade, upon whose raw materials we can draw, from which we know that a military attack against us is unthinkable—such a Latin America is vital to our existence as the pre-eminent power in the free world. This statement, which may sound dramatic, could be documented.

The security of the continental United States for the last 150 years has, in a crucial sense, been based on our hegemony in the Western Hemisphere. Now, as an indirect result of the Cuban Revolution, that hegemony is being challenged.

Latin America has been our sphere of influence. In the world of power politics it is our area, and we have the Monroe Doctrine to prove it. We are the Colossus of the North, and no European nation has been allowed to exercise political influence, let alone power, south of the Rio Grande.

Can we lose that hegemony now? The fact that the question has to be asked, that there is even a possibility of our position being lost or seriously weakened, proves in itself how grave a challenge we are facing from the forces unleashed by the Cuban Revolution.

When Premier Khrushchev made his flamboyant threat in July, 1960, to use nuclear weapons against the United States if we intervened militarily in Cuba, he knew that we had no intention of sending American troops into Cuba and we knew that he had no intention of waging a third world war, with all that it means, because of Cuba. The significance of his gesture—which he, himself, later called symbolic—was that a Latin American country was for the first time accepting military protection from a European power, not from the United States or the Inter-American System.

Those of us working in the Latin American field and seeking to grasp the real, the profound, the historic forces at work feel almost tempted to brush aside these surface manifestations, of which communism is one. That, of course, would be idiotic, but the impulse is based on a legitimate desire to get at the root of the trouble in Latin America, at the causes of a phenomenon like the Cuban Revolution.

Let me repeat that the basic cause of the revolutionary ferment in Latin America is social. It is the demand for what we are conveniently labeling social justice that is pressing upon the political and economic structures in such a way as to endanger their solidity, to distort them, to give them new and dangerous directions.

These are nations seeking the answers to their insufficiencies, their maladjustments, their distortions, their injustices. These are people striving for material betterment, but also for human dignity and, to an extent we do not grasp in the United States, for national sovereignty, for independence from domination or dictation by outsiders.

"In a real sense," as Professor Frank Tannenbaum of Columbia University has written, "the United States and the non-industrial areas, including Latin America, live in separate worlds, and matters of most concern to one lie beyond the basic preoccupation of the other."

It is hard for Americans to realize the extent to which we live in a world of our own, with ideas and values that others do not share. This is as true of Europeans as it is of Latin Americans. In any event, what counts in the relations between nations is not common ideas or moral values, but, as Lord Palmerston pointed out a long time ago, common interests. I would not feel at all sure that our way of life—our democratic, capitalistic, free-enterprise system—is applicable to Latin America in its present stage of underdevelopment, and considering all the historical, traditional, social, religious and racial factors at work.

As Latin Americans search for the answers to their problems, we say to them: "You will find the answers as we have found them. It is our example that you should emulate."

The real meaning, and the real importance of the Cuban Revolution is that it challenges this contention. It says:

"You will find the answers in a totalitarian system reached through a social revolution. Your examples are to be found in the East, not in the West. With their methods and their help we will make a Cuban Revolution, a Latin American revolution."

For the first time, Latin Americans do not need to look abroad for something different. It is in their midst.

It is important to us—and we believe to Cuba and Latin America—that this type of revolution should fail. Yet it is even more important to realize that its failure would ultimately solve nothing. Kill Fidel Castro and overthrow his regime, and this particular revolution, in this form, would be over in Cuba, but we would have exactly the same forces to contend with, the same searching for answers and solutions that we have today. Meanwhile, Cuba would be suffering the horrors of bloodshed and anarchy.

We would cure the patient by killing him—as we tried to do with the invasion of April, 1961. There are no easy answers to our conflict with Cuba, because the answers that have to be found for the island off our shore are the same answers that we need for the whole vast area of twenty countries and a continent and a half.

CHAPTER SIX

The United States

UNITED STATES POLICY toward Cuba since early in 1960 has been to destroy the Castro regime. This is the key factor around which relations between Cuba and the United States have revolved.

This statement is not made to absolve Fidel Castro and his Government of their share of the responsibility for carrying events to a point where such a decision seemed necessary to the Eisenhower Administration. I think the decision was at least made too soon. It was certainly made without a correct understanding of what was happening in Cuba, why it was happening, how strong the Castro regime was, and how much all of Latin America would resent United States intervention in Cuba and anywhere else.

The Kennedy Administration carried on the Cuban policies of the preceding Administration. The policies were bad and they led to the incredible and inexcusable fiasco of the invasion of April, 1961. None of this is wisdom after the event. None of it—let me repeat—is intended to excuse bad, ignorant and often inexcusable policies on the part of the Castro Government. It was as if a curse had been put upon both our countries.

In some curious way, the Cuban Revolution aroused an emotionalism in the United States that had not been seen since the Spanish Civil War. The history of Cuba began on January 1, 1959, for virtually all Americans. They did not know what had happened before; they did not understand the real reasons for the summary executions of "war criminals"; they were told that the Communists were taking over, although at that time they were of little importance.

The Cubans on their part had always been convinced that the Administration in Washington was out to destroy the Revolution. They really believed that the hostile press in the United States, the distortions and falsities, as well as the facts being printed here, the welcome given by Congressional committees to Cubans known to have been sadists, assassins and thieves in the Batista regime, the frequent raids by little planes from Florida, the discouragement of tourism during all the months when Havana was safer than New York and Americans warmly welcomed—these and other factors had convinced the Cuban leaders that the United States was preparing to take action, and there was no reason to doubt that they even feared the possibility of American military intervention—with good reason, as it turned out.

Some students place the definitive turn in American

policy—that is to say, the decision that we could not get along with the Cuban Revolution—in May, 1959, when the terms of the agrarian reform were divulged. It was, indeed, a tough, extremely radical land reform and it resulted in the resignation of five Cuban Cabinet Ministers, including the Minister of Agriculture, Humberto Sorí Marín, whose own more moderate proposals were rejected. This was the first major break in revolutionary unity.

The agrarian reform law, in fact, was much more radical than the Cuban Communists were suggesting. This was ironical considering that the law, which was promulgated on June 3, 1959, was immediately and generally labeled as communistic in the American press and by many American businessmen and Congressmen.

The decision was Fidel Castro's, and it was typical of a paradoxical feature of the Cuban Revolution: *Fidelismo* is more radical than *comunismo*.

On June 11, 1959, the day the Cabinet Ministers resigned, U.S. Ambassador Philip W. Bonsal handed Minister of State Roberto Agramonte (who, incidentally, was one of the men who resigned) a note from our State Department. The key passage read:

"The United States recognizes that under international law a state has the right to take property within its jurisdiction for public purposes in the absence of treaty provisions or other agreement to the contrary; however, this right is coupled with the corresponding obligation on the part of a state that such taking will be accompanied by payment of prompt, adequate and effective compensation."

The law provided for compensation in twenty-year bonds bearing 4½ per cent interest. No bonds ever materialized, nor was there compensation at any time for American mines, public utilities, factories, refineries and property of all kinds seized as the conflict between us worsened. These had a capital value of at least $800,000,000.

Fidel and his associates insisted that Cuba was in no position to pay compensation after the colossal peculations of Batista and his cronies—which was true enough—and that bonds would have been issued for expropriated lands if we had been patient enough. I was not so sure of that, but it was true that the revolutionary government was too disorganized and had too few technicians to issue the bonds quickly.

A crucial question began to take shape at that time: How much patience could or should the United States exercise toward the Castro regime? Before that question could be answered with a proper degree of wisdom, common sense and understanding, history, the character of the Cuban people and the long intimate background of Cuban-American relations had to be studied, as well as the phenomenon of the Cuban Revolution.

I do not believe that such a study was made or was considered necessary. Perhaps it would have been an intellectual exercise too confusing and too paralyzing for men concerned with the security and power of the United States. Only the intellectuals can safely indulge in the luxury of seeing both sides. It need hardly be pointed out that in similar circumstances Premier Khrushchev would have acted sooner and with complete ruthlessness—a simple fact that Fidel Castro and his associates did not seem to have considered.

However, the United States is not a Communist or Fascist State. "In a free society like ours," Walter Lippmann was to write after the abortive invasion, "a policy is bound to fail which deliberately violates our pledges and our principles, our treaties and our laws."

So, with regard to Cuba, we have been performing the classic maneuver of sitting down between two stools.

Unhappily, we are ill prepared as a people and a nation to understand and meet the problems that face us in Latin America. We start with a great handicap. The ignorance of Latin America in American official and public life and in the press, radio and television of the United States is quite simply appalling. There are many first-rate Latin Americanists in our universities, but not nearly enough. None specialized or kept up with Cuban affairs and as a result there has been no history of Cuba in English since 1936.

There has been no Secretary of State since Cordell Hull who has made a close study of Latin American affairs (Dean Rusk is no exception) and Hull was narrow minded, unsympathetic and lacking in understanding.

One of the most frequently heard complaints in Latin America was that we "neglected" the area and concentrated all our attention and an overwhelming percentage of our aid on Europe and Asia.

There was no logical reason for our neglect. On the contrary, the importance of Latin America to the United States is paramount. Our private investments outside of Cuba, for instance, exceed $8,000,000,000 compared to about $5,300,000,000 in Europe. About one quarter of all our exports go to Latin America and one third of all our imports come from the area. Of seventy-seven articles listed as strategic materials for stockpiling in the Second World War, thirty are produced in large quantities in Latin America. We get more than 90 per cent of our quartz crystals, two thirds of our antimony, more than half of our bauxite, half of our beryl, a third of our lead, a quarter of our copper from the area. Zinc, tin, tungsten, manganese, petroleum and iron ore are some other important raw materials we get from Latin America.

The trade between the United States and Latin America, both ways, exceeds $8,000,000,000 a year. United States receipts for exports of goods and services and for net long-term investments are in the neighborhood of $7,000,000,000 yearly. The figure for payments by the United States to Latin America for imports of goods and services, net donations and investments in excess of liquidations or repayments is roughly the same.

It should be remembered, incidentally, that we get nearly all our coffee and most of our imported sugar from Latin America. These may not be strictly "strategic" materials, but one would hate to live without them.

What all this adds up to can be stated simply. Latin America is our most important trading and investment area. Latin American raw materials are essential to our existence as the pre-eminent world power. A friendly Latin America is necessary to our military security.

These are the facts of life, and yet we see the paradox of Latin America being taken for granted, neglected and misunderstood. While the United States poured aid into other parts of the world to forestall social revolutions or communism, or threats to the security of the West, Latin America has received only about 2 per cent of direct American aid since 1945. In 1955, Latin America occupied first place among the major regions of the world in new United States private investments; in 1959 Latin America was in last place, and she stayed there in 1960.

The pent-up feelings exploded with a tremendous shock when Vice President Nixon made his now famous trip to South America in April and May, 1958. Virtually all students of Latin American affairs agreed at the time that Mr. Nixon drew the right conclusions from his experience—that the hostility was not directed against him personally but against the United States policies toward the region, especially economic policies, and the favoritism shown toward Latin American dictators.

Among the dictators who had been especially favored was General Batista of Cuba. This policy came at the end of a century of policies that Cuban patriots resented generation after generation. Yet we started in 1959 by blandly ignoring the past.

The Cubans had longer memories. A conflict between Cuba and United States had been built into Cuban-American relations by past history and it overflowed in

1959, from which time it was aggravated to the point of a bitter form of cold—and nearly hot—warfare.

The two events which precipitated an open break were the seizure of the American and British oil refineries in Cuba when they refused to process Soviet oil in June, 1960, and the decision of the Eisenhower Administration to punish Cuba by eliminating her sugar quota.

The arguments as to whether the Castro regime deliberately followed the general line it has taken, or was forced to do so by American policies and the attitude of the American public, could be endless. There is no way of settling the issue, for these are matters of opinion.

I am sure that Fidel Castro, Che Guevara, Raul Castro, Raul Roa, Armando Hart and the others sincerely convinced themselves that the United States was the aggressor from the beginning, and gave them no alternative. It is also possible, if not probable, that they were only too willing to go the way they did and often followed policies that deliberately provoked American reaction.

History, which ends up by holding an impassive balance, will no doubt say that both sides were to blame, that each provoked the other, that action was met by reaction in an almost compulsive chain or (to change the figure of speech) in a vicious circle.

An example of Fidel Castro's deliberately provoking an American reaction was his demand that the personnel of the huge American Embassy in Havana be cut to eleven persons in forty-eight hours. This was on January 3, 1961, and President Eisenhower had no choice but to break diplomatic relations.

In any event, I do not see how a confident judgment can be passed blaming either Fidel Castro or the United States for the bitter and irrevocable conflict that developed between us. Neither side can be absolved of mistakes, misunderstandings, injustices and stupidities. Let history decide who was guilty of more sins of omission and commission. I will not, as I remarked before, quarrel with history.

Granting United States patience in 1959, it could be argued that the situation required some positive American policy and economic initiative toward Cuba and certainly there was neither of these.

The inevitable was not recognized as early as it could and should have been, and the supreme importance of Fidel Castro was also missed. One can only speculate as to what differences a recognition of Cuban realities by the White House, State Department, Congress and perhaps, above all, by the American press, radio and television would have made. The Revolution could never have been defeated or destroyed, as so many American officials and businessmen believed.

In diplomacy, as in boxing, there is such a thing as rolling with the punch. We never seemed to be able to do that with Cuba; we just traded punches, and since our opponent was outweighed and desperate he tried to hit back harder for every blow he received.

In Cuba we are seeing an extreme form of the ineradicable, all-pervading, ubiquitous Latin American emotion of anti-Yankeeism. Because so many Americans became aware of anti-Yankeeism when Fidel Castro began attacking the United States, we thought he invented it. Because the Communists are anti-American, we thought anti-Yankeeism in Latin America must be synonymous with communism, and we blamed Vice-President Nixon's unhappy experience in 1958 entirely on the Reds.

There are few North American attitudes more dangerous or more self-deceptive than labeling all these manifestations of anti-American feeling, from Japan to Latin America, as Communist.

A Havana newspaper once put in double 8-column headlines: "HATRED OF NORTH AMERICANS WILL BE THE RELIGION OF CUBANS."

This was not in 1959 or 1960. It was in June, 1922, four years before Fidel Castro was born, and it was a typical reaction to the long period of ruthless control of the Cuban economy for the profit of United States companies and a small group of corrupt Cuban businessmen and politicians. Professor Robert F. Smith of Texas Lutheran College, who quotes these headlines, has documented this period with overwhelming evidence in his recent book, *The United States and Cuba.*

"As long as the Cuban Government would meet the payments on its foreign debt," he writes, "and maintain stability, the United States did not press the issue of honesty and democracy in government."

That, one might say without too much exaggeration, sums up United States policy toward Cuba in the six decades that ended with the Castro Revolution.

We must recognize that just as we are fiercely and emotionally anti-Communist, many Latin American politicians, students, intellectuals and industrial workers are anti-Yankee. The commencement of wisdom in this field is to recognize that there are some natural and legitimate reasons for anti-Yankeeism in Latin America. The sentiment is used with great effect by the Communists, but it is an instrument, a weapon that they pick up. They did not forge it.

When we ask what we Yankees have got that so irritates and frightens the Latin Americans, which the Russians have not got, the answer is that we are there and have been there for 150 years. We are the Devil that they know.

There has been anti-Yankeeism in Cuba for a long catalog of reasons going back to its struggles against Spain throughout the nineteenth century. We think the Cubans should be grateful for our intervention in the Spanish-American War. They resent the way we intervened, how we fought the war, and what we did afterwards.

They had fought for ten desperate, bloody, destructive years for independence from the Spaniards, 1868 to 1878. We stood by, and sold arms to the Spaniards. They rose again in 1895 and had been fighting hard and, they think, successfully for three years when we decided to intervene. We fought for 114 days with total casualties of less than 2,500 and of those nearly 2,000 were from disease, not combat.

With the war won, we would not let the Cuban troops share our triumphant entry into Santiago de Cuba. After the war, we occupied the island for five years, a fairly good occupation, but what country likes to be militarily occupied by a foreign power? Then we forced the Cubans to put the Platt Amendment into their Constitution. Its key Article III read as follows:

> The Government of Cuba consents that the United States may exercise the right to intervene for the preservation of Cuban independence, the maintenance of a government adequate for the protection of life, property, and individual liberty. . . .

We started intervening in 1906—a shameful administration under Charles E. Magoon. We landed the Marines in 1912 and 1917. Even when there was not physical, military occupation there was a more or less complete economic domination. A series of crises in the autumn of 1929, for instance, bankrupted the Government and people of Cuba, but permitted Wall Street to get economic control.

Finally, with the advent of Franklin D. Roosevelt's Good Neighbor Policy, the Platt Amendment was abrogated in 1934. Yet, it still rankles and Fidel Castro, who was only seven years old in 1934, resents it as do all his compatriots.

Cubans blame us for the overwhelming role that sugar has played in their economy, with the imbalances it brought, the social inequities of profits going to a few people, many of them North Americans, and the unemployment it caused during the eight or nine months of the year between harvests.

Nationalism is a powerful force in the modern world and is exceptionally strong in Latin America. Is it any wonder the demand for "sovereignty and independence" from the United States was so insistent in Cuba from the beginning of the century?

Add to all this the culminating horror and indignity of the Batista dictatorship of 1952–59, during which the United States favored Batista, and one has, in schematic form, the reasons for Cuban anti-Yankeeism. In many respects the Cubans were wrong, unreasonable and unfair to us, but the important thing is that this is the way a great body of them felt for three generations.

History often depends on the point of view. Like politics, it is an art, not a science. Whether the reasons were good or bad, Fidel Castro, as I said before, is taking revenge for generations of Cubans.

This anti-Yankeeism in Latin America has nothing to do with the attitude toward individual North Americans. Latin Americans are invariably as friendly, cordial and hospitable to us as they can possibly be. This has always been true of the Cubans and there was no excuse for the American press campaign depicting Havana as a dangerous, hostile city, or for the U.S. State Department ban on tourism to Cuba—except as a move in our cold war with the Castro regime. There is no excuse now for preventing American students and teachers from going to Cuba to study the situation there.

However, nothing could be more foolish or less productive than to beat our breasts and take the blame for everything that goes wrong in the hemisphere. The failure of the ruling classes in Latin America to grasp what was happening, to see the handwriting on the wall, to make social and economic reforms, to move from Spanish

243

colonialism and feudalism into the 1960's is appalling to contemplate. Whom the gods would destroy they first make mad—and these people are going to be destroyed if they do not come to their senses. We can only help them to help themselves.

Moreover, it would be folly to ignore the fact that along with the criticism and antagonism there is also a great fund of respect, admiration, good will and friendship toward us in Latin America. These are also assets that we can draw upon. The anti-Yankeeism has a good deal of the exasperation and disappointment one feels toward a friend who has let one down.

History, geography and economics have always acted to link Cuba to the United States and our people to each other. The present break between us cannot last. I had occasion to write Fidel in December, 1959, when the quarreling was getting acute.

"We were sorry to miss seeing you on our vacation in Cuba last month," I wrote, "but as it was a vacation I did not feel it was fair to be bothering you. Afterwards I wished we could have had a talk, as I am perturbed by the conflict between our two countries. I foresee a period of great strain and difficulties which will require careful management on both sides. There is much misunderstanding, in the United States of Cuba and in Cuba of the United States. I wish we could all forget the past and only remember what Lord Palmerston once said: 'We have no perpetual allies and we have no perpetual enemies. Our interests are perpetual.' Cuba's interests are bound to ours and ours to Cuba's and no policy in Havana or Washington that forgets this can succeed."

Statesmanship was lacking on both sides. We had no right, on our part, to feel self-righteous.

It is hard for us North Americans to understand that people can dislike and resent intensely the things that we do or have done in the past, when we have meant well or do not know what our predecessors did. It did not seem to have occurred to Americans, in the press or in Congress, that the Cubans had any right or reason to be hostile toward the United States. We should have made the effort to realize that they had a number of reasons, some of them good, and that their feelings were sincerely held and not the result of perverseness, wickedness or communism.

"We are getting into trouble," as James Reston wrote in *The New York Times*, "because we are not seeing ourselves as others see us and not seeing others as they actually are."

The "Apostle" and hero of Cuban independence, José Martí, warned his people seventy-five years ago that they must achieve freedom both from Spain *and* the United States. They did not do so until 1959—and it remains to be seen whether they can make it stick.

"Colonialism," the Puerto Rican official who is now Assistant Secretary of State in the U.S. State Department, Arturo Morales Carrión, wrote, "does not merely subsist under a colonial status. Countries enjoying full sovereignty on paper may suffer from colonialism in their economic life, their political action or their intellectual outlook. Colonialism, among other things, is a condition in which basic policies involving a people's economic existence, political organization or cultural and spiritual life, are dictated from afar, by a power remote and different, and implemented by local representatives of that power, not directly responsible to the people."

This was the condition with Cuba. In 1958, United States interests controlled 80 per cent of Cuban utilities, 90 per cent of the mines, 90 per cent of the cattle ranches, all of the oil refining and distribution (with the Royal Dutch Shell) and 40 per cent of the sugar industry.

There has been a great deal of nonsense written and spoken about the United States sugar quota system and the "generous" subsidy that we are supposed to have provided Cuba by paying about two cents a pound above the world price of sugar for our imports from Cuba. This higher price was a subsidy for the American domestic sugar producers in order to protect their internal markets. They could not produce profitably at the Cuban price.

It is true that Cuba benefited, of course, but as a counterpart the United States obtained substantial tariff advantages for its exports to Cuba. Moreover, the sugar policy in general saddled Cuba with a distorted, one-commodity economy at the mercy of the American Congress. At best, it was a mutually beneficial arrangement that did not call for self-righteousness on our part. Any future arrangement should be, and doubtless will be, bilateral in scope.

Sugar was more than an industrial commodity to the Cubans; it was a symbol of their subjection to the United States and of American power over them. When we wanted to punish Cuba in the worst possible way, we cut off the sugar quota. This was a foolish move, which made matters worse for both of us, but it seemed an obvious thing to do. It was a power move and was typical of the fact that not only Cubans, but all Latin Americans are subject to the ubiquitous power of the "Colossus of the North."

Naturally, as a tactic anti-Yankeeism was useful to Premier Castro in sustaining the popular fervor for the Revolution and in winning support around the hemisphere. A revolution is like a fire. It blazes as long as there is something to feed on. Fidel has to keep throwing things on the fire to make a good blaze, and nothing is so inflammable as "Yankee imperialism." Jean Paul Sartre pointed out that if the Yankees had not existed, Fidel would have had to invent them. We have played a role, for Castro, somewhat similar to that played by the Jews, for Hitler.

As early as February 20, 1959, Fidel angrily declared that the United States had been "interfering in Cuban affairs for more than fifty years" and that now was the time for Cuba to "solve its own problems."

The day before—on February 19—Philip Bonsal arrived to take up his post as American Ambassador in succession to the unfortunate and amateurish Earl E. T. Smith. Bonsal was one of our most expert career officers, with a fine record in Colombia and Bolivia. He was sympathetic to the ideals of the Cuban Revolution in their early democratic, non-communistic form. But as an Ambassador he failed.

It was a curious quirk of history that Bonsal should have been a direct descendant of Gouverneur Morris, who was United States envoy to Paris during the French Revolution. As it happened, this did not give Philip Bonsal the mentality or temperament to understand or sympathize with the sort of revolution Cuba was experiencing. Moreover—and this was the real handicap—the aristocratic, precise, rational Bonsal was the last person in the world to strike up a friendship with a wild young revolutionary like Fidel Castro. Bonsal could not do in Cuba what Josephus Daniels did so successfully with President Lázaro Cárdenas in Mexico.

Bonsal could see only the American point of view. The Cuban point of view not only made no sense to him, he found Fidel Castro positively "sinister." Fidel on his part could not remotely understand and appreciate a person like Philip Bonsal. This was typical of what was happening, on a national plane, between Cubans and Americans.

Nietzsche has his mythical seer, Zarathustra say: "That is my truth; now tell me yours." There has been a Cuban truth about this Revolution and an American truth, and the two often differed. There was also an inability to understand that a revolution has a logic of its own.

Governor Muñoz Marín of Puerto Rico, although he and his Government were under attack from the Fidelistas, warned Americans from the beginning not to let themselves become enemies of the Cuban Revolution.

The man who, to me, is the wisest, most understanding, most clearheaded of all American journalists, Walter Lippmann, wrote back in July, 1959:

"For the thing we should never do in dealing with revolutionary countries, in which the world abounds, is to push them behind an iron curtain raised by ourselves. On the contrary, even when they have been seduced and subverted and are drawn across the line, the right thing to do is to keep the way open for their return."

This was always good advice, but it was never taken. President Eisenhower, himself, has given us a date when a war to the finish was decided upon. After the ill-fated invasion attempt of April, 1961, he confessed that he had given orders for the training and equipping of the Cuban refugees on March 17, 1960.

Theodore Draper reminds us that former Vice-President Nixon advocated training Cuban guerrilla forces to overthrow Castro as early as April, 1959. This is typical of the hopeless ignorance of all the factors at work which has motivated so much of American policy toward Cuba. In April, 1959, only the worst type of Batistiano exiles could have been used for such a purpose.

Eisenhower's decision could hardly have been a sudden one. It may have been a reaction to the visit to Cuba by Anastas Mikoyan, the Soviet Deputy Premier, in February, 1960. A trade pact was signed in Havana between the Soviet Union and Cuba. In any event, I would feel sure that from the beginning, the overriding consideration in our hostility to the Castro regime was connected with communism.

The President's decision was naturally kept secret. The work was entrusted to the Central Intelligence Agency, thus setting in motion what was to prove the most futile,

stupid and costly blunder ever made in the course of
United States relations with Latin America. It was, incidentally, President Eisenhower's contention that American armed forces would be required—at the very least,
some air cover for the invading elements if they were
sent in.

So far as any of us knew during that spring of 1960,
the decisive act against the Castro Government was the
cutting of the sugar quota, which came early in July,
1960. In June, Fidel had demanded that the American
and British refineries in Cuba handle Soviet oil, which
he could get cheaper than the Venezuelan oil and without
having to pay precious dollars. Since the Cuban Government already owed the companies more than $50,000,000,
and since the Americans and British were in a global
petroleum "war" with the Russians, it was not unreasonable for the oil companies to refuse. The Cuban operation
was a very small one for these colossal organizations. It
may have been thought that Cuba could not get along
without Venezuelan oil. If so, this was a miscalculation.

The really important decision was the punitive action
taken afterwards by President Eisenhower. It is true that
there had been almost intolerable pressure from Congress
to do something. American feelings against Fidel Castro
and his Government were intense.

There were two policy calculations. The first was that
if the United States went on doing nothing in the face
of Cuban provocations like the confiscations of American
property, a dangerous example would be set for the rest
of Latin America. In this respect, I would say that taking

economic sanctions against Cuba in violation of our treaty obligations under the Bogota Charter counteracted any positive effects we may have gained. On the other hand, some of the Latin American sugar-growing countries— Mexico, Brazil, Peru—benefited by increased or new quotas.

The second calculation was that Cuba had to export her sugar to us and would suffer so greatly that the Castro regime would be fatally weakened. This was typical of the constant underestimation of the Castro regime's strength and the determination of Fidel Castro to carry on, whatever the cost.

Cutting the sugar quota once and for all threw the Castro Government irrevocably into the Communist camp. There are only two doors through which an under-developed country can go in the present world. When we shut and locked ours, Cuba had to become dependent on the Soviet bloc. Without Soviet oil and without the extra sales of sugar to the Iron Curtain countries the Castro regime would have collapsed in a matter of weeks. With Communist help it could go on indefinitely.

As the months passed and as it became clear that Fidel Castro was carrying on, no recourse was left to Washington except to try to arrange for the overthrow of the revolutionary Government by arms, which is to say, an invading force that we would train, equip and send into Cuba.

This seemed to the United States Government to be all the more necessary because Fidel was in process of getting arms from behind the Iron Curtain. One of our earliest and most foolish decisions had been to prevent Fidel from getting some jet planes from the British. When that happened, he naturally went where he could get arms.

All though the latter half of 1960 exiles were pouring into Florida from Cuba. It became possible to build up an invading force that did not have to be largely Batistiano.

The full story of the invasion fiasco requires no retelling here. For the purposes of calculating United States relations with Cuba and, indirectly, with the rest of Latin America, it is only necessary to keep certain salient facts in mind.

The decision to support an invasion, as stated above, was first made by the Eisenhower Administration. It was a foolish decision, based on misinformation and a failure to understand the effect of such an act on hemispheric relations.

Every student of Latin American affairs recognized that the era of military interventions by the United States had to end. We are still paying a high price throughout Latin America for the "Big Stick" policies. The doctrine of non-intervention is considered almost sacred by Latin Americans. They struggled for nearly fifty years to get it. Even our indirect intervention in Guatemala in 1953–54 has done us great harm.

Of course, we argue that the policy of non-intervention was never meant to condone intervention in the hemisphere by international communism. Even if that argument is granted, the reaction should be collective, not unilateral.

President Kennedy also favored building up and sending in a Cuban armed force. He said so in the presidential campaign—and was dishonestly attacked for it by Vice-President Nixon who knew all about the preparations for invasion being made and who favored them, as he boasted later. In any event, Mr. Kennedy both spawned the monster and inherited it. What he did realize was the danger and folly of using American air cover and naval support.

Yet by that time (the final decision was made on April 4, 1961) only American military intervention could have succeeded.

The most important feature for historians to recognize in the whole sorry business is that the invasion could not possibly have succeeded. I know of no one inside or outside of the United States Government who has been able to make any sense out of this truly incredible adventure.

This is what was frightening about it. The Central Intelligence Agency was making the most obvious mistakes and we all knew that in adavnce. The whole operation seems to have been entrusted to one Frank Bender. Allen Dulles and his deputy, Richard Bissell, do not seem to have known what was happening in detail. The intelligence section of the CIA was not in close contact with Bender and the operational sector. In any event, the CIA's information could not have been more mistaken. It was an appallingly perfect example of intelligence agents making their "information" conform to the plan they were determined to work out.

Anybody who really knew what the true situation was in Cuba could have told the CIA and the Kennedy Administration that there would not be a popular uprising in Cuba. Fidel Castro still had popular support and had built up a powerful army and militia. To cap the climax of their folly, the CIA refused to allow the underground organization of Manuel Ray and his *Movimiento Revolucionario del Pueblo* (MRP) to take part in the attempt. Yet the MRP had the only efficient underground in Cuba!

The reason for this was that Frank Bender, and whomever he worked for and with, considered the MRP to be "Leftist." It was formed at the top by men who had worked with the Castro Government in the beginning and broke with it over the Communist issue. They were anti-Communist, liberal, democratic and therefore slightly Left-of-Center. Apparently, that is considered a dangerous position by the CIA.

Bender would not give Ray and his associates money or help. Almost everything went to the *Frente Revolucionario Democrático* (FRD), composed of admirable but pre-Batista and rather conservative men.

The folly of the CIA was compounded still more by putting Batistiano military officers in command positions despite what was announced as orders from the White House that no Bastista followers were to take part in the invasion. On the contrary, so far as can be seen, the CIA intended to install a Batista-type regime in Cuba at the first opportunity.

In all this, I do not consider it fair to blame the Cuban exiles. They should not be held accountable. Their emotions naturally blinded them. They believed what they passionately wanted to believe. They risked everything and paid the greatest price. The United States Government did not back them as strongly as it had promised. What was inexcusable was for Americans to accept their information and their hopes as valid.

Let it be noted in passing that the Cubans could not keep what they were doing secret. The Castro Government obviously knew just what was shaping up and so, in a general way, did we newspapermen from late 1960 onwards. When I was in Cuba in August, 1960, I was closely questioned by Fidel Castro and others about an American intervention they believed we were preparing. Knowing nothing at the time, I could even deny any belief that we would be so foolish as to prepare for an invasion by Cuban exiles. Looking back later I realized that Fidel had some information about the preparations.

In this connection, since I believe that the bitter draught of this whole dreadful business should be drunk to the dregs, it has to be noted that our Government lied to us about the invasion even after it had started. That anyone who means so much to the United States and to our image abroad as Adlai Stevenson should have been led to give a false picture to the United Nations of what we had done and what had happened is sad to contemplate.

Afterwards we learned that only Senator William Fulbright, Under Secretary Chester Bowles and White House aide Arthur Schlesinger, Jr. opposed the adventure, but Schlesinger seems not to have felt himself important

enough to protest vigorously and Bowles was not consulted. Not a single other major figure tried to dissuade
the wavering President Kennedy.

Thus, history will record a list of men at the top of the
United States Government, all of whom have respon-
sibility in an act that could not succeed and that was
bound to do enormous damage to the United States.
These men are President Kennedy; Secretary of State
Dean Rusk; Secretary of Defense Robert McNamara;
Secretary of the Treasury Douglas Dillon; General Lyman
Lemnitzer, Chairman of the Joint Chiefs of Staff; Admiral
Arleigh Burke, Chief of Naval Operations; Adolf Berle,
head of the Latin American Task Force; Allen Dulles,
head of the CIA; his assistant, Richard Bissell; Assistant
Secretary of Defense Paul Nitze; and the White House
adviser, McGeorge Bundy. Perhaps we should include
former President Eisenhower and former Vice-President
Nixon.

One can exaggerate the importance of Cuba to us and
of this fiasco to our general status. We will recover from it,
somewhat damaged to be sure. But if the most important
men in the United States Government can make such a
blunder, what protection have we all got against other
and perhaps more important blunders?

Let us return to Cuba and our relations with that
dramatic island.

The future of Cuba will not be in the hands of the
exiles if the experience of other nations, like Italy, Germany and Spain is a criterion. Those who stay and live
and suffer through revolutions are the ones who pick

up the pieces later and forge a new nation. The exile loses touch; he ceases to be representative; he will not have the confidence of the people or of the underground resistance.

The country changes while he is gone. It moves on to something else. The clock cannot be turned back after a social revolution as drastic as Cuba's.

This does not mean that forward-looking, capable, patriotic Cuban exiles will have no role in the future of their country. The men of the past will go—and that includes the pre-Batista past of Presidents Grau San Martín and Prío Socarrás. If the United States had succeeded in putting them into power in April, 1961, they would not have lasted. They are anachronisms; they represent a Cuba that has gone into history.

The men who might be representative of what Cuba now wants and needs, the men who were repudiated by the CIA, were those who had helped to make the Cuban Revolution, who served it in its early hopeful non-communistic stage and who want to make a new Cuba. These were men like Manuel Ray, who was Minister of Public Works; Rufo Lopez Fresquet, Minister of the Treasury; Raul Chibás, the educator and Felipe Pazos, President of the National Bank of Cuba.

None of these men may get their chance. Social revolutions normally take a long time to work themselves out. The French Revolution lasted from 1789 to 1815; the Mexican from 1910 to 1940; the Russian (I would say) from 1917 to the death of Stalin in 1953; the Italian Fascist Revolution ran from 1922 to 1943; the German Nazi from

1933 to 1945. The Chinese Revolution began in 1949 and is still going strong. The Bolivian Revolution started in 1952 and is far from over.

In modern times, the mechanism of the totalitarian state is almost impregnable. The Fascist and Nazi regimes had to be overthrown by military invasions. The Franco and Salazar regimes have gone on for decades. No government within the Sino-Soviet bloc has been overthrown. The nearest thing to the defeat of a totalitarian regime by counter-revolution occurred in Argentina in 1955, when General Juan Perón was driven from power. However, Argentina did not have a real totalitarian structure.

The weakness of the Castro regime in Cuba lies in its dependence on Fidel Castro. The totalitarianism is still a façade although it may be getting a basis in the new unified political party. In this respect Cuba resembles Italy in the early stages of the Fascist Revolution. Had Mussolini been eliminated before 1926, by which time the Fascist State had been constructed, fascism would have collapsed.

This does not mean that the Cuban Revolution would end or that Cuba would return to pre-Castro days if Fidel were to be assassinated. It is too late for that. The eggs have been scrambled. Whatever came out of the chaos and bloodshed which would follow the elimination of Fidel Castro would be different from the Cuba of 1903–59.

This is what American policy makers did not—perhaps still do not—realize. The attempt to turn Cuba back to the era of Batista was utter folly.

President Kennedy, Secretary of State Rusk and other officials and advisers are paying lip service to the ideal of social reforms in Cuba. All we have done so far is to try to overthrow the Castro regime by every means in our power short of using American armed forces in order to install a regime that the White House believed would recreate the pre-Batista era and that the CIA intended to turn into a neo-Batista era.

At best there would have had to be a regime, imposed by the United States, nominally headed by José Miró Cardona and the Revolutionary Council, but actually kept in power by American economic aid. A long period of guerrilla—perhaps civil—warfare would have followed. The effect on our position in Latin America and on our relations with the hemisphere would have been catastrophic.

One has to end by saying: "Thank the Lord for the United States and for Cuba that the invasion of April 17, 1961, failed!"

With the collapse of the invasion President Kennedy was faced with the realization that the Cuban problem was greater than ever. Fidel Castro's regime was stronger; so was the Communist apparatus in Cuba and throughout Latin America; the Cuban exiles were defeated beyond any possibility of a comeback for a long time; the underground opposition in Cuba had been badly weakened; the reputation of the United States in Latin America had been severely damaged. More capital left Latin America in two weeks after the invasion than in the previous two years. As Theodore Draper wrote: "The ill-fated invasion of Cuba last April was one of those rare politico-military events—a perfect failure."

For a day or two there seems to have been something approaching panic in Washington with the hotheads urging President Kennedy to throw in the American forces. The President wisely resisted these pressures, but he did make some tough pronouncements. The most important came in an address to the American Society of Newspaper Editors on April 20 when the magnitude of the disaster had just been realized. In a masterly understatement he conceded that "there are, from this sobering episode, useful lessons for us all to learn."

"Any unilateral American intervention in the absence of an external attack upon ourselves or an ally would have been contrary to our traditions and to our international obligations," he said. "But let the record show that our restraint is not inexhaustible.

"Should it ever appear that the inter-American doctrine of non-interference merely conceals or excuses a policy of non-action; if the nations of this hemisphere should fail to meet their commitments against outside Communist penetration, then I want it clearly understood that this Government will not hesitate in meeting its primary obligations, which are the security of our nation."

Two days before, there had been an exchange of messages with Khrushchev in which the Soviet Premier had said: "We shall render the Cuban people and their Government all necessary assistance in beating back the armed attack on Cuba," and the President replied that "the United States intends no military intervention in

Cuba." This statement has been reiterated by Mr. Kennedy and by Secretary of State Rusk and it should be taken as definitive in present circumstances.

However, the speech to the A.S.N.E. contains a clear threat to use the Monroe Doctrine if the other Latin American States do not join us in preventing "Communist penetration."

As a matter of fact, one of the casualties of the Cuban Revolution may prove to be the Monroe Doctrine, although there is unlikely ever to be an official repudiation of it. The Doctrine is woven too firmly and too emotionally into the fabric of American history and psychology ever to be thrown away.

It is worth recalling the key phrase in President James Monroe's message to Congress on December 2, 1823:

"We should consider any attempt on their [the European powers] part to extend their system to any portion of this hemisphere as dangerous to our peace and safety."

In this post-war period we stretched the meaning of Monroe's phrase, "to extend their system," to subversion and control by international communism. This has been a bipartisan policy and has been clearly expressed in the Truman and Eisenhower, as well as Kennedy Administrations.

In a press conference on July 13, 1960, answering a question on Cuba, Premier Khrushchev said: "We consider that the Monroe Doctrine has outlived its time, has outlived itself, has died, so to say, a natural death."

The State Department lost no time in rejecting this interpretation. A statement was issued the next day which said: "The principles of the Monroe Doctrine are as valid today as they were in 1823 when the Doctrine was proclaimed. Furthermore, the Monroe Doctrine's purpose of preventing any extension to this hemisphere of a despotic political system contrary to the independent status of the American States is supported by the Inter-American security system through the Organization of American States."

In theory, the latter statement is true; in reality the Latin American nations have never liked the Monroe Doctrine. Any exercise or threat to employ power made by the Colossus of the North was invariably resented—and the Monroe Doctrine is a unilateral document that forever holds such a threat over the hemisphere. The Doctrine cannot be invoked by a Latin American country; we are the ones who decide when and if it applies.

When President Kennedy threatened in his speech to the A.S.N.E. to invoke the Monroe Doctrine, he sent a figurative shiver of distaste through Latin America. There is agreement with us in wanting to oppose the intervention of the Sino-Soviet bloc in the Western Hemisphere, but Latin America is not asking us to lead a crusade against communism. The concentration of American policy on anti-communism at any price is always criticized in Latin America, except by those dictators and demagogues who profit by this American obsession.

If it is granted that we are within our right in saying that intervention by international communism is a violation of the Monroe Doctrine, then there is no doubt that Fidel Castro and Nikita Khrushchev are flouting the Doctrine. It has been challenged before, but the only power capable of nullifying it—Great Britain in the nineteenth century—was concerned with trade and investments in the hemisphere, not territorial or political conquest.

It was, however, an Englishman who put a finger on the legal and logical weakness of the Monroe Doctrine. This was Lord Salisbury, then the British Foreign Secretary, during a dispute over Venezuela and British Guiana in 1895. "The Government of the United States," he wrote, "is not entitled to affirm as a universal proposition with reference to a number of independent States for whose conduct it assumes no responsibility, that its interests are necessarily concerned in whatever may befall those States simply because they are situated in the Western Hemisphere."

This, put in much less diplomatic language, is the position that Khrushchev and Castro take—in other words, that Cuba has a right to work out her own political and economic destiny and that so have all the other Latin American States. In theory we do not deny this right; in practice we have put all Latin American countries on notice that we will not permit any of them to go largely or wholly Communist.

But we have thus far failed to put this policy into effect with regard to Cuba! This is one of the many extraordinary developments that have come out of the Cuban Revolution. As a general proposition, the ability of the small powers to defy the large, even on their doorsteps, is a new fact of life in the world today—a hard one for the United States to digest.

Of course, we have not heard the end of the story. There are influential elements on the American scene (the whole powerful conservative Republican movement headed by Senator Barry Goldwater, for instance) who want to send the American Marines in to "clean up" Cuba. We can, of course, conquer Cuba. Many American lives would be lost, as well as Cuban lives; the island would suffer fearful destruction; there would be guerrilla warfare for as long as the American Army was in occupation; and the Good Neighbor policy, not to mention the Organization of American States, would be destroyed for many years. Still, we could do it.

President Kennedy wisely has no intention of committing that folly. In fact, he made a pronouncement about the Monroe Doctrine while he was campaigning for President which sounds curious in the light of his post-invasion statements. There should be, he said, "an administration that realizes that neither the Monroe Doctrine nor the old Good Neighbor policy of Franklin D. Roosevelt, is adequate for the Latin America of 1959–60. We need now a new policy."

The concept of accepting the existence of a Communist or pro-Communist regime in Latin America was not contemplated by John Kennedy either as a Senator or as President. Nevertheless, it is one that students of the area are discussing, and it has been put forward by a number of European commentators. In Europe, where nations live with Communist countries as neighbors—and between the wars with Nazi and Fascist countries—this idea is not startling.

It may be that the present strength and influence of the Russo-Chinese Communist bloc, which are increasing, could not be contained short of World War III if they intensify political and economic intervention in Latin America. It may also prove too dangerous in present circumstances to act to prevent a Communist regime's arising in Cuba if the Cuban revolutionaries should try to install one later.

The moment has not yet come when a decision has to be made on this problem, but we must be prepared for it. If the choice be acceptance of some Communist regimes in Latin America and of greater penetration by the Sino-Soviet bloc, or a Third World War, it is hard to see us making the decision for a holocaust. This dreadful choice will not have to be made, as stated before, if the United States with Latin American cooperation tackles in a positive way the social and economic demands of the Latin American peoples.

Moreover, to be practical, we should recognize the obvious fact that Latin America is too far away from the Sino-Soviet bloc to be regarded as vital and therefore as a cause for war. The Russians think in terms of spheres of influence, and Khrushchev would in a pinch accept the fact that Latin America is vital to us. He would also understand, better than anybody, that we are unlikely indefinitely to put up with a hostile power on our doorstep. When that time comes Fidel Castro, Che Guevara *et al.* are going to discover that so far as the Soviet Union is concerned, Cuba is expendable.

Meanwhile, this argument is getting ahead of the facts.

The Castro regime is not yet Communist, despite Washington's propaganda, and in any event, its communistic connections and coloration do not constitute the chief danger to the United States. *Fidelismo* is what should frighten the powers that be in Washington, not communism.

We are afraid of communism, but fear is not the best defense against an enemy. Communism exists; it has its historic roots, its popular support and a nation of enormous power and wealth behind its drive, just as capitalism has. Communism cannot be destroyed or conjured away any more. The United States must learn to live with it, perhaps even in the Western Hemisphere, or fight a nuclear war.

Fidel Castro has carefully refrained from provoking the United States to a point where we would have had justification to take military action against him. He obviously never had the slightest intention of attacking our naval base of Guantánamo Bay in the eastern end of the island because he knew we would fight for it. The American press never seemed to grasp this fact.

Sooner or later we are going to have to give up Guantánamo Bay because in the modern world it is not possible indefinitely to hold a military base in a foreign country against the wishes of the people of that country. France, Britain and Spain were unable to hold on to their bases in the Middle East and North Africa, and we are having to give up our air bases in Morocco.

However, we have the power to hold Guantánamo and Fidel knows it. One may also be certain that he has no intention of sending military expeditions against any other country in the Caribbean or in Central America; and there is no need or reason for Soviet missile bases. Cuba did not invade us. We—by proxy—invaded Cuba, having used American bases to train and transship Cuban troops with the connivance of our virtual satellites, Guatemala and Nicaragua. We are the ones who broke our treaty commitments and violated the Bogota Charter, which is the basis of the Inter-American System. This is not going to be forgotten quickly in Latin America.

Our policies, however, have not changed just because we made a fearful mess of the Cuban affair. We still say that we will accept a Cuban revolution—that is to say, social reforms—but that we will not accept communism or negotiate with Cuba unless it repudiates its Communist connections. Since, as I pointed out before, this would be the end of the Cuban Revolution, and since Fidel Castro and his associates will die before they give up their Revolution, we have reached an impasse.

We can continue to argue that it is unrealistic to apply the doctrine of non-intervention only to the United States. It should not and must not, we say, protect the Soviet Union and Red China when they intervene in the hemisphere. This is a logical argument and the Latin American Governments seem to agree with it in principle. What they do not accept is our contention that the Castro regime is Communist and that Cuba is a satellite of the Communist bloc.

Besides, they do not take the same attitude toward communism that we do. The cold war has only just begun to affect them. They are not in a life-and-death struggle with communism, as we are. They do not—and never will —accept our extreme position of anti-communism at all costs, even at the cost of supporting brutal and predatory military dictatorships in Latin America. They will support us against the Communists only when they are convinced that we believe in political liberty for them as well as for ourselves.

We have not yet made it clear to Latin Americans how far we would be willing to see them go in making their social reforms. We have made it clear, by our Cuban policy, that if we can help it we will not permit them to try to solve their social and economic problems the Cuban way. Perhaps there is no middle way—peaceful, democratic, evolutionary—such as we want to see. Perhaps we will be faced with the choice of one of the two evils— the Left-wing, socialistic, Fidelista way, or the Right-wing, reactionary, military dictatorship way. If so, our record shows that we would choose the Right-wing, if only because it is anti-Communist, and would hold out for "stability" and the status quo. Such regimes would not hold out long.

There is no quicker or better way I know of to demonstrate the type of traditional policy that must be abandoned than to cite a brief passage from Professor Robert F. Smith's book, *The United States and Cuba.*

"The late John Foster Dulles told a Senate Committee about Venezuela under the dictator Pérez Jiménez:" Smith wrote.

"'Venezuela [said Dulles] is a country which has adopted the kind of policies which we think the other countries of South America should adopt. Namely, they have adopted policies which provide in Venezuela a climate which is attractive to foreign capital to come in.'

"[Dulles] concluded by saying that if all Latin American countries followed the example of Venezuela, the dangers of communism and social disorder would disappear."

Dulles was then, of course, Secretary of State and he was testifying to the Senate Committee on Finance. This was in 1955 at a time when Venezuela, under General Pérez Jiménez, was suffering from as brutal and corrupt a tyranny as Latin America has ever seen, and when the dictator's policies were clearly leading Venezuela into bankruptcy. Our Ambassadors of that period were intimate friends of Pérez Jiménez.

This is the sort of American attitude and policy that must be abandoned. We have no proof that it has been abandoned.

All our Administrations have paid lip service to the cause of democracy in Latin America, and the Kennedy Administration is no exception. In his inaugural address Mr. Kennedy promised "to assist free men and free Governments in casting off the chains of poverty." The "Alliance for Progress" plan is intended to do this. The real tests are yet to come, and they will be severe tests.

It is vital that we permit the impetus for change to come from within the countries and not impose change upon them, even if we could. Yet how are we going to keep international communism out of the Western Hemisphere, and *Fidelismo* out of the other countries of Latin America, without intervening? This is one of the most serious dilemmas that we face in our Latin American policies.

If the Cuban Revolution succeeds as a social revolution, if it raises the Cuban standard of living, diversifies the economy, industrializes, brings schools, hospitals, homes, land to till and jobs for city workers—if it does these things or even partly achieves them, we will lose a major battle in the cold war. Yet, these are splendid goals, the very goals we want to see reached. We contend that they cannot be achieved by totalitarian methods or if they are, as in Russia, that the price paid will be degrading. Besides, anywhere in Latin America the aims would be achieved at our expense and would represent a grave danger to our security.

Therefore, if one wants to be logical, the Cuban Revolution, from the point of view of American policy, must fail. At least, *this* revolution, the Castro Revolution, must fail. At best, we applaud its ideals but not its methods. Yet we must have something far, far better to offer the Cubans than the pre-Batista or neo-Batista alternative we were preparing to foist upon them with the April invasion.

To Cubans, the policies followed by the United States in the first decade of this century or in the early 1930's, or during the Batista dictatorship, are vivid, burning realities which they deeply resent. Hardly one American in a million would know about these policies or agree that he should be held responsible for them. And if he did know about them and were in the Government, he would have the deeper responsibility of protecting the security of the United States.

However, it is to be hoped that Cuba really has taught us some lessons, as President Kennedy ruefully confessed. They are painful, as lessons often are.

The traditional policy of the United States toward Latin America, it must be repeated here, has been to seek stability, under which there could be profitable trade and investments, safe supplies of vitally needed raw materials, political support in the international organizations against the Communist bloc, and a friendly strategic zone in a geographic area of vital importance to our continental security. In the past, when instability developed we moved in with Marines or with the manipulation of economic and political weapons, or with both, as we often did in Cuba.

Let us grant that it is the business of any government to look out for its own security and economic strength. It is even arguable, in terms of practical power politics, that our policies paid off well enough in the past and that they were within the range of the normal, expected behavior of great powers in their sphere of influence.

But times have changed. The dynamism of the contemporary world is turning the concept of stability into an oppressive reaction. The ruling classes in Latin America, who maintain what stability there is, are trying to stop the tide from coming in. There must be change. As I am continually pointing out, either it comes by social and economic reforms made voluntarily by the governing

classes in Latin America with our aid and encouragement, or it will come through Leftist revolutions that will
resemble the Cuban upheaval.

Evolution or revolution, as President Eisenhower put
it in 1960. (Incidentally he got the phrase from an editorial in *The New York Times*.) As a policy, it is going to
be infinitely more difficult and costly than anything we
faced in the past. The Good Neighbor policy is not enough
any more. It consisted mostly in ceasing to do things we
had no right to do. And it cost nothing.

What is good for the United States is not necessarily
good for El Salvador, for Ecuador or for Brazil, and we
certainly do not think that what is good for Russia and
China is good for Latin America.

Countries like Brazil are showing pretty clearly that
they want to work out their own destiny in their own way.
Brazil is one of the future giants of the world, one of the
countries which is transforming our bipolar world of the
United States and the Soviet Union into a multilateral
world with many first-rate powers.

If we insist that Latin American nations be like us,
copy our economies and political systems, and be on our
side against the Communist bloc, we will lose allies. We,
as well as the Communists, face resistance in Latin America. It differs, in our case, in form and quality from the
resistance to communism but it has a historic, persistent
base in the nationalistic emotion of anti-Yankeeism.

Yet, we have a basic advantage, too, for Latin America
belongs to the West by history, tradition and ideals.

The changes taking place in Latin America are inevitably bringing a new generation of younger, more radical, iconoclastic men into power, men who will respond to mass pressures for social and economic betterment and who will resist United States leadership.

History does not flow backwards, as I have already remarked. We will not recapture the past. We will never again exercise the degree of power or economic domination that we used to have.

The forces that have brought about this change were at work for decades before the Cuban revolution. As has been said, that Revolution is a result of long pent-up historic forces and of social ferments at work everywhere in the contemporary world, especially in the underdeveloped areas.

One might say that Fidel Castro was like Pandora. The box was there and all the troubles were in it—and he opened the box.

Latin America is moving fast, and not necessarily with us or toward us. The social and economic pressures have revolutionary possibilities. Our policies to date have not been successful. They have been too negative, too little, too closely tied to dictators and to small ruling classes who will become victims of the new social pressures if they do not move quickly and make necessary reforms. Stability and the status quo are dreams of the past.

We have lost the Cuba we knew and dominated, or influenced so greatly. Our relations with Cuba will never be the same, even when they become friendly again, as they must.

As I have said repeatedly, January 1, 1959, when Fidel

Castro triumphed, began a new era in Latin America. It will be an era of challenge and conflict and danger. The New World is no longer new in our United States. We represent an older, a mature, a conservative world. This is not the world of Latin America. Their world is young; it is dynamic; figuratively or literally, it is revolutionary.

The challenge has come out of Cuba in the voice of Fidel Castro. It has been taken up by the Communists, but also by the youth, the intellectuals, the oppressed, the poor, the ill, the illiterate. It is not the challenge of communism; it is the challenge of people—ordinary people—for a better way of life, a fairer share of the wealth they produce. We, the North Americans, will win or lose to the extent that we satisfy these demands, not to the extent that we prevent communism or frustrate *Fidelismo*.

This Revolution has struck deeply, not because its strength comes from Moscow and Peiping, but because it comes out of the deep wellsprings of Cuban and Latin American history, because it holds a promise as well as a threat, because it seeks an answer to questions that are tormenting the minds and hearts of all Latin Americans today.

We say it is the wrong answer. Well and good! But then, we must give a better answer. Not an old answer for a new era.

We can do it, of course. This is still the Western Hemisphere, our hemisphere. We belong. We have power, wealth, ideals, freedom, democracy, things to give, things we need. We must shape all this to better purposes than in the past.

A truly astonishing feature of the conflict between Cuba and the United States lies in the fact that Fidel and his associates are counting upon the defeat of the United States in the cold war. They see us as a declining power, approaching the fall of our "Empire" just as the Romans did in olden times and the British and French in the postwar era. They have no illusions about the disparity in strength between them and us, but they believe that they are riding the wave of the future and will share the triumph of the "Socialist" forces over "Yankee imperialism."

"Cuba is just a small incident," Che Guevara said to me the last time I saw him. "You will lose everywhere in the world."

The danger to us in such beliefs is obvious. These young men, after all, do control Cuba, have considerable influence in the hemisphere, and are permitting Cuba to be used as a base from which communism, as well as *Fidelismo* can operate to stir up revolution and play the Communist game throughout Latin America.

Whether this was unavoidable or whether our policy blunders were to blame has long ceased to be a problem to Washington. This is where an academic approach is meaningless. Whatever sins North Americans may have committed or condoned in Cuba since the Spanish-American War, however responsible our policies—economic and political—may have been for bringing on the Cuban Revolution, even if it were our fault that the Castro regime had ended up in the arms of Khrushchev,

Washington would still say that we will not stand for the Communist domination of Cuba.

By this I presume we mean a Cuban regime actively playing a role on the side of the Sino-Soviet bloc against the United States and engaged in subverting and stirring up anti-American, Leftist social revolutions throughout Latin America. If this is what Fidel Castro represents, then he and his regime will have to be destroyed. No amount of sympathy for Fidel Castro and for the ideals and genuine accomplishments of his Revolution could lead an American to any other decision.

On the other hand, an American policy so stupid as to seek to restore the pre-Revolutionary situation, as we tried to do with the invasion of April, 1961, is no answer. It would bring about a state of affairs as damaging to us and to Cuba in the long run as the Castro Revolution.

The hope, surely, must be that the Cuban Revolution will run a course that brings social and economic benefits to Cuba and that meanwhile can be isolated. Cuba is a small, weak, poor country which could be allowed to work out its own destiny, even if its government is socialistic or communistic. It will not subvert the hemisphere or any countries in it if American policies are wise and sensible.

Allowing for all the weapons and power that a totalitarian regime puts in the hands of a modern government, I still think that communism could not survive in Cuba. The Cuban people are too violent and brave, as well as too individualistic, to put up with a totalitarian regime indefinitely. In the long run, the Cubans will rid themselves of communism, and they are more likely to do so if we let them do it and do not try any more foolish stunts like the invasion of April, 1961. Cubans did not make good use of their liberty when they had it, but they love and crave liberty.

The answer to *Fidelismo,* as everyone knows and keeps saying, is to help bring about the positive social, economic and political reforms in Latin America that will make the Cuban Revolution seem unnecessary, irrational, undesirable and too costly in terms of human liberty.

The outcome of the cold war will then be decided on more crucial battlefields than Cuba—or for that matter, Berlin. If our way of life is the better one in the field of power politics and in a material as well as moral sense, we will win, and the Cuban Revolution will have played a role similar in our century to that of its many predecessors in modern times.

This will have been a great role, and a worthy one. I could never bring myself to condemn it and to condemn Fidel Castro outright for what he has done, and especially for what he has tried to do. At worst, the role that he and his young associates will have played, would resemble that of the Jacobins of the French Revolution who applied a surgical knife to the body politic, wounding and painful, but salutary.

The French Revolution was a terrible experience for France and for Europe, but we of later generations have lived and profited by it. The Cuban Revolution, in its different way, is proving a harsh and painful experience for Cuba and Latin America, but I believe that its ultimate effects will have been beneficial for the hemisphere. Mexicans make a similar, and impressive, argument in favor of their long and costly social revolution of 1910 to 1940.

In this analogy (and I do realize how tricky historical analogies can be) the United States would be playing a role somewhat similar to England's in the French Revolution. I first felt this in reading a passage from Louis Kronenberger's *Kings and Desperate Men* about the French Revolution: "At the fall of the Bastille most Englishmen rejoiced, assuming that the French would now take to themselves a constitution and form of government minutely patterned on the English. But the pent-up passions, the accumulated abuses of many generations imposed a less graceful outcome. Excitement in France turned to confusion, and confusion to terror; the French encouraged other nations to revolt, and began a campaign of aggression which produced Napoleon and subsided only at Waterloo."

By substituting Cuba for France and the United States for England we do get a striking parallel, except that there is no Cuban Napoleon in sight. Those in the United States who condemn the Cuban Revolution for its excesses, it violence and its tyranny are like Edmund Burke, who so brilliantly saw what was wrong with the French Revolution and who predicted its excesses—but who failed so signally to *understand* the French Revolution.

It was so much more than he thought or realized! Its ideals were transforming Europe and did, indeed, transform the modern world. The Reign of Terror and even the conquests of Napoleon went into history—pages that we turned and left behind. But "liberty, equality, fraternity," like "life, liberty and the pursuit of happiness," were ideals that lived on and that changed the world, even though in this latter half of the twentieth century they are still unattainable ideals.

I would not try to predict what will come of the Cuban Revolution or what will remain of it. I only know that it will not die; that for all its faults and excesses it contains ideals and hopes and aspirations for which men and women in Latin America will struggle. However it ends— and all revolutions must end—it will not have been made in vain.

CHAPTER SEVEN

Journalism

"IN ALL MY thirty-eight years on *The New York Times*," I said, "I have never seen a big story so misunderstood, so misinterpreted and so badly handled as the Cuban Revolution."

This ill-tempered, but carefully pondered and earnestly meant judgment, was made to the annual conference of the American Society of Newspaper Editors in Washington in April, 1960. As a matter of fact, I had said much the same thing as early as the end of January, 1959, to my colleagues in the Overseas Press Club. That was apropos of the uncomprehending way the execution of the "war criminals" was being handled and the abysmal ignorance of Cuba and Cuban history that was being displayed.

Nothing else I said about the Cuban affair has been so widely quoted. It was—and continues to be—picked up by those who favor the Castro regime and who therefore agree with me. It was also used by those who feel I have misled the American public about Fidel Castro and who wax sarcastic.

I have now been on *The Times* thirty-nine years and will repeat what I said for posterity since I am as firmly convinced of it today, as I was from the beginning. I never made the charge lightly. I am not a quarrelsome man and I value the respect and friendship of my colleagues more than anything in my career. I simply believe it is important to put the judgment on record and I am certain it is one with which future students of the Cuban Revolution and of American journalism will agree.

By a strange coincidence, this is the second time that the American press has played a major role—and a bad one—in Cuban-American history.

Dr. Joseph E. Wisan, now head of the History Department of the City College of New York, devoted his doctoral thesis back in 1934 to "The Cuban Crisis as Reflected in the New York Press." The "crisis" he referred to was the rebellion against Spain that began in 1895 and ended with the Spanish-American War in 1898.

"The principal cause of our war with Spain," he wrote, "was the public demand for it, a demand too powerful for effective resistance by the business and financial leaders of the nation or by President McKinley. For the creation of the public state of mind, the press was largely responsible."

I am sorry to say that my predecessors in the newspaper profession in the 1890's were turning out some of the wildest fakes that the human mind could conceive and the gullibility of readers absorb. I am not talking of the fighting stage, during which we had some superb war corresponding. I am referring to the preliminary period when the New York publishers, headed by the young William Randolph Hearst and his *Morning Journal,* sent correspondents down to Cuba with orders to get stories about the heroism of the Cuban rebels and the atrocities of the Spanish rulers.

I am sure that Walter Millis, in his book, *The Martial Spirit,* was right in saying that much of this so-called news was collected in Havana bars and hotel lobbies.

This was a case where journalists were not providing the material for history—I would feel sorry for any student who believed what they wrote—but, nevertheless, the newspapermen made history. They provided the decisive push behind public opinion, which, in its turn, forced the McKinley Government into a war that need not have occurred.

Bad journalism made Cuban-American history then, and bad journalism has been making it again. We have been seeing an intricate mechanism of news coverage and editorial opinion operating to create and heighten tensions and antagonisms between Cuba and the United States and, at the same time, building up a hostile public opinion which, in its turn, has brought pressure on Congress and the White House to force American policies into unavoidable channels.

Of course, many other factors were operating besides the mass communications media. There were also the inexcusable distortions and misunderstandings of the

Cuban press with regard to the United States, even before freedom of the press was crushed in Cuba.

In general, I think that this Cuban story represents one
of the most fascinating and important chapters in the
history of American journalism. It comes to me in the
twilight of a long career when I can look back on other
big stories in faraway places. I have worked in my time
with just about all the important newspapermen of the
last four decades—many great ones, and many from other
countries. I know good journalistic work when I see it,
and I know poor work.

I have a reputation in my profession which I value, and
I staked it on the Cuban story. The verdict, however, is
not one for my contemporaries to make. It will have to be
the verdict of history, say fifty years from now, and I will
not hear it.

For a very long time through 1959 and 1960, I felt like
Horatio at the bridge. No one else seemed to be able or
willing to present the Cuban side of the story except those
who went so far and so unreservedly and unrealistically
to the Fidelista side that their testimony lost value.

The greatest failure of the American press was its lack
of balance and objectivity. From the time of the executions in Cuba in the early months of 1959, the American
press, radio and television were emotionally and overwhelmingly hostile. Once the label of communism was
pinned on Fidel and his regime—and this, too, was early
in 1959—the hysteria that accompanies the American
attitude toward communism worked its poison.

This was not a question of sympathy or criticism, praise

or blame. The failure was in a lack of understanding, and it was a tragic failure because it contributed greatly to the developing conflict between Cuba and the United States. In my opinion, it also helped to drive Fidel quicker and deeper into the Communist embrace.

Fidel and his associates were always convinced that the reasons for the hostility toward him and his Revolution lay in the subservience of the American press to the State Department, the business interests and in the conservatism of newspaper publishers.

We are so used to a free press that we cannot realize that outside of the Anglo-Saxon bloc of countries there is no conception of how the press operates in our type of democracy. This is as true of the French and Italians as it is of the Latin Americans. They do not understand, even when the press in their own countries—as in France and Italy—is free to a very considerable extent. The press works differently in these countries and, especially, is much more easily bought and controlled by business and political interests.

Our own press is not 100 per cent free, just as we do not have a pure and complete democracy. Everything is relative in this imperfect world. By reasonable and practical standards we do have a free press, and it was not hostile to Cuba because it was paid to be or ordered to be. I don't know how often I tried to persuade Fidel and his colleagues of this fact. They could not believe it, partly because they had no genuine conception of what freedom of the press meant, and partly because they were so passionately convinced of the righteousness of their cause that criticism to them was immoral and evil.

The logical conclusion of such reasoning was the suppression of criticism in Cuba. Cuban "freedom of the press" was always a relative matter. With some honorable exceptions, newspapers, magazines and journalists were subsidized by successive Governments, as they were by the Spaniards during the colonial era. This was true of the Batista dictatorship, as it was of preceding regimes.

"Freedom of the press" in Cuba meant that even though newspapers would take money from President Batista, they still felt free to criticize him, so much so that he was compelled to keep a tight lid of censorship on the press during most of the period of the Castro insurrection. He did not and could not force the newspapers to conform to a single Government line, as Fidel Castro came to do.

Fidel understood enough about freedom of the press to realize that he killed it in Cuba, but that does not mean he understands how the American press works. He always, and very bitterly, resented the hostility of the American press and he could not believe it was a sincerely felt, and not a directed, hostility.

He was wrong, but there was no dissuading him. My own criticisms of the American press lie in other directions. I do not doubt that many of my colleagues are writing what they know their publishers and readers want them to write, but to me the basic problem still lies in a failure of understanding.

Consider the ideal qualifications a journalist required

to understand what was happening in Cuba and, above all, why it was happening.

A newspaperman ought to have had a knowledge of Cuba and the Cuban people, some grounding in Cuban history, especially the recent history of the Batista dictatorship, a knowledge of Spanish, some idea of the Latin American picture as a whole and (this was the most difficult of all) an understanding of what communism really is and of the mechanism of a social revolution.

This last point is one in which I find myself in agreement with Professor C. Wright Mills, in his *Listen Yankee.*

"I believe another source of trouble," he writes, "is that most journalists simply do not know how to understand and report a revolution. If it is a real revolution—and Cuba's is certainly that—to report it involves much more than the ordinary journalist's routine. It requires that the journalist abandon many of the clichés and habits which now make up his very craft. It certainly requires that he know something in detail about the great variety of Left-wing thought and action in the world today. And most North American journalists know very little of that variety. To most of them it appears as all just so much 'communism.' Even those with the best will to understand, by their training and the habits of their work, are incapable of reporting fully enough and accurately enough the necessary contexts, and so the meanings, of revolutionary events. In all truth, I do not know that anyone has all the necessary capacities; it is an extraordinarily difficult task for any member of an overdeveloped society to report what is going on in the hungry world today."

All in all, I know of no story in my career so difficult to cover with understanding and competence as the Cuban Revolution. This has been especially true for American journalists who were so ill qualified to tackle the story when it broke. The problem was not that there were so few American newspapermen with all the qualifications I listed. Nearly all the correspondents and editors handling the story could not fill a single one of the qualifications.

It was a story that began on January 1, 1959 and that was then interpreted in terms of our own Anglo-Saxon way of life and our economic and political philosophy.

One of the most difficult tasks for a journalist, as it is for a historian trying to understand a past age, is to put himself in the place of the other man or of the people being studied. The Greeks had a word for it—empathy. If there was no feeling for the Revolution, there was no understanding. The understanding could—and would—leave an American highly critical of much that was happening, but only the understanding gave the right to criticize. American coverage was, instead, distorted, unfair, ill informed and intensely emotional.

Besides, it missed the main point of what was happening. The French Revolution, for instance, was not simply the fall of the Bastille, the guillotining of a lot of people and the Battle of Waterloo. It was a dynamic process and development whose really great significance lay in its social and political ideas.

The American coverage of the Cuban Revolution concentrated almost wholly on executions, guerrillas, the seizure of American property, sabotage, communism, trade embargoes, diplomatic quarrels, bitter speeches and considerable attention to Fidel Castro's beard.

The Cuban Revolution has not been described in the American mass media of communication for what it truly is, for its real significance in Cuba and in Latin America. The concentration should have been on the fact that this was a social revolution of great importance. Its gradual development toward totalitarianism and socialism is its most significant aspect, internally. All the other events connected with it—the speeches, the sabotage and the like —are news, of course, and deserve attention every day, even front pages, but these are the surface manifestations of the Revolution. What the story has lacked is coverage in depth.

It has been an interesting feature of the journalistic aspect of the Revolution, that the European newspapermen did a much better job, generally, than the Americans. They were not prejudiced in advance, not emotional and they did not regard the issue of communism with the hysteria that characterized the American coverage. As a result, there has been some distinguished coverage in the British, French and Swiss press.

(Incidentally, I would not want to leave the impression that there has been no distinguished work at all by American correspondents. There has been some, but the good work has been done by a few and it has not made its mark on the general picture of United States coverage.)

American writers greatly oversimplified what was hap-

pening. One could always say of Cuba what the Middle
East correspondent of *The Economist* wrote about Iran
this summer—"Anyone who knows what is really going on
in Persia [Iran] must be grossly misinformed." We have
had, and still have, in the United States innumerable
newspapermen who tell you confidently what is happening in Cuba. They are quite sure of themselves, but if
any situation called for humility, doubts and an open
mind, it was the Cuban Revolution.

I have never seen a situation so dynamic. To be away
from Cuba for a month or two was to lose touch. The
truth at one period would no longer hold for a later
period. This did not make it any the less the truth when
it was written, as so many Americans seem naïvely to
believe.

In my case, for instance, a great play has been made
of the fact that on July 16, 1959, I wrote: "This is not a
Communist revolution in any sense of the word and there
are no Communists in positions of control. . . . Premier
Castro is not only not a Communist, but decidedly anti-
Communist."

It so happens that was true when it was written, and it
will, therefore, always be true. It also happened that Fidel
afterwards changed his mind and his policies. The truth
in the late summer of 1961 is therefore different, and
writing today I would write what is true today. This is the
proper function of journalism.

Prophecy and prediction are not its proper functions,
although they have their fascination. A newspaperman
calculating the course of a story like Cuba's resembles a

businessman calculating the market. The gamble might or might not come off. The guesswork might be clever, but it will be guesswork.

Nobody could have known in 1959 what was going to happen in Cuba because an extraordinary complex of men and forces was at work, because those who were making the Cuban Revolution—and especially Fidel Castro—were young, inexperienced, emotional and rash, because they were responding to each day's problems as they came along. Meanwhile, the United States was responding to its own complex and powerful pressures and to the vicious circle of provocations and reactions in both our countries. Add the crushing, tearing, stormy effects of the global cold war, which gradually engulfed Cuba, and you can realize that there was no safe way of predicting what was going to happen.

I am not arguing that a journalist should have no opinions about what was taking place, and still less that he should have had no feelings or emotions or even bias about a story like the Cuban Revolution. This is not only asking the impossible; it would be bad.

One of the essentials of good newspaper work is what F. Scott Fitzgerald called "the catharsis of a powerful emotion." A catharsis is the escape hatch of the emotions that a drama arouses. But it should be a controlled catharsis. It should never prevent the newspaperman from seeing and presenting the whole picture.

This is not the place to analyze the press coverage of the Cuban Revolution in detail.

One could begin at the very beginning when the Associated Press, on December 31, 1958, the very night Batista fled, sent its famous despatch telling of a decisive Batista victory at Santa Clara and the rebels being driven back eastward. The United Press International was not doing much better at the time.

However, one example of fundamental importance to Cuban-American relations and therefore to the course of the Revolution should suffice for our purposes. This was the treatment in the American press of the executions of Batistiano "war criminals" in the first few months of the Revolution. I have had occasion already to explain these executions and the psychology behind them. The slap-dash, summary methods used were very bad, of course, but the reasons for the executions, the fact that the Cuban people approved, that rioting and personal vengeances were forestalled, that Batista had killed, often after torture, thousands of Cubans, and that something else was happening in Cuba—a remarkable social revolution was, in fact, getting under way—all this was virtually ignored in the American press.

Lest I be accused of using Left-wing opinion or some special reasoning of my own on this, let me cite two of the most respected voices in the hemisphere on this subject.

Dr. Henry M. Wriston, President of the American Assembly, ex-President of Brown University and former Government official, gave an address in Colorado Springs on April 3, 1959, on "Revolution and the American Citizen" which sums up much of what I have been trying to say in this book.

In a revolutionary situation, different rules apply. The opposition is not a mere political competitor; often it is the enemy. ... When these new governments seem to sacrifice freedom for "internal security," we would do well to remember our own Alien and Sedition Acts during the administration of John Adams. . . .

It required all our political maturity and sophistication to treat Mikoyan [on his visit to the United States] not as the author of savagery in Hungary, but as the First Deputy Premier of a great power with whom the realities required us to deal. If it is so hard for us, we ought to be able to understand the over-sensitiveness of a weak, new government, menaced by an opposition unwilling to seek power by ballots and ready to resort to bullets at the first hope of success. . . .

No one need feel regret at the overthrow of Batista. His tyranny was scandalously corrupt, viciously brutal. Add adverbs and adjectives to taste, and you will hardly do violence to the facts. Fidel Castro was everything a revolutionary should be: a man of good family and fortune, well educated. He abandoned comfort and career to gamble his life on a military adventure which any knowledgeable strategist would immediately have branded as hopeless. He lived in the wilderness, was hunted like a wild animal; yet his own life was marked by unusual self-discipline. He imposed a control upon his followers which was astoundingly strict. He never repaid torture with torture; he refused to copy his enemy's practice of killing prisoners.

If we recall these facts, it is equally clear that after years of hanging on by the slenderest margin, Castro had a sudden success which developed enormous momentum, and ran beyond his control. Even so, the number of executions [of "war criminals"] was a fraction of the Batista murders. Despite procedural deficiencies, the revolutionary trials were far less lawless than the midnight murders of his predecessor. Yet nearly all American newspapers and commentators gave the impression that there was an orgy of blood. . . .

Is it any wonder that Castro felt he was misunderstood? The plain fact is that he was misunderstood and misinterpreted in quarters, supposedly "liberal," whose imaginations should have made them more understanding. I have used Castro as an illustration because events in Cuba are close at hand, recent, and so fresh in mind. Remember, then, that revolutions develop a dynamic of their own, and no one can predict just how far they will go.

At the time the executions started, José Figueres, ex-President of Costa Rica, was asked by a friend to condemn the Cubans. Instead, he wrote a long letter that was published in the Havana press on January 22, 1959. He wrote in part:

In my country, the death penalty does not exist, nor have we felt the need of it in this century, by good fortune. But each society and each historical moment has its own necessities of survival, which usually tend to be the least of various possible evils. In the present circumstances of Cuba, which I know quite well, severity may be a lesser evil than impunity. . . .

No one who knew the extremes of barbarism to which the recent tortures in Cuba, Venezuela and other "republics" have gone, will be able to deny in conscience that the corrective methods must be extreme. . . .

Those who today advocate that the criminals of Cuba's war be granted civil justice are disconnected from the circumstances of the moment. There is not the slightest doubt, in each city and each town, who were the principal assassins. . . .

If the Provisional Government does not execute the most noted criminals quickly, public passion will overflow, outraged at the impunity or the delay, and then the number of dead will be many, many thousands.

It was astonishing and exasperating to me that Americans could not see these obvious facts. I know of no one in the American press corps who understood what was involved or, if he did understand, who was able to present a proper interpretation to his readers. This was the time —January 22—when I went before the Overseas Press Club and first said that I had never in my career seen a big story so badly handled.

The next week I wrote an article explaining my point of view for the house organ of the O.P.C.

"The good and the bad make up the picture," I ended. "The distortion and falsity of the Cuban coverage, in my opinion, came because the whole truth was not presented and because a small part of the truth was presented in a twisted, inadequate, misleading way."

From that time on I was making myself unpopular with my colleagues. I thought then, and I still think on the whole, that one of the worst jobs of coverage of the Cuban Revolution was being done by *Time* magazine. I said so publicly and wrote a strong letter to one of its top editors in May, 1959, saying I thought their coverage was slanted deliberately to present the most unfavorable picture possible of the Revolution. Their coverage was also inaccurate, which will not surprise any professional newspaperman who knows how *Time* operates. It has first-rate correspondents who send straightforward copy, and I am sure this would have been the case with Cuba in the early weeks, but what correspondents send and what comes out in the magazine are two different things.

I am not saying that the other news weeklies were appreciably better. *Time* happens to be the most widely read of all United States news publications and it has more influence on the people of the country as a whole than any other publication, even *The Times*, which hits a much higher intellectual and official level. Consequently, what *Time* printed about the Cuban Revolution was of considerable importance. This is why I feel it requires discussion.

A delightful description of *Time*'s methods, given just at this period—March 4, 1959—came in a speech made by John O'Rourke, Editor of the Washington *Daily News*. He referred to unhappy experiences he and John S. Knight, Publisher of the Knight Newspapers, had just had with *Time*.

"I have met an astonishing number of people who have had experiences similar to those of Mr. Knight and myself," O'Rourke said. "It leads me to think that perhaps we are taking the wrong approach as we read *Time*.

"*Time* lives, I find, in a higher keyed, wittier, more brightly colored world than the real world I am forced to inhabit. Therefore, I enjoy *Time*. It is nice to escape once a week from mundane reality and gaze at the wild, improbable place around me, through *Time*'s kaleidoscopically colored glasses.

"Mr. Chairman, there are many forms of fiction. There is historical fiction, called the historical novel. There is the fiction called science fiction. Why not news fiction?"

Time took its revenge on me—or did its best to—in an article under its section "The Press" on July 27, 1959.

"In already choosing sides in Cuba's conflict," *Time* wrote among other things, "Herb Matthews, 59, was following a well established pattern."

It then went on to say how in a trip to the Orient in 1929 I "felt more sympathy toward the Japanese than the Chinese," how I supported the Italians in the Abyssinian War, how I was a "partisan for the Communist-backed Loyalist forces" in the Spanish Civil War, leading to my sins in the Cuban Revolution. A photograph was printed of me standing with Faustino Pérez and Liliam Mesa (who had taken me and my wife to Oriente Province for the original interview with Fidel Castro). There was a sneering caption.

Allowing for the customary mistakes, distortions and quotations out of context mixed into the article, what might have interested *Time* readers was that every word "exposing" me was taken from my own books, chiefly *The Education of a Correspondent.*

This is my main reason for citing *Time,* among a host of critics of my Cuban work. A newspaperman, like any other man, lives to learn. Moreover, he will make his quota of mistakes. In nearly forty years of newspaper work I have written millions of words. If I had not made errors I would be a calculating machine, not a journalist.

The important thing is to correct the errors when they are brought out. Beyond that, what matters is to give all the facts, whether they support one's point of view or not, and if a situation changes to describe the changes. These are basic tenets of journalism, by my credo, and no one can say that I have not followed them throughout my career.

Everything about my work has been open for everyone to see and read. When Senator McCarthy was at the height of his outrageous smear campaigns, he claimed there were many "Reds" on *The New York Times*. Considering my record in the Spanish Civil War it would have seemed natural for him to pick on me. He could not and did not, for the simple reason that there was nothing to pick on. I never belonged to any Communist front organization, let alone any Communist group or party. I have considered myself a liberal, and liberalism—not fascism, McCarthyism, John Birchism or what Senator Fulbright calls "Right-wing radicalism"—is the real opposite and enemy of communism.

During this Cuban excitement, my critics and enemies would love to find something in my career to fasten upon and expose. The egregious Eastland-Dodd Subcommittee of the Senate Judiciary Committee has heard frequent and interminable attacks on me, as I mentioned before, but it can find nothing worse than what it would consider mistaken judgments.

Nevertheless, the attacks on me—and through me on *The Times*—have been and continue to be fierce. They are especially so from my former Cuban friends and admirers who are now exiles in Miami. I regret the way they feel and wish I could find myself in agreement with men whom I respect like Felipe Pazos, Rufo Lopez Fresquet, Raul Chibás, Manuel Ray, José (Pepín) M. Bosch.

Pepín Bosch wrote me on March 15, 1961: "To Fidel

you are the equivalent of an army division, so winning you away will be quite a victory."

All that could "win me away" are the facts, the truth, the real developments in Cuba, and the extent to which I have drawn away should be clear in this book. This still leaves me seeing the Cuban situation differently from the exiles, for I see what is good about it, how important it is, and I retain my sympathy and, in many respects, admiration for Fidel Castro.

The attitude I have taken throughout often left me standing virtually alone among the United States editors and newspapermen. I had some precious encouragement. Now that he is dead, I can divulge that one who stood by me at all times was Ernest Hemingway, as did his wife, Mary. My last letter from Ernest, written in the late summer of 1960 while he was in Spain, was to assure me that the reports saying he had "gone sour" on Fidel and the Cuban Revolution were false.

It is not easy to be a dissenter in the United States in a highly emotional period like the present when McCarthyism has been reborn, with its special emphasis on Cuba.

There was a passage in an article by John Strachey in the English magazine, *Encounter*, for December, 1960, which seemed apt to me.

"Britain is the traditional land of dissent," he wrote, "of dissent not only in its original connotation but of dissent itself: of—if you will—dissent for dissent's sake. In this respect there seems a persisting difference between the mental climates of Britain on the one hand and Russia and America on the other. It has been well said that both

Russia and America are 'unanimous countries.' The consensus of opinion at any one time is so strong in each of them that it is difficult indeed for an individual to swim against it."

Allowing for the exaggerated comparison of the United States with Russia (after all, nobody is going to send me to the salt mines for dissenting) there was much truth in what Strachey wrote.

The problem was a difficult one for my newspaper, and since the principles involved went to the heart of what might be called the philosophy of journalism, they deserve consideration.

The sensational impact of my Sierra Maestra interview with Fidel Castro in February, 1957, set the stage. The problem of what to do about it came up soon after in connection with the coverage of the closely related Dominican situation in *The Times*. Because of the censorship there and the complete, brutal and tyrannical nature of the Trujillo dictatorship, we had been unable to get an adequate job done for a long time. Yet the Dominican Republic was much in the news then—July, 1957—because of the dramatic case of the disappearance of the Columbia University teacher, Jesús de Galíndez, and the murder of Gerald Murphy, the American pilot.

I was in a position to do the job for *The Times*, but it would have had to be a strongly personalized job. It could not be anything else, after the Cuban sensation, with my name meaning what it does in Latin American affairs and since I was known by Generalissimo Trujillo and all Dominicans as the man who was writing the editorials that were always so critical of Trujillo. The Dominican press and radio were constantly attacking me.

The problem that *The Times* had to face was whether there were not particular cases in which a personalized type of journalism would be of value—perhaps of great value—to the paper. As a general proposition, I have been as strong an adherent of impersonal journalism as anyone on the staff. I always said I would have been content if our *Times*, like *The Times* of London, never used by-lines, or names of correspondents.

I was the first one to call attention to the dangers and embarrassments inherent in the spectacular Cuban reaction to my Fidel Castro stories. I always tried to discourage every kind of manifestation, and by coincidence there had been a big demonstration of tribute by Cubans in the street in front of the Times Building at the end of June, 1957, while I was away. (In 1960 and 1961, as I have mentioned, the demonstrations were of an opposite nature.)

In the case of the Dominican story, it seemed to me that the paper had a remarkable opportunity if we wanted to take advantage of it. Had I gone to Ciudad Trujillo in July, 1957, or at any time thereafter, it is no exaggeration to say that the atmosphere would have been electrified. The fact that I was there would have been immediately known, not only in the Dominican Republic, but all over the hemisphere. *The Times* could have had some articles afterwards that every newspaper, magazine and news agency in the hemisphere would have reproduced and commented upon.

I did not go to the Dominican Republic, and I have cited the incident only as an example of the type of problem a newspaper like *The Times* has in dealing with stories which, as in the case of Cuba, become supercharged with a personality factor.

I always respected *The Times*'s problems and understood its reasoning—and the paper respected my attitude. There are many satisfactions in working for *The New York Times*. None is greater than the fact that it permits a man to retain his integrity.

It is a curious and paradoxical feature of *The Times*'s great reputation that it is based, on the one hand, on the impartial, objective, uneditorialized thoroughness of its news coverage and, on the other hand, on the work of individuals whose names give a special quality and fame to the newspaper. These men (and women, too, for I am also thinking of the late Anne O'Hare McCormick) have helped to make the paper great precisely because they possessed unique qualities. When they die or retire they are irreplaceable; whoever takes their places may be as good or better, but they will be different.

So far as Cuba was concerned, any news story I would do had to have a personal angle. At the same time, the information I was in a unique position to get, the ideas that would have a special authority, the impact of my stories, the fact that whatever I wrote would have a historic value—these features provided journalistic assets that might or might not have outweighed the liabilities (as a newspaper like *The Times* would see it) of a special, individual imprint.

Competent men, having no involvement, can do a technically adequate job in such circumstances, and, of course, the reader would never know what he missed. The editors would have nothing to worry about. No one would complain about what was printed—or praise it, either, for that matter. The danger to a newspaper in playing safe lies in discouraging individual initiative and penalizing a correspondent for the results that inevitably follow the performance of dramatic, or especially outstanding, work. This *The Times* naturally does not want to do.

The principle at stake from *The Times*'s point of view (and it would apply to all newspapers with similar standards) is that the news columns—not the editorials, of course—should be kept as neutral, impartial and objective as possible. We do our best to keep editorializing out of the news. When a correspondent becomes personally involved in a situation, his stories are bound to have a special coloration.

My argument on that score—and I began arguing back in the Abyssinian and Spanish Civil Wars—is that all correspondents are human, and being human, cannot help having a bias. If a man's work is rejected or distrusted for that reason, one would also reject the only things that really matter—honesty, understanding, compassion and thoroughness. A reader has a right to the truth and to all the facts, to the best of the writer's ability to find them; he has no right to expect or demand that a correspondent agree with him.

Charles Pelham Curtis, Jr., the distinguished Boston

lawyer, put the problem in better words than I could in his *A Commonplace Book*.

"There are only two ways to be quite unprejudiced and impartial," he wrote. "One is to be completely ignorant. The other is to be completely indifferent. Bias and prejudice are attitudes to be kept in hand, not attitudes to be avoided."

There were frequent occasions during the Cuban insurrection and since Fidel Castro's triumph when the American press did not get stories because there were no correspondents close enough to the men and events to find out what was happening. One example of many was the illness of Fidel Castro in the summer of 1960. The American press indulged in the wildest speculations, whereas anyone like myself, who would have been in personal contact with Fidel or his entourage, could have ascertained the truth easily and quickly.

Another important problem for a newspaper is that even though the editors would know and trust the work of a correspondent, a number of readers would be suspicious.

There has also long been an unresolved conflict on *The Times*—and I suppose on other newspapers—about letting editorial writers contribute to the news columns. It is a little like the problem of permitting intelligence agents to gather information for an operation. The tendency for an editorial writer might be to get or to send information that would fit an editorial line.

As with all these arguments, it depends on the individual. Working for a big institution like *The Times* is not unlike working for the Government. It is hard to assert one's individuality and not to be merged with the smoothly working mass as it rolls forward day by day. Yet the "good, gray *Times*" has long ceased to be "gray," except to those who do not know how to read a newspaper or whose prejudices make them color blind.

All the same, there are, and there no doubt have to be, limits. *The Times* has a style, a pattern and a responsibility that impose certain restraints. And if the man gets bigger than the paper in a certain field or in a certain way, or looms too large on the smoothly rolling horizon, there is uneasiness.

The maverick can be a fine animal, welcomed, admired, appreciated—but an embarrassment and a worry at times. However, the owner does not get rid of such a maverick; he might even treasure him.

At the height of the controversy over my role in the Cuban story, and at a time when Americans had reached the peak of hysteria about Fidel Castro and the Revolution, word got around that I had been forbidden by *The Times* to write anything more about Cuba. C. Wright Mills put this in his best seller, *Listen Yankee.* There were many whose wishful thinking led them to believe a widespread report that I had been discharged. I have delivered many lectures on the Cuban situation, mostly at colleges and universities, and I hardly recall any place where I was not asked why I was no longer writing on Cuba.

The answer to that question was simple. I am an editor, I would point out. While our editorials are the anonymous expression of the newspaper's opinion, it was divulging

THE CUBAN STORY

an open secret to say that except when I was away from New York or having my days off, I have written all the editorials in *The New York Times* on Cuba. If *The Times* had not trusted me to do them and accepted my opinion as I accepted the newspaper's traditions and responsibilities, I would not still be on *The Times*. But, then *The Times* would not be the great institution that it remains if it did not show loyalty to its staff, as it always does.

Having said that, I want to repeat my point, modesty aside. Newspapermen are not turned out like Fords on an assembly line—at least, not the top-flight ones. They are unique works of art, not cogs in a machine. When they go, others come along to do just as good or better work, but it will be different work.

The fact that my work has always been recognizably mine has been a source of pride to me, as it has been both an asset and an embarrassment to *The Times*. Those looking back on the coverage of the Spanish Civil War in *The Times* will see *me*—and so it will be with the Cuban Revolution.

The criticisms and the smears one receives for doing controversial work on controversial events are easy to take. They almost always come from those emotionally involved on one side or the other (and I respect such criticism) or from the ignorant, the crackpots, the knaves, the reactionaries.

I consider it almost an honor to be attacked by the Eastland-Dodd Committee, by writers like the columnist George Sokolsky and William Buckley of the *National*

Review, by publications like *The American Legion Magazine* and the Brooklyn *Tablet.* If such people did not attack me I would feel that there was something wrong with my work.

In my day I have been accused of taking Fascist gold and Moscow gold. When I went back to Cuba after the Castro interview in 1957 there were two contradictory slanders being circulated in pro-Batista circles. One was that I was being paid by ex-President Prío Socarrás, then in Miami. I believe the figure of $100,000 was mentioned. The other was more subtle. It was that I was writing editorials and articles harmful to Batista in order to induce the President to pay me a great sum to stop doing so.

The extraordinary thing about slanders of this type is that so many people believe them, or have a gnawing doubt that there may be a grain of truth in them. Cubans do not have a high opinion of their own newspapermen.

Pity the poor Latin American dictator! It is baffling for men like Perón of Argentina, Pérez Jiménez of Venezuela, Trujillo of the Dominican Republic, Batista of Cuba, who believe that every man has his price and who have no grasp of the concept of a free and independent press, to have to sit back helplessly when a newspaper of the power and influence of *The New York Times* consistently attacks them.

When I was in Cuba in June, 1957, someone said to me: "Batista would gladly give Mr. Sulzberger (our Publisher) $1,000,000 if you would go home and stop writing articles and editorials about Cuba."

Of course General Batista would have paid that and much more if he could have silenced *The Times*, and it would have been worth every penny of it to him. Naturally, he was too intelligent to try.

The late Generalissimo Trujillo, who did not have the slightest scruple about assassinating those who annoyed him—and he killed some men with impunity in the United States—would undoubtedly have taken an exquisite pleasure in getting me killed. It would not have paid him.

Curiously enough, dictators (and I have been up against many of them in my career) are almost always sensitive to criticism. As I said, one can almost sympathize with them because in these cases they are dealing with ideas they cannot grasp and forces outside their control.

Those of us who work for *The New York Times* use arms that, metaphorically speaking, are the equivalent of nuclear bombs. An editor in Oshkosh or Peoria or Asheville could be the most brilliant editorial writer in the world with the most expert knowledge of Latin American affairs, and it would not matter much what he wrote or if he did editorials on the area every day.

The Times is the most powerful journalistic instrument that has ever been forged in the free world. It is not the mouthpiece of the State Department, nor a "semi-official organ," as so many people believe. It is an independent institution and those who work for it, especially we editors who give expression to its opinions, have a sobering responsibility.

I was always conscious of that responsibility in the case of Cuba. On June 18, 1957, when I came back from a visit to Havana where I wrote some news articles, I circulated a memorandum to the Publisher and editors.

"As a postscript to my Cuban trip," I wrote, "I would like everyone to understand that we have both an extraordinary opportunity and responsibility, and also an extraordinary problem in handling the subject in the news columns and on the editorial page. Certainly, I have been up against nothing comparable in my career and it is really no exaggeration to say that the role we have been playing since February is of far greater importance to Cuba than that of the State Department. The articles on Fidel Castro and the Cuban situation which I did in February have literally altered the course of Cuban history, and the job I have just done has also had a sensational impact on Cuban affairs. As I am sure you realize, the earlier articles and our editorials also were primarily responsible in ending the diplomatic career of Ambassador Arthur Gardner and in changing the State Department policy toward Cuba. [Not for long, let me insert as an aside!]

"I have insisted to all Cubans I met, and I will always insist, that the job we did was a purely journalistic one. It consisted in the legitimate procedure of throwing a searchlight on a situation that the dictatorship has been trying to keep in the dark. However, as is always the case, when the truth hurts it affects a political situation profoundly, and this is what has been happening in Cuba.

"At the same time I believe that because of the truly extraordinary effect of anything that I do or anything that we print editorially on Cuban affairs at this extremely critical moment, we must be very careful to remain within the bounds of strict journalism. I believe we must not go out of our way at any time to write things about Cuba which are not called for by the requirements of the news situation and legitimate comment. . . .

"I think we can feel proud of the extraordinary power which *The New York Times* possesses in a situation like this, but just because we have that power we also have a responsibility that must be carefully considered at every step."

So it was. As my career draws to its close, I say now what I have said from the beginning. Nothing matters more than the search for truth and its complete expression. The journalist can say with the Psalmist: "Judge me, O Lord . . . according to mine integrity."

The truth is to be found where the history is being made. In my long years of war corresponding what mattered, I always felt, was to be at the front, with the fighting. Those who stayed at headquarters and got the whole story could have the front page. It meant more to me to get that one little moment and place of truth, where men were fighting and dying—and making history.

The truth has a palpable, sentient quality when you live with it. Those of us who lived, and felt and suffered through the Spanish Civil War—we know what it was. Now, they are writing *histories* of the Spanish Civil War, like the superb job of scholarship which the young Englishman, Hugh Thomas, has done. He consulted every document, visited all the places, spoke to whom he could.

It is all there—everything but the living truth. It is not the Spanish Civil War; it is the *history* of the Spanish Civil War.

There are those who are already writing history about the Cuban Revolution, reading the documents, what Fidel Castro said one day and Che Guevara another, adding them together like an accountant toting up a column of figures.

"What is history?" a modern Pontius Pilate might well ask. Those of us who live with history and try to relate it know how inaccurately it is chronicled when it happens, how much of it is colored by the point of view, how many different truths there are, what a complicated world we live in.

One makes mistakes, but they will be corrected by time. The truth that one relates will endure. Those who come after cannot take from us the reality of having lived the events—lived the Cuban Revolution as those who made it lived it.

Ralph Vaughan Williams, the composer, once wrote: "Whether my music is good or bad, it is always honest, and by that I mean I could not put down on paper a line which I did not first feel in every part of me."

The only monument I want to leave on earth is for some student years from now to consult the files of *The New York Times* for information about the Spanish Civil War, the Cuban Revolution, or other events and places, and find my by-line, and know that he can trust it.

Index